KEATS

KEATS

A Brief Life in Nine Poems
and One Epitaph

LUCASTA MILLER

ALFRED A. KNOPF New York

2022

THIS IS A BORZOI BOOK
PUBLISHED BY ALFRED A. KNOPF

www.aaknopf.com

Library of Congress Cataloging-in-Publication Data
Names: Miller, Lucasta, author.
Title: Keats : a brief life in nine poems and one epitaph / Lucasta Miller.
Description: First American edition. | New York : Alfred A. Knopf, 2022. |
Includes bibliographical references and index. |
Identifiers: LCCN 2021020620 (print) | LCCN 2021020621 (ebook) |
ISBN 9780525655831 (hardcover) | ISBN 9780525655848 (ebook)
Subjects: LCSH: Keats, John, 1795–1821—Criticism and interpretation. |
Keats, John, 1795–1821. | English poetry—19th century—
History and criticism. | Poets, English—19th century—Biography.
Classification: LCC PR4837 .M55 2022 (print) | LCC PR4837 (ebook) |
DDC 821/.7 [B]—dc23
LC record available at https://lccn.loc.gov/2021020620
LC ebook record available at https://lccn.loc.gov/2021020621

Front-of-jacket painting: *John Keats,* 1818, by Joseph Severn / Granger
Jacket design by Gabriele Wilson

Manufactured in the United States of America
1st Printing

To my mother

Contents

KEATS

Prologue

Body and Soul

THIS IS A BOOK by a reader for readers. It takes nine of Keats's best-known poems—the ones you are most likely to have read—and excavates their backstories, looking behind their popularity as anthology pieces to the context of their creation. Reproduced at the beginning of each chapter, the poems are arranged chronologically in the order in which Keats wrote them. They are used as entry points into telling his life story, although this is not quite a conventional biography. Instead, my aim has been to get under the skin of those now famous poems, to see how he made them and to answer the questions about them, and him, that have always intrigued, inspired or irked me. The close readings are my own, but they are informed by a long tradition of Keats scholarship and draw on the most recent research and critical currents.

As I write this, in lockdown London in 2020, the two-hundredth anniversary of his death in 2021 is approaching. I want to foreground those aspects of the poet's life and work that haven't always made it into the popular imagination, which still tends to make him appear rather more ethereal than he actually was. It's hard, for example, to imagine that the Keats in the award-winning romantic biopic *Bright Star* (2009)—which focuses chastely on his relationship with Fanny Brawne, with whom he fell in love toward the end of his short life—could have taken medication for syphilis. Or that he could have had radical and heterodox political and religious opinions. Or that he had experienced a painfully dysfunctional childhood, taken drugs, inserted a scalpel into a man's head or extracted a bullet from a woman's neck. Or that he had gone on to die with his lungs so ravaged by tuberculosis that the doctors who performed the autopsy could not believe he had lived as long as he had.

Most important, the film does not explain how he could have grabbed established English verse by the scruff of its neck and shaken it into something utterly fresh, while inventing strange new words, such as "surgy," "palely," "soother" and "adventuresome"; and creating phrases, including "tender is the night," "negative capability," and "A thing of beauty is a joy for ever," that went on to have an afterlife divorced from their original context. According to one critic at the time, Keats rejected "prescriptive language" in pursuit of his "own originality." His contemporaries bridled. In 1820, the *Literary Chronicle and Weekly Review* complained that Keats's work was "unintelligible" and urged him to "avoid coining new words." For that reason, the *London Magazine* opined that some might regard him as "a subject for laughter or for pity." Keats has had the last laugh.

The urge to imagine dead poets into life is something that John Keats understood. On the evening of Friday, March 12, 1819, he depicted himself in the momentary act of writing, as he scribbled a new installment in a long journal-letter, written over several weeks between February 14 and May 3, to his brother George and sister-in-law Georgiana, who had recently immigrated to America:

> the candles are burnt down and I am using the wax taper—which has a long snuff on it—the fire is at its last click—I am sitting with my back to it with one foot rather askew upon the rug and the other with the heel a little elevated from the carpet . . . Could I see the same . . . of any great Man long since dead it would be a great delight: as to know in what position Shakespeare sat when he began "To be or not to be."

We can't satisfy Keats's curiosity about Shakespeare, but this vignette brings John Keats himself vividly—and, to posterity, voyeuristically—to life. He was twenty-three at the time and, though he didn't know it, had a little less than two years to live.

Nothing much has surfaced about Shakespeare's day-to-day existence since 1819, even after a further two hundred years of increasingly in-depth scholarship. Although the posthumous impact of his works on culture—including, electrically, on Keats himself—is more recorded and expansive than that of any other English writer, Shakespeare the man remains resolutely disembodied, despite the efforts of his biographers, owing to the lack of surviving contemporary letters and diaries. His context can be—and has been—reconstructed in ever more fascinating detail, but Shakespeare as a subjective individual remains for us a nonentity. He indeed seems the ultimate chameleon poet, as Keats put it, who has "no self" (or "camelion Poet," to quote Keats in his original spelling, which is often quite idiosyncratic, as is his punctuation).

We have a lot more detailed, time-specific, personal information about John Keats. We know, for example, exactly where he was when he wrote to George and Georgiana, by the dull light of a taper and with his back to the fire: at Wentworth Place, the house on the edge of Hampstead Heath where he was then living as the lodger of his friend Charles Armitage Brown. It's now a museum called Keats House. You can visit it today and see the very fireplace where those dying embers "clicked."

These days, Keats House sits on a street renamed Keats Grove in which the other houses are now prestigious properties, affordable only by international bankers, from which most twentysomething writers in the London area would be priced out. It's a world away, economically, from that of the insecure Regency middle class to which Keats and his friends belonged, though the instability they lived through was not that far away from the experience of today's urban millennials.

In 1819, Keats House was a pretty but modest suburban new-build, finished less than three years before he moved in, and architecturally a bit of a cheat. From the front, it looked like a symmetrically proportioned single villa, with a central front door and windows on either side, like a child's drawing of what a house should look like. But the facade hid the fact that it was designed on the inside to house two small independent semidetached dwellings, divided by a party wall, each with its own individual staircase: a symptom of the way in which Regency taste often had more to do with aspirational appearance than reality. In the later nineteenth century, the house was remodeled. The front door used by Brown and Keats—which was around the side—no longer exists; nor does their staircase. But the rooms where they lived—

each had a study on the raised ground floor and a bedroom above—are the same.

In the case of Keats's works, in contrast to those of Shake-speare, there are instances where testimony has survived to tell us something about the actual, physical moment of com-position. Most famously, his "Ode to a Nightingale" was said by Charles Brown to have been written one spring morning in 1819. According to Brown's later recollections, Keats took a chair out into the garden after breakfast to sit on the grass under a plum tree, where a nightingale had built a nest. He came back into the house a couple of hours later with some scraps of paper which he then proceeded, in Brown's account, to try to hide by thrusting them behind some books.

In Brown's memoir of Keats, written more than a decade after the poet died, although not published until 1937, this becomes a parable of Romantic unworldliness, of a Keats supremely uninterested in anything beyond the moment of inspiration. As Brown depicts it, it is he, Brown, who res-cues the scribbled sheets—"four or five in number"—and gets them into shape: a job of work, he tells us, as the "writing was not well legible." Happily, as Brown puts it, "With his [Keats's] assistance I succeeded . . . Thus I rescued that *Ode*." It's hard not to suspect that it was Brown's prying eyes that Keats was trying to circumvent when he thrust the papers behind the books, if that is indeed what happened. He was certainly not shy about publishing the ode, which was printed in *The Annals of the Fine Arts* in July 1819, then again, a year later, in the *Literary Gazette* on July 1, 1820, as a pre-puff just prior to its inclusion in his collection *Lamia, Isabella, The Eve of St. Agnes, and Other Poems,* the third and last of the books he published in his lifetime.

The posthumous shaping of the Keats myth by his contemporary acquaintances—and their occasional desire to claim complicity in his creativity—has proved both an inestimable resource and an ambivalent legacy since his death at twenty-five in Rome, where he had gone in the vain hope of arresting his terminal tuberculosis. His traveling companion, the young painter Joseph Severn, who oversaw Keats's medical treatment, took on an extraordinary burden. Both were only in their twenties at the time and Severn's father had, understandably, tried to stop him from going, as he thought it a rash course. Severn's written account of Keats's final days remains biographically priceless, though it's not uncontroversial. The famous portrait that he made of the dying Keats, which shows the poet's hair plastered down with sweat, combines documentary candor with eerie symbolism, the face silhouetted against a dark disc that looks like a setting sun about to make its slow disappearance behind the bedclothes.

It's a strange thought that Keats's intimate friends—as an orphan, friendship was important to him, as indeed was the kindness of strangers—knew him so briefly, though that's inevitable given he was only twenty-five when he died in 1821. Severn first met Keats at the earliest in late 1815, so their acquaintance was only around five years, though it subsequently colored the rest of the painter's life, during which he produced endless posthumous portraits of the poet, none as intimate as the deathbed sketch. When Severn finally died, aged eighty-five, in 1879, he was buried next to Keats in the foreigners' cemetery in Rome under a matching gravestone of his own design.

Brown, by his own account, first met Keats in the late summer of 1817. Although the pair went on a bonding eight-week hiking holiday to Scotland in 1818, they were housemates at Wentworth Place for less than eighteen months. Since becoming a museum, Wentworth Place is the house with which Keats is most associated today. The flat above the Spanish Steps in Rome, where he died, and which is also now a museum, comes a close second. Keats himself was restless and rootless, never staying long at any address to the extent that it's a challenge to keep track of all the different places where he lived or stayed.

In his "Ode on a Grecian Urn," Keats refers to "slow time." Time certainly plays tricks when you're looking at his brief life. It balloons—both in terms of the documentation and in terms of his lasting achievements—in his so-called living year, 1819, during which he wrote most of his best poetry, including his now famous odes. There's much less known about his early childhood and he left little direct testimony about his experience during his final months, when he was too ill to write.

The epitaph Keats wrote for his own gravestone—"Here lies One Whose Name was writ in Water"—seemingly damned him to oblivion. And yet Keats also told his brother George, in a confident if throwaway aside on October 14, 1818, "I think I shall be among the English Poets after my death." The latter prophecy—fittingly for a poet who was so interested in the poets of the past, especially Shakespeare, and their continued reach into the present—has come to pass. There are Keats scholars alive today who have spent longer studying his works than his twenty-five-year life span.

The vast corpus of commentary Keats has inspired can seem intimidating for anyone trying to get close to him for the first time today. The first full *Life and Letters* of Keats was published in 1848, over a quarter of a century after he died, by the poet and politician Richard Monckton Milnes (Lord

Houghton). It put a significant part of the poet's private correspondence on record for the first time, though not all. Keats's letters to Fanny Brawne, the woman whom he loved, were not included, and Milnes omitted any reference to her name. He also toned down Keats's voice.

By the twentieth century, Keats's biography had become a genre in its own right as succeeding generations added to the sum of information and interpretation. Over the course of the last hundred years, more than twenty lives have been published, including landmark works such as *John Keats* by Amy Lowell (1924), *John Keats* by Robert Gittings (1968) and, most recently, Nicholas Roe's monumental *John Keats: A New Life* (2012). Their titles can be found in the bibliography. It's something of a relief that Roe concludes, in an essay titled "Undefinitive Keats," that coming to grips with the dead poet represents a "cumulative process of collaboration across the years in which fresh understandings will continue to provoke new questions."

Alongside the biographies are the myriad and ever-burgeoning critical studies now available. Essay topics plucked at random from the *Keats–Shelley Journal* range from "Keats's Post-Newtonian Poetics," to "The Etymology of Porphyro's Name in Keats's 'Eve of St. Agnes,'" to "Which Letters Did Keats Take to Rome?" You can add to that the vast number of book-length monographs on offer. Their titles range from the neutral (such as *Reading John Keats*) via the determinedly abstract (*Keats and Nature; Keats and Philosophy*) to the unabashedly physical, from *The Dying Keats: A Case for Euthanasia?* to *Keats, Modesty and Masturbation*.

Then there are the other books that include explorations of his life and works but don't have his name in the title, from *The Monstrous Debt: Modalities of Romantic Influence in*

Twentieth-Century Literature to the worrying-sounding *Weakness: A Literary and Philosophical History.* Added to that are the websites, blog posts and tweets that, since the internet revolution starting around 2000, have added a further layer to the public construction of "Keats," which continues to replicate through culture.

One of the most famous twentieth-century critical commentaries remains that by Christopher Ricks, *Keats and Embarrassment,* first published nearly fifty years ago, a brilliant book-length essay whose title alone is enough to trip you up. Taking in everything from the nineteenth-century physiological science of blushing to a rather tasteless practical joke played by Keats himself, it muses on the moral value of embarrassment—uncertainty, self-consciousness—as a human experience. Anyone who has even a glancing acquaintance with the scholarly literature will feel embarrassed at the prospect of daring to approach Keats directly, given the riches on offer by previous commentators, a literature so vast that it seems it could almost suffocate the poet even as it illuminates him.

As early as 1924 the Keats biographer Amy Lowell feared she was already telling a "tale twice told." But the fact remains that every new reader coming to his poems is coming to them afresh, perhaps with something like the sense of discovery that he himself experienced in his own reading of past poetry. John Keats's work has by now become a pillar of the canon across the English-speaking global scene, taught in schools or universities wherever "English Literature" is an established subject, from India to Australia, from the United States to China. And yet his writing still has the capacity to astonish with its individuality. Keats refused to bow to conventionalities in his lifetime. His voice, marginal and avant-garde in his own day, retains its vertiginous originality. Despite the fact that he has been posthumously accorded the role of poetic influencer and canonized as a dead white European male, he remains an eloquent outlier.

At the same time, his voice, which still speaks across the generations, was a product of its own historical moment and was, moreover, fed by the influence on him of other writers. To read him is to participate in an invisible web that has connected human beings over millennia via the literary imagination. Keats was inspired by earlier poets from Virgil to Shakespeare, and he himself went on to inspire creativity in others, from poets such as Oscar Wilde, Thomas Hardy and W. B. Yeats to the science fiction novelist Dan Simmons. For Keats, who came from outside the establishment, the idea of participating in a literary tradition seemed democratic and forward-looking, not conservative or hidebound.

Although Keats's short but intense existence is more richly documented than Shakespeare's longer life (the latter died at fifty-two and wrote his first play at around the age Keats died), gaps remain in the biographical record. Even the precise date of his birth in 1795 has been disputed. The painstaking work of editors and textual scholars over the years means that all his known writings, and the testimonies of his friends, are available in print. The best record of his experience as an individual is to be found in his extant letters, which cover the period of his greatest creativity. To redeploy his own self-description, they show him "young[,] writing at random—straining at particles of light in the midst of a great darkness," as he put it in the long letter to George and Georgiana in which, inter alia, he depicted himself writing with his back to the fire and wondering about Shakespeare.

In that carelessly punctuated phrase, Keats was describing

his own philosophical speculations, but his words could just as easily be applied to the letters themselves, which are among the best ever written in English, though they weren't written for publication. Certainly, among Romantic period letters, only Byron's come anywhere close. (It's a tragedy that so many of Jane Austen's were destroyed.) Byron, no doubt, had a more self-consciously tuned eye to posturing for posterity when he wrote them. An aristocratic megastar at the time, he mocked "Jack Keats or Ketch or whatever his names are" in his correspondence as a lower-class literary wannabe whose poetry was no more than "a sort of mental masturbation." Byron's manner was superciliously de haut en bas. Posterity has since leveled them up.

Even if he had never written a line of poetry, Keats's letters would make you gasp with their in-the-moment, sinewy, free-flowing stream of consciousness, which shows his elastic mind on the move, whether he's inventing new philosophical concepts such as "negative capability" or making crude jokes. (The coarse sexual references were excised in Richard Monckton Milnes's Victorian edition.) They promise, to quote Hamlet's advice to the players, "to give the very age and body of the time his form and pressure." One moment, we're in the midst of gossipy news about his friendship group, or the latest play he's seen, or his current-affairs take on Napoleon Bonaparte, or the contemporary financial crisis, or his chance meeting with the celebrated poet Samuel Taylor Coleridge on Hampstead Heath, or what he's been eating and drinking. The next, he's tumbling into poetry, sometimes into a masterpiece.

The earliest extant draft of Keats's iconic ballad "La Belle Dame sans Merci" pops up, for example, in the same long letter to George and Georgiana that was written in fits and starts between February 14 and May 3, 1819. He jots down the poem—which didn't make it into his last collection—just after he's described how he's enjoyed a trip to see the "Panorama," a popular visitor attraction in Leicester Square in which paying customers could see a Regency virtual-reality representation of the "north Pole—with the icebergs, the Mountains, the Bears the Walrus—the seals the Penguins—and a large whale floating back above water."

Though it was never intended to become a museum piece, the original of Keats's long letter to George and Georgiana is now preserved in state in the archive at Harvard University, its black ink on white paper faded to brown on sepia. Most readers will, however, have encountered it in the medium of print, perhaps in what remains the standard scholarly edition, edited by Hyder E. Rollins in two volumes, first published in the 1950s and bristling with explanatory footnotes. Keats's reference to "To be or not to be," when he wonders about Shakespeare's bodily position when he wrote it, is, for example, formally glossed "*Hamlet,* III.i.56."

My own copy of Rollins's edition of Keats's letters, a pair of faded blue-gray hardbacks that I sourced secondhand online for a song, is stamped "WITHDRAWN: MISSOURI BAPTIST COLLEGE LIBRARY . . . ST. LOUIS." Since Keats's death, "English Literature" as a cultural project has grown and, more recently, at least in the West, has begun to contract, though the latest academic literature reveals how many readers around the world are appreciating Keats today. On August 16, 2019, *The Guardian* reported that fewer and fewer British high-school students are opting for English A level, preferring STEM subjects over literature, as they "don't see the value" of a subject that has no obvious economic application in the jobs market. Keats's legal guardian Richard Abbey, who took over responsibility for him and his siblings after their parents and grandparents died, would have concurred. But Keats himself continued to cleave idealistically to poetry over economic prudence, even after his own "cash-recourses" had been "stopp'd." Two centuries to the day before that recent *Guardian* report, on August 16, 1819, Keats told Fanny Brawne that he "thought very little of these matters," although perhaps he should have.

Victorian grandees such as Keats's first biographer Richard Monckton Milnes turned English—which wasn't available as a university option in Keats's day—into an establishment discipline. The downside of that was that literature was pressed into the service of mainstream Victorian morality, as is only too visible in Milnes's editorial suppressions, which silence references in Keats's letters to sensitive subjects from sex, to drinking, to religion. The upside was that "English Literature" enshrined—albeit in denial of the fact that it was doing so on the back of a burgeoning capitalist Empire—the non-economic value of individual human creativity.

The material, economic underpinnings of Keats's own brief career aren't often at the forefront when we read his poems, but they were not always secure, although his grandfather made a good living running a livery stable in the City (perhaps comparable in today's terms to being a small-business owner with a successful garage and car dealership). Keats was not born poor, but his social status later became a topic of invective and subsequently of hot dispute, with the *London Magazine* in 1820 dismissing him as limited by his aspirational, lower-middle-class metropolitan milieu, his work fit to appeal to readers only "on Primrose Hill . . . or by the Paddington canal." To his late Victorian biographer Sidney Colvin, writing in the 1890s—by which time Keats was widely recognized as a genius—the poet's low birth seemed proof of the strange inscrutability of nature. Keats was certainly far down the social scale from the upper-class Shelley and aristocratic Byron. However, he was just as far from being an untutored peasant poet like his contemporary John Clare.

At fourteen, Keats was apprenticed to an apothecary and later studied at Guy's Hospital. It comes as a surprise to realize that he actually spent longer at his medical training than he did devoting himself to poetry full-time. Medicine represented a solid, if neither adventurous nor glamorous, middle-class career choice. Keats was subsequently able to give it up to devote himself to writing because he hoped to have just about enough money from his inheritance, without earning, to go traveling abroad for a couple of years and to give himself over to exploring his poetic ideas. They crowded into his brain to the extent that at times he thought they were "my only life," as he put it in September 1818. He did not expect to make his fortune from his pen, and often expressed scorn for the literary marketplace, although he was not at times averse to considering the demands of commercial taste.

Keats subsequently found himself strapped for cash, "possessed of much less than I thought," as he put it on April 13, 1819, realizing his funds might in a pinch make only a "moderate two years subsistence." The travel plans—a projected simulacrum of the Grand Tours made by his more entitled, better-heeled contemporaries—never made it to fruition. He did not travel beyond the British Isles until his final trip to Rome was ultimately necessitated by illness, at a time when the Mediterranean climate was considered potentially lifesaving for consumptives. By the time he got there, he was too ill to appreciate the Italy that featured so vividly in the English Romantic imagination.

Like Shakespeare's texts, Keats's letters and poetry exist

today, for most people, in the black-on-white of print held between book covers or, increasingly, on-screen. That disembodies them, unlike his original, now faded, manuscripts. Their pen-work betrays the touch of his hand, that almost seems to be referenced in what remains of one of his most startling poems, an eight-line fragment in iambic pentameters, probably written sometime in November or December 1819:

> This living hand, now warm and capable
> Of earnest grasping, would, if it were cold
> And in the icy silence of the tomb,
> So haunt thy days and chill thy dreaming nights
> That thou would wish thine own heart dry of blood
> So in my veins red life might stream again,
> And thou be conscience-calmed—see here it is—
> I hold it towards you.

Biographers formerly speculated that these lines were addressed to Fanny Brawne, whom Keats first met in 1818 and with whom he had fallen in love by 1819. But according to the current Penguin edition of his works, edited by John Barnard, they are now "generally supposed to be a fragment meant for later use in a play or poem," and they certainly have a Shakespearean feel. "Thou" was a half-archaic use of English in Keats's time for a metropolitan like him, though it continued in usage in provincial dialect and in self-conscious literary language. It's the old medieval singular, used in contrast to "you" which, on analogy with French, was originally the "*vous*" form, plural or polite. This is thus an intimate and yet at the same time stagey poem, never published in Keats's lifetime, though it's since been reproduced ad infinitum. Who is its projected reader? In 2022, that reader can only be us.

Unlike Shakespeare, Keats has a body, and not just a severed "living hand." Everyone who met him, even glancingly, seems to have paid testimony to his physical charisma, although he was only five foot tall and thus sometimes referred to by contemporaries as "little Keats." Edward Holmes, who was at school with him, recalled that, "from his extraordinary vivacity & personal beauty," Keats was someone who was obviously going to become "great"—though he remembers him as a physically demonstrative boy whose "*penchant* was for fighting" rather than for "literature." Leigh Hunt, the radical journalist who was one of his first mentors, described him thus:

> He was under the middle height; and his lower limbs were small in comparison with the upper, but neat and well-turned. His shoulders were very broad for his size: he had a face in which energy and sensibility were remarkably mixed up.

The imprint of Keats's actual face survives in the plaster cast made of it by the artist Benjamin Robert Haydon in December 1816, around the time that Keats was making his first steps into the wider world of Regency artistic bohemia and public recognition. Haydon—whom Keats hero-worshipped for a time—was a decade older and lived much longer, though his talent didn't live up to his ambitions and he finally slit his own throat in 1846 after a career of monumentally heroic failure. His life mask of Keats—along with a surviving profile drawing he made around the same time as a study for one of the faces in the crowd in his huge and otherwise wooden religious history painting, *Christ's Entry into Jerusalem*—remains, with Severn's deathbed image, one of the few contemporary portraits that speak as in-the-moment records of a real, visceral body.

Haydon's drawing, with its thrust-out chin, captures the sitter's pent-up energy. His three-dimensional cast shows Keats's wide mouth held uncomfortably closed and unnaturally rigid as he keeps his face as still as possible while it's being pasted with bandage strips soaked in wet plaster. Haydon was in the habit of making casts of famous, or (in Keats's case, then) potentially famous, faces. In 1815 he'd made one of the by-then-celebrated Wordsworth.

In his painfully self-aggrandizing yet addictively readable diaries, Haydon describes making a cast of someone's face as if he's acting a music-hall turn. He loves the fact that his sitter—in this case, Francis Jeffrey, the editor of the *Edinburgh Review*—seems to regard the process with anxiety levels more appropriate to a public beheading, as do Jeffrey's wife and friends, who are eagerly looking on. In fact, it takes only five minutes or so for the plaster bandages to harden. I know, as I had it done myself years ago by a friend when we were students. It feels a bit tickly and, as you can neither scratch your face nor move a muscle, it seems to go on for eons.

The cast of Keats's face, made by pouring plaster into the face-made mold, gives his every nook and cranny, arrested in unnatural stillness. In the early version, now in the National Portrait Gallery, you can see how the individuated hairs of the eyebrows and lashes clump. Later reproductions are all based on Haydon's skin-close original, but the version you can buy as a souvenir in Keats House today for £90 is smoother and more marbly.

As soon as Keats died, Joseph Severn called in someone to make a death mask, in which the departed poet's face looks a bit more bony. The eyelids—that were held in uncomfortable suspension in the life mask—sag. In his sonnet on sleep, probably written in late April 1819 but not published in his lifetime, an insomniac Keats begs the "soft embalmer of the still midnight" to shut his eyes with careful fingers. Body parts—whether eyelids or the cut-off head of the murdered Lorenzo that's buried in a pot plant and tended by his lover in *Isabella; or, The Pot of Basil*—feature frequently in Keats's poetry. Shortly after Keats died, Shelley transmogrified him into a disembodied Romantic saint in his poetic eulogy *Adonais*. But the Keats of the letters is a resolutely bodily presence, whether he's talking about roast beef or barmaids or primroses or claret, or perhaps, as he did on September 22, 1819, "a Nectarine—good god how fine—It went down soft pulpy, slushy, oozy—all its delicious embonpoint melted down my throat like a large beatified Strawberry."

The plum tree under which Keats wrote "Ode to a Nightingale" is long gone. The life span of plums is at the most around forty years, as I am only too well aware, following the sad demise of the one in my garden, which was already mature when I inherited it nearly twenty years ago. All my life, I have lived in Keats's stomping ground, on what has always been the less fashionable side of Hampstead Heath, a short walk across from Wentworth Place, now "Keats House." As a child in the 1970s I used to borrow books from the Keats Community Library next door, which was set up as a public amenity in the 1930s at the same time that Keats House was turned into a museum. Keats was the first poet I ever heard of. I knew where he had lived long before I was able to read his work.

When, as an adult, I moved into a house close to my childhood home, I continued to take the same familiar walks across the Heath. One sunny late-spring morning, when my daughter was a toddler, my husband and I took her over to Keats House in her stroller. I left them on the lawn outside while I went in search of coffees from a local café. When I came back, he was still sitting on the grass engrossed in his book, but she was wandering free-range with—to quote "Ode to a Nightingale"—a "purple-stainèd mouth." She had clearly been bursting joy's grape against her palate fine, as Keats put it in his "Ode on Melancholy." Terrified that she might have got hold of some poisonous berries from one of the bushes in the garden, I scooped her up and ran into the house, but was relieved to discover from the custodian that whatever she had ingested could have been nothing more toxic than mulberries.

Mulberry trees are much longer-living than plums and can easily take a century or even two in their stride. Some individuals are capable of legendary life spans. The mulberry tree whose fruit my daughter had gorged on—its ancient, stumpy, bifurcated trunk lolling exhaustedly on the grass, its dark bark knobbled and gnarled, yet still shooting leaves and making berries—is believed to have been there in Keats's day. Outliving him by two hundred years, it symbolizes a natural bond with the dead poet that two centuries of critical commentary can't compete with, on an emotional level, despite the intellectual riches they offer.

The idea of forbidden fruits—of luscious but dangerous eating—is a repeated image in Keats's poetry. In "La Belle Dame sans Merci" the knight is given "roots of relish sweet / And honey wild, and manna-dew" by a femme fatale who lures him to eternal exile on the "cold hill's side." In "The Eve of St. Agnes," it's a female character, Madeline, who's seduced by an intruder. His sexual predations are likewise depicted in terms of food imagery, when he sets out a feast

> Of candied apple, quince, and plum, and gourd,
> With jellies soother than the creamy curd,
> And lucent syrups, tinct with cinnamon.

And on it goes in increasingly exotic measure—manna and dates from Fez, "spicèd dainties" from "silken Samarkand" and "cedared Lebanon." These were places that Keats had never visited but that occupied the far-flung orientalist compartment of his imagination, symptomatic of his restless desire to overreach his physical limits as a body, that's also seen in his frequent relocations from house to house. (One contrasts the Brontë sisters with their lifelong attachment to Haworth Parsonage.)

Keats was as restless in his friendships, constantly refocusing from one intimacy to another, if his letters are anything to go by. One of the poems in his first collection (*Poems,* 1817) is, for example, addressed to a young man called George Felton Mathew, a keen amateur poet who was one of Keats's intimates for a while, though it seems they subsequently lost touch. Aged twenty-three, Keats considered in general (in a letter to his brother written on September 21, 1819) that "men who had been bosom friends, on being separated for any number of years, afterwards meet coldly, neither of them knowing why." Yet he might have felt differently had he lived into old age. For all we know, he might have reestablished contact with George Felton Mathew, who himself lived on until 1854, and a few years' noncommunication over the course of a long life might, in the end, have proved meaningless.

Those jellies soother than the creamy curd, to which Keats refers in "The Eve of St. Agnes," have always made me gag a bit. It's not just the creamy curd, but that neologism "soother"—half smoother, half soothing, yet ultimately not either, because Keats jerks you, with his linguistic creativity, into something unexpected, less easy to digest. Despite the glutinous sweetness, there's a tangy discomfort in the phrase. It's perhaps not surprising that one recent scholar, on investigating the early nineteenth-century pharmacopoeia, concludes that some of the ingredients mentioned in the poem were used at the time in what he robustly calls "cures for clap."

Ever since Keats's death, those left behind have been trying to make sense of the way in which he brings body and soul together. Soon after he was eulogized by Shelley as a spiritualized essence, his memory was attacked by the cynically materialistic *Literary Gazette,* which unfairly dismissed him as a "foolish young man" who had written some "indecent" poems merely to make money. By 1847, the Quaker writer William Howitt, in an attempt to promote Shelley's idealized vision, tied himself in knots. In trying to praise Keats for his spirituality in a popular book with the cozily Victorian title *Homes and Haunts of the Most Eminent British Poets,* Howitt alluded, in somewhat startling terminology, to Keats's "orgasm of . . . intellect."

Keats continues to confound, his writings simultaneously regarded as the peak of abstract poeticism and as the ultimate in language's capacity to represent material bodily experience. This book is an attempt to trace that fissure, while drawing out his human complexity as a living person. Few people's personalities have yet solidified into an inexorable form by the time they are twenty-five, the age at which he died. The Keats who remains for us, in sometimes intimate, sometimes distant historical fragments, is never a fixed entity. He's always in motion.

"On First Looking into Chapman's Homer"

Much have I traveled in the realms of gold,
    And many goodly states and kingdoms seen;
    Round many western islands have I been
Which bards in fealty to Apollo hold.
Oft of one wide expanse had I been told
    That deep-browed Homer ruled as his demesne;
    Yet did I never breathe its pure serene
Till I heard Chapman speak out loud and bold:
Then felt I like some watcher of the skies
    When a new planet swims into his ken;
Or like stout Cortez when with eagle eyes
    He stared at the Pacific—and all his men
Looked at each other with a wild surmise—
    Silent, upon a peak in Darien.

THE EARLIEST POEM Keats wrote that has since been routinely anthologized is his sonnet "On First Looking into

Chapman's Homer." Written in 1816, just as he was turning twenty-one, it was his breakthrough poem, the first to get him truly noticed, though it wasn't the very first he published (it was his second). The cumbersome title doesn't say that much to the reader coming to it for the first time today. But the contents do. It's a poem about the potentiality of reading to inspire creative thought.

In it, Keats describes the sensation of new horizons opening up that he experienced when he first encountered Homer's Greek epics in the translation made by Shakespeare's contemporary George Chapman, who, in the early seventeenth century, had been the first person to render the whole of the *Iliad* and the *Odyssey* into English verse. Keats depicts his mind unfolding into what becomes geographical and indeed astronomical space. The sheer expanses depicted—a far-off planet, the other side of the world—reflect the grand scope not just of Keats's imaginative response to reading but, implicitly, to his own self-propelled ambitions as a poet.

Even today, Keats's popular image tends to underplay the conscious drive and determination he brought to his writing. The schoolfellow who remembered his predilection for fisticuffs, and marked him out even then as destined for greatness, had no inkling that it would be in the sphere of literature. He thought Keats would find fame in the military. The idea of a sensitive poet leading the charge on the battlefield seems a contradiction in terms. But this fugitive memory gives an insight into the sheer vigor with which Keats, in fact, approached literary creativity.

Keats must have been born with a particular ear for, and propensity to delight in, language. Practically the only vignette we have of him at the pre-school stage—in fact, one of only two anecdotes—is from a childhood neighbor, a Mrs.

Grafty, who recalled how "when he could just speak, instead of answering questions put to him, he would always make a rhyme to the last word people said, and then laugh." As a child, he was probably picking up on the popular Regency parlor game bouts-rimés. He went on, as a poet, to develop that innate proclivity through determined, exhilarating practice.

The film *Bright Star* has Ben Whishaw's Keats mockingly dismiss the idea of mere "craft," instead promoting a Romantic myth of poetic inspiration without perspiration by rhapsodically telling Fanny Brawne that poetry should come as naturally as the leaves to a tree. That phrase is indeed the real John Keats, though it originates not in a conversation with his girlfriend but in a letter to his publisher John Taylor of February 27, 1818, in which he wrote, "If Poetry comes not as naturally as the Leaves to a tree it had better not come at all." What Keats meant, perhaps, was that the best lines were those that came to the mind unimpeded. By 1819, Keats was able to draft something as formally, imagistically and emotionally complex as "Ode to a Nightingale" in a couple of hours. The evidence shows that such free flow did not drop miraculously from heaven but came as the later upshot of prior, intensive application, fueled by reading.

"On First Looking into Chapman's Homer" was itself written at speed, but it was the result of much more backstage literary labor than one brief look at Chapman. As with "Ode to a Nightingale," it is also one of those poems whose actual moment of composition is recorded. We know when it was written, where it was written and even who its very first reader was—an uncanny thought, given that it's a poem about reading that has subsequently been read by millions, undoubtedly by more people than have ever read the book that inspired it, *The Whole Works of Homer, Prince of Poets, In his Iliads, and*

Odysses, Translated according to the Greeke By Geo: Chapman (1616).

Keats composed the sonnet in the early hours one morning in October 1816, almost certainly that of Saturday, October 26, according to the dating established by his most recent biographer Nicholas Roe. The address at which he wrote it was 8 Dean Street, Southwark, located in a densely built-up district on the south side of the Thames, which Keats had called a "jumbled heap / Of murky buildings" in an earlier sonnet. It was a far more urban neighborhood than Hampstead, the bucolic suburb with which he is most associated today. He had moved into rented rooms at Dean Street only the previous month with his two younger brothers, George and Tom, and their dog Wagtail. They chose the address because it was conveniently close to Guy's Hospital, where Keats was at that time studying medicine and working long hours as a junior doctor.

Keats had spent the previous evening a couple of miles away on the other side of the Thames at Warner Street in Clerkenwell. He'd gone over to see an old friend, Charles Cowden Clarke, who was living there with his sister and brother-in-law. House-sharing was as common then as it is now among young Londoners.

Clarke was the son of Keats's old headmaster and, as such, had known him for around a decade. He must have first caught a glimpse of the future poet as an eight-year-old boy in the playground soon after the latter started at Clarke's Academy. Eight years Keats's senior, Charles went on to teach in his father's school and became a mentor figure to the fledgling poet, sharing books, ideas and eventually literary contacts. With literary aspirations of his own, Clarke later pursued a minor career as an editor, writer and public speaker, whose published works included a popular volume on Shakespeare and the nineteenth-century sports classic *The Cricketers of My Time* (Keats himself was a cricket player and got a black eye during an amateur game in 1819). Having married the daughter of the successful music publisher Vincent Novello in 1828, he went on to have several children, move to Italy, and live into advanced old age, dying in 1877 at ninety. Keats, meanwhile, remains for us a young man caught in the fragile and jittery amber of the Romantic era.

On the evening of Friday, October 25, 1816, Keats and Clarke had supper together, drank wine and eagerly turned over the pages of a borrowed vintage edition of Chapman's Homer. Their interest in a two-hundred-year-old poetry book wasn't a sign of dusty academicism. Poetry itself was then at the height of its Romantic cultural capital, which had been growing since Wordsworth and Coleridge created a literary revolution by publishing their landmark *Lyrical Ballads* in 1798. By 1816, the poetry craze was everywhere, seen at all levels of cultural endeavor in British society: in the increasingly establishment figures of Wordsworth and Coleridge; in the cult of celebrity surrounding Byron; in the bestselling verse romances of Walter Scott; in the amateur albums kept by fashionable young ladies; in advertising copy; and, at a time of increasing government clampdown on free speech and democratic ideas, in the political counterculture.

The latter was embodied at that time in the flamboyant figure of Leigh Hunt, a high-profile public presence in the literary world, and a man with whom Charles Cowden Clarke was already personally acquainted. Hunt was the editor of *The Examiner,* and known both as a poet and for the radical politics he promoted in his paper. His fame (or notoriety) had soared in 1813, when he was jailed for two years for libeling the Prince Regent. The content of the libel—it featured the phrase "a fat Adonis of forty"—was less significant than the political motivation of the court. With the Napoleonic Wars not yet won, anything that smacked of republicanism or rebellion was ruthlessly stamped on. During his well-publicized incarceration, Hunt cocked a snook at authority, decking out his cell with trellis-patterned wallpaper, installing a piano, receiving celebrity visitors including Byron, taking deliveries of luxury foodstuffs from well-wishers—and continuing to edit *The Examiner.* A line from his 1816 poem "The Story of Rimini" sums up his attitude: "strike up a blithe defiance to mischance."

Keats, who had been reading *The Examiner* with Charles Cowden Clarke since his schooldays, regarded Hunt as "Libertas," a heroic martyr on the altar of free speech. In 1815, he had written a sonnet, as yet unpublished, celebrating the editor's release from prison. In May 1816, he had managed, presumably through Clarke's influence, to get another sonnet, on the topic of solitude, published in Hunt's paper: the first time Keats had seen his work in print. He had long been hoping to be introduced to the editor in person, but Clarke, perhaps aware that his charismatic protégé might outshine him, had dragged his feet.

On Saturday, October 19, 1816, the longed-for meeting with Libertas had finally occurred, when Clarke took Keats along to a party at Hunt's Hampstead home. It was a "red letter day" in Keats's life, Clarke recalled as an old man, by then not unpleased with his own go-between role in forwarding Keats's career. The ambitious Keats was under no illusion as to the networking significance of the moment: it was a chance to socialize at the heart of avant-garde literary London and perhaps to join it.

Keats was still in a buoyant mood the following weekend when he joined Clarke in Clerkenwell for their Chapman evening, on October 25. Far from being backward-looking, their retro interest in a seventeenth-century poet was a statement of radical modernity. Hunt himself was in the vanguard when it came to championing the writers of the past and disparaging the eighteenth-century giants who still represented the establishment, such as Alexander Pope, who, in Hunt's view, mistook "mere smoothness for harmony." Earlier English writers were admired for their freer, looser style of versification: Chaucer, Spenser, the republican hero Milton, and above all Shakespeare. It was an aesthetic preference with a political edge, a desire to return to mythic old English liberties by freeing the English language itself from conservative shackles.

Keats himself was drawn to Shakespeare, Spenser, Milton, Boccaccio and Chaucer, all of whom seemed to his mind to get closer to the complexities of the human condition than the polite writers of the eighteenth century. He also admired contemporaries, including Wordsworth and Coleridge, both of whom he later met, and Byron, to whom he wrote an early sonnet, although the latter privately went on to mock him. But the admiration Keats and Clarke felt for Chapman's grittily Shakespearean style was a conscious rebellion against the old guard, in the shape of Pope, whose elegantly poised verse translation of Homer still represented the gold standard.

After the Chapman sonnet was published, Keats was mocked by conservative critics for supposedly knowing Homer only from Chapman. It was true that Keats never learned ancient Greek. However, he himself makes it clear in the poem that this was not the first time he had traveled in Homer's "realms of gold." At a remove, he was already acquainted with Greek literature not just through the medium of Pope's English translation, but through the Latin authors whose work he had read in the original. What he was recording was not a first encounter, but a first meaningful encounter, via Chapman, which gave him a sudden, elated sensation of connecting with the oldest known poet in the canon and going beyond that abyss into uncharted futurity.

Clarke's memoirs pinpoint precisely one of the passages he and Keats read that evening, and compare it with Pope's version, just as they had done together. It's from Book Five of the *Odyssey*, depicting the moment when the shipwrecked Odysseus crawls up onto a beach, half-dead. In his memoirs, Clarke quotes the passage from Chapman, italicizing the line that really struck them:

> Then forth he came, his both knees falt'ring, both
> His strong hands hanging down, and all with froth
> His cheeks and nostrils flowing, voice and breath
> Spent to all use, and down he sank to death.
> *The sea had soak'd his heart through;* all his veins
> His toils had rack'd t' a laboring woman's pains.
> Dead-weary was he.

He then goes on to quote just two lines of Pope's version of this same passage to emphasize the contrast, italicizing, with added exclamation marks, the line that he and Keats had found most risible:

> From mouth and nose the briny torrent ran;
> *And lost in lassitude lay all the man* [!!!]

You can see how Chapman's passage showcases his verbal muscularity; his physical directness, in the visceral metaphor of the sea-soaked heart, which yokes the emotional and the bodily in one; and the way he nonchalantly allows the syntax to cross the line boundary as he plunges forward. In contrast, Pope provides impersonal itemization of mouth and nose, prissily static end-stopped lines, and that weirdly abstract and circumlocutory "lost in lassitude lay all the man," which isn't improved by the alliteration. In his own context, Pope was a genius as a cut-glass satirist, moralizer and inspired technician of the "heroic couplet" (indeed, it was Byron's admiration for Pope that was partly responsible for his dislike of Keats). Clarke and Keats seem to have alighted, not quite by chance, on his two worst lines.

The two young men talked long into the night, and then, in the early hours, Keats walked back to Southwark across London Bridge. Once home, still surging with energy, he didn't fall straight into bed, but sat up writing. When Clarke surfaced for breakfast in Clerkenwell around ten the following day, he opened a letter addressed to him in Keats's handwriting that had been delivered earlier that morning. (Messengers crisscrossed London at all hours, making communication on paper as randomly delivered as today's texting and almost as speedy.) Only it wasn't a letter. All it contained was the manuscript of "On First Looking into Chapman's Homer."

———

JOHN KEATS, who proved so hungry for language, had been born in London in 1795. The fact that the exact date of his birth was later disputed—and, in addition, that no one has ever established the precise address at which he was born— seems surprising, given how much we know about when and where many of his best poems were written. It reflects a level of anxiety, both his own and that of his memoirists, concerning his origins.

In an early memoir, Leigh Hunt claimed that Keats was born on October 29, 1796. But that was out by a year according to Charles Cowden Clarke, who dated the poet's birth to October 29, 1795, the date then enshrined in Richard Monckton Milnes's 1848 *Life and Letters.* Clarke was right about the year but perhaps not the day. Keats's baptismal record, in the register of St. Botolph's Church, Bishopsgate, where he was christened, gives it as October 31, 1795, the date subsequently accepted by modern biographers. Oddly, when Keats turned twenty-one in October 1816, he had no record of the fact that he had reached his majority and was therefore legally entitled to access his inheritance. He had to apply to a former servant for confirmation of his birth date so that he could provide legal proof that he had actually come of age. Clearly, he had kept few family papers.

Keats's letters offer a resounding silence on the topics of his background, his childhood experiences and his family. A fellow medical student who knew him well in 1816 recalled that Keats never said a word about his parents, and concluded, accurately, that he must have been an orphan. The loss of documentation reflects Keats's own history of loss: the fact that his early life had been marked by family breakdown and multiple bereavement.

Keats's class origins have been a matter of dispute, perhaps made harder to pinpoint because he lived at a time of unprecedented social mobility and flux. Leigh Hunt, a republican with egalitarian principles, said that Keats's background was of "the humblest description" but that he never spoke about it owing to his "personal soreness" on that score. In contrast, the eminently Victorian gentleman Richard Monckton Milnes was so keen to establish his subject's respectability that he described him as having been born into "the upper rank of the middle class." That version did little for the poet W. B. Yeats, who preferred the story of rags-to-poetic-riches. He famously called Keats "the coarse-bred son of a livery stable keeper" who was "shut out from all the luxury of the world" but nevertheless miraculously able to make "luxuriant song."

The truth about Keats's background was ambiguously in between, more nuanced, and certainly less impoverished, than Yeats's line implies. His father, Thomas Keats—or Keates— began as a lowly ostler, or stable-hand. But his mother, Frances, was better off and much more bourgeois. She was the daughter of John and Alice Jennings, who owned and ran the Swan and Hoop Livery Stables where her future husband Thomas was an employee.

Situated in Moorgate in the City of London, the Swan and Hoop was a well-run, prosperous concern, offering horses for hire at a time when that was the standard method of transport. The business left John and Alice Jennings wealthy enough to invest their hard-earned money in stocks and shares. The stables were arranged around a spacious yard, while the ground floor of the main building housed a taproom, which brought in added income. The Jenningses lived over the shop in comfortable, genteel surroundings.

Although the original building doesn't survive, there is still a pub, the Globe, on or near the site, housed in a Victorian building at what is now 83 Moorgate. Its website claims, somewhat Messianically, that the poet Keats "was born in a stable next door—quite the claim to fame!" That may not have been exactly what John Keats had in mind when, on May 10, 1817, as yet almost unknown, he mused, in a moment of idealistic

poetic ambition, "What a thing to be in the Mouth of Fame."
Then again, poetry and pubs were not mutually exclusive
Keatsian ideas. His "Lines on the Mermaid Tavern" celebrate
the drinking hole frequented by Shakespeare.

Unlike Jesus Christ, Keats was not born in a stable, though
it's possible that he was indeed born in his grandparents'
home at the Swan and Hoop. However, the first sure reference shows that by 1797, when he was two, his mother and
father were living close by, at 12 Craven Street. That we don't
know where Keats spent his infancy reflects the atmosphere of
secrecy that surrounded his parents' marriage.

All the signs suggest that the ambitious ostler Thomas
Keates eloped with his boss's rebellious daughter. Frances
was underage when, at nineteen, she married Thomas, then
twenty-one, without her parents' consent, on October 9, 1794.
No family member attended the wedding, which did not take
place locally, in the mercantile City where they lived, but at
St. George's, Hanover Square, in the more aspirational—and
anonymous—West End. It was the sort of place where louche
high society wed. The following month, the Earl of Morn-
ington married his illegitimate French actress mistress there.

However, John Jennings and his wife Alice accepted the
marriage after the event, as Thomas turned out to be reliable.
When they retired to the country in 1802, John was happy
for his son-in-law to take over the business, which thence
became the "Keates" livery stables. The fact that Thomas
renamed it after himself is indicative of his desire to make
his mark, a characteristic inherited by his eldest son. Only
then did Thomas and Frances move in above the livery stables with their young family: John (born 1795), George (born
1797), Tom (born 1799) and Fanny (born 1803). Another son,
Edward (born 1801), died in infancy, making Keats only just

seven years old when he had his first close-up experience of death.

In 1803, Keats was sent away, along with his younger brother George, to boarding school at Clarke's Academy, where Charles Cowden Clarke's father was headmaster. It was located twelve miles out of London in the then bucolic village of Enfield, now a dormitory suburb of London. At eight and six, the brothers were very young to be sent away from home, but their grandparents, John and Alice Jennings, could keep an eye on them as the couple had retired to the area.

Then, on Saturday, April 14, 1804, disaster struck when Keats's father Thomas was killed in a fall from his horse on his way home from visiting his young sons at the school. The circumstances of his death—he was found on the pavement at Bunhill Fields, close to the Swan and Hoop—have never perhaps been adequately explained. As a man who had worked with horses all his life, he would have been an expert rider.

The tragedy exposed what biographers have concluded were already underlying problems in the nuclear family. As soon as Keats's father is found dead, his mother, then twenty-nine, does not pull her children close but disappears, leaving the elder two at school and the younger two with their grandparents. Only in June does the recently widowed Frances resurface on the record, when she marries William Rawlings, a banker's clerk nine years her junior, again at St. George's, Hanover Square, and again without her parents' presence.

John and Alice Jennings clearly did not approve of this hasty new match, which promised to make the twenty-year-old Rawlings, who had no experience or expertise in the livery profession, the new manager of the Swan and Hoop. When John Jennings died in 1805, he was still unreconciled with his daughter, who went on to bring a legal action against his estate, complaining that she had inherited too little from it—one small strand in the convoluted wrangles over money that went on to form the backdrop to Keats's poetic career.

Frances's second marriage was not a success. She and Rawlings later parted and she appears to have taken up with another man. She ended up "without money" and "probably an alcoholic," in the words of Keats's most recent scholarly biographer. By December 1809, she was on her own and seriously ill with tuberculosis, the illness that later killed her famous son. She took refuge with her mother Alice Jennings, who was by then a widow. Keats, then fourteen, spent that Christmas holiday at his grandmother's; he was a daily witness to his mother Frances's sufferings, and did all he could to try to alleviate them.

Frances had abandoned her children at the moment of their father's death. They never lived with her and her new husband Rawlings as a family. But when she reappeared, gravely ill, it only made the fourteen-year-old Keats cleave to her more closely, as if her life depended on his care. He "sat up whole nights in a great chair, would suffer nobody to give her medicine but himself, or even cook her food." In her "intervals of ease," he read her novels. He may not have accepted that her illness was terminal, so shocked was he when he received the news of her death.

At the time his mother finally died in March 1810, Keats was back at boarding school for the term. Some bereaved fourteen-year-olds might clam up in the presence of their teachers and peers. Keats, however, could not contain his desire to demonstrate his devastation. Instead, he crawled under a desk and refused to come out. His complex attitude toward women, evinced in poems such as "The Eve of St.

Agnes" and "La Belle Dame sans Merci," was rooted in his fleeting relationship with his prodigal mother.

By the time he was in his fifteenth year, Keats had lost his infant brother, his father, his mother and his grandfather John Jennings. Those deaths would be followed by those of his grandmother Alice Jennings, who died in 1814 at the age of seventy-eight, and of his brother Tom, who succumbed to tuberculosis, like his mother, at the age of nineteen in 1818. His maternal uncle Midgley Jennings had also died from the same disease in 1808. As Keats put it to Fanny Brawne in 1819, "I have never known any unalloy'd Happiness for many days together: the death or sickness of someone has always spoilt my hours."

Keats was well aware of the effect on his own character of the traumas he experienced in early life. Throughout his brief existence, periods of energy and elation would counterpoint with phases of lassitude and despair, though he tried practical ways of countering depression. "Whenever I find myself growing vapourish," he wrote on September 17, 1819, "I rouse myself, wash and put on a clean shirt brush my hair and clothes, tie my shoe strings neatly and in fact adonize as I were going out—then all clean and comfortable I sit down to write. This I find the greatest relief."

It would be reductive to overexplain Keats's creative drive as a compensation for his childhood losses, but there's an element of truth in the idea. It's also true that he was able to make the most of what nurture was available. Until her death when he was nineteen, his grandmother Alice Jennings, with whom he stayed at the holidays, offered some familial warmth and stability. But it was Clarke's Academy that really held Keats together and enabled him to grow. Unlike his fellow Romantics Byron (Harrow) and Shelley (Eton), Keats did not attend an elite public school. He did not go to Oxford (where Shelley later studied prior to being expelled) or Cambridge (Byron's university). Yet he probably received a more inspiring and humane education at the lesser-known Enfield establishment, though he left it without studying Homer in the original Greek.

Under the inspirational headship of John Clarke, the school offered unparalleled opportunities for intellectual development in a contained and compassionate environment. It had been started by a Baptist as a dissenting academy, one of the numerous educational establishments founded in the eighteenth century to provide high-quality teaching for those outside the religious mainstream at a time when entry to Oxford or Cambridge required swearing an oath of allegiance to the established doctrine of the Church of England. Such schools remained what we might call "alternative," but many developed such scholastic reputations that they attracted a wider clientele than bona fide dissenters, including the Keatses.

Into the nineteenth century, nonconformist religion continued to go hand in hand with liberal politics of the sort Keats encountered at Clarke's Academy, where he first read *The Examiner.* A raison d'être of dissenting religion remained the right to question the status quo, even when it came to questioning the basis of religious belief itself. Keats was baptized an Anglican but grew up a freethinker. Conventional Christianity held no attraction for him, as evidenced in a reference to "the sermon's horrid sound" in his early sonnet "Written in Disgust of Vulgar Superstition." An atheist by early-nineteenth-century definitions of the term, he spent his brief career grappling with the problem of what it is to be human, in a mortal body, when there may be no magical promise of Christian resurrection. At the same time, he charted the value of the human need to aspire beyond the actual by exploring that hunger—imagination, creativity—as a spiritual and moral end in itself.

John Clarke was, in the view of his son Charles, a man with a liberal pedagogic vision far in advance of his time. At a period when corporal punishment was the norm, for example, he refused to use the birch and instead instituted a system whereby pupils' work and conduct were given positive or negative marks in a book. Those who accrued the best score at the end of term were given rewards.

Unlike the traditional narrow syllabus followed at the public schools, which focused almost solely on Latin and Greek, the curriculum was wide and flexible. Although there was no ancient Greek tuition, pupils were taught Latin and French and encouraged to open their minds by reading as broadly as possible. They were introduced, for example, to news of the latest scientific knowledge, such as William Herschel's discovery of the planet Uranus in 1781, alluded to in "On First Looking into Chapman's Homer." The school had its own telescope. Nicholas Roe describes how astronomy was imaginatively taught to young children, who were invited to mimic the solar system by standing in the playground in the position of the planets.

Clarke's Academy was, moreover, set in an idyllic spot. The handsome main building, erected in the seventeenth century, had a facade ornamented with flowers and fruits. Outside was not just an ample playground but a paddock and an orchard, where the boys were allowed to ramble at will. There were strawberry beds and a rustic seat under an arbor. Swans swam along the stream that bordered the grounds. Many of these images would recur in Keats's later poetry, as he sought to rework the poetic pastoral mode, that he encountered at school in Latin authors and later in Spenser, into something modern and personal.

In his early years at the school, Keats was not particularly academic. He was more pugilistic than intellectual, with his diminutive but broad-shouldered frame, but with a strong sense of natural justice. On one occasion, Clarke recalled, when one of the younger teachers boxed George Keats's ears, Keats flew at him in defense of his brother. (John Clarke's principled ban on corporal punishment was clearly not wholly successful.) On another occasion, George himself, who was taller though younger, had to help hold the excitable John down when he was, in Charles Cowden Clarke's phrase, "in one of his moods."

Yet Keats eventually began to channel his energies into his classwork, to a quite remarkable degree. The headmaster John Clarke gave prizes for evidence of extra, voluntary study. According to his son Charles, by the time Keats was thirteen the future poet was at work before 7 a.m., continued at it during playtime, and kept going after school hours, laboring away on some French or Latin translation long beyond the moment when others had given up.

If there was a prize, Keats won it. A silver medal awarded to him at school in 1810 is yet preserved. He even occupied his mealtimes in reading, if Charles Cowden Clarke is to be believed. Far from being a rebel or a dreamer, the young Keats became, at least in the atmosphere of the Academy, a compliant high-achiever.

At fourteen, he left school to be apprenticed to an apothecary, Thomas Hammond, the family doctor who had attended his own mother in her final illness. Hammond's home-cum-surgery, where Keats would lodge, was located not far from the school or from his grandmother's house in Edmonton, where the latter had moved after being widowed. Fourteen sounds young, but one has to remember that future naval officers of the period were often sent to sea as midshipmen at twelve. Medicine, not yet being a university subject, was taught by training on the job.

Without quite the academic or social kudos it has today, medicine was the lowest of the professions, in contrast to the church or the law, which attracted upper-class entrants. In Jane Austen's *Emma,* the local apothecary—what we'd now call a GP—is not considered the social equal of the landowner Mr. Knightley, or his younger brother, who is a barrister in London. Nevertheless, the apprenticeship represented the first step on a secure middle-class career ladder for John Keats.

There is no direct evidence as to how much say Keats had in the decision. But we do know how much care he showed toward the dying Frances. Hammond must have witnessed this, perhaps concluding that the adolescent Keats had an aptitude for healing. However, the formal decision to bind him over must have been made by his widowed grandmother Alice Jennings in consultation with the businessmen friends she had by now appointed as legal guardians for the Keats children, John Nowland Sandall and Richard Abbey. Given her years, she was thinking ahead to the children's future after her death. Keats's relations with Abbey, who was left sole guardian after Sandall died in 1816, would subsequently become fraught when he decided to give up medicine to pursue poetry full-time.

At Hammond's, the intellectually brilliant school performer Keats was set to dull, practical tasks, such as preparing pills. He later quarreled with his apprentice-master and left, though he then went on to Guy's Hospital to pursue medicine more intensively. While it lasted, his apprenticeship was made more bearable by the fact that he was able to keep up contact with Clarke's Academy, which wasn't far away, and especially with Charles Cowden Clarke, with whom he had begun exploring English poetry.

According to Charles, *The Faerie Queene,* by the Elizabethan poet Edmund Spenser, had Keats "ramping" through it "as a young horse would through a spring meadow." The conventions of pastoral poetry and the tamed ruralism of Enfield chimed. Keats meanwhile continued to work in his free time on his own translation of Virgil's epic the *Aeneid,* an ambition pursued for its own sake. Sadly, it doesn't survive, but it shows that Keats must have had some experiential insight when it came to assessing Chapman's art as a translator.

Clarke's contribution to Keats's poetic apprenticeship was more focused than mere enthusiasm. Long before English Literature became a formal academic subject, he encouraged Keats not just to appreciate but to analyze, as they sat together on the garden seat. It was under his influence that Keats wrote his first surviving poem, "Imitation of Spenser," in 1814. In a verse letter "To Charles Cowden Clarke"—composed in September 1816, not long before he wrote "On First Looking into Chapman's Homer"—Keats paid tribute to him as the mentor who "first taught" him the rudiments of English verse.

Written in rhyming couplets, and steeped in the literary pastoral mode, the piece is on one level a version of a traditional trope: the formal tribute to a patron. But it's detailed and personal, intimate and emotional:

> Ah! had I never seen,
> Or known your kindness, what might I have been?

Pastoral becomes a delightfully physical, not just a literary, posture when Keats depicts the glee he'll feel if Charles likes his "rhymings": "I shall roll on the grass with two-fold ease."

Keats acknowledges Clarke for having taught him the differences between the poetic genres, including the ode, the epic and (particularly relevant to "On First Looking into Chapman's Homer") the sonnet. Charles is thanked as the man

> Who read for me the sonnet swelling loudly
> Up to its climax and then dying proudly

—a reference to the formal divide between the first eight lines of a sonnet (the octave), which traditionally set out a proposition, and the last six (the sestet) which, equally traditionally, are supposed to respond and conclude.

Keats went on to describe his long-standing habit of confabulation with Clarke—which shows that the evening of October 25, 1816, was not an isolated occurrence. They were accustomed to have

> revelled in a chat that ceasèd not
> When at night-fall among your books we got:
> No, nor when supper came, nor after that—
> Nor when reluctantly I took my hat . . .

Those lines are good-humored and touching and confidently informal, rather than straining after "poetic" effect. Their mood itself shows the influence of Leigh Hunt, for whom informality, and domestic and sentimental tropes, were charged with antiestablishment undertones at a time when radical voices were being silenced in the public sphere. But, in sheer technical terms, the lines are nowhere near the flying level Keats achieved only a month or so later in the Chapman sonnet.

Although sincere in his gratitude to Charles Cowden Clarke, Keats may also have wanted to achieve a particular effect in addressing a poem to him: the introduction to Leigh Hunt which came soon after, on Saturday, October 19, and whose confidence-enhancing effects are felt in "On First Looking into Chapman's Homer." By then Keats had moved, to rework the metaphor of the sonnet itself, on to another planet.

———

THE SONNET FORM, which originated in medieval Italy, had been an established poetic mode in Europe since the Renaissance, the most famous English example being Shakespeare's set of 154 sonnets. Fourteen lines long, with five main beats to the line and a prescriptive rhyme scheme, it's a small-scale but technically demanding formula. Keats's preferred mode at this stage was the "Petrarchan" sonnet, named after the Italian Renaissance master, rather than the "Shakespearean" sonnet which, unlike the former, sums up at the end with a rhymed couplet. He later adopted the latter scheme in sonnets such as his Shakespearean meditation, "On Sitting Down to Read *King Lear* Once Again," with its brilliantly coagulated metaphor for the human as "impassioned clay."

"On First Looking into Chapman's Homer" was far from being the first sonnet Keats had attempted. By the time he published his first book, *Poems,* in March 1817, he had written and kept thirty, twenty-one of which made it into that volume. He may have attempted others that do not survive. Nor was "Chapman's Homer" the first of these to have been explicitly inspired by other poets. In 1814, for example, Keats had written a sonnet to Byron, who had shot to literary superstardom in 1812 with *Childe Harold's Pilgrimage*. It began:

> Byron! how sweetly sad thy melody!

In 1815, he had addressed another to Thomas Chatterton, the English outsider poet with a taste for medievalism who had killed himself in a garret in 1770 at the age of seventeen and thence went on to became an icon for the Romantics. It began:

> O Chatterton! how very sad thy fate!

These two examples of first lines strike because they are so fenced in by their exclamation marks that they are drained of the very emotion they purport to express. Both are uncomfortably end-stopped—the punctuation prevents the line from running over into the next. "On First Looking into Chapman's Homer" could have begun something like

> Chapman! how very great thy Homer's power!

In contrast, it shows Keats breathing freely, taking the risk of beginning with an extended metaphor, confidently inserting his own "I" into the first line, and achieving structural mastery in the space of two serpentine sentences.

Unlike his static paeans to Byron and Chatterton, this is sinewy and fluid like the letters, a record of an authentic personal response. He does not address Chapman from a respectful distance as a discrete and detached individual, but instead gets inside the poetic space of his Homer translation and feels it expand around him. It's also as if this sonnet is contained in a structure and a rhyme scheme that the poet no longer feels to be restrictive but regards as elastic, winged and capacious.

Such simultaneous flexibility and control allow the poem to open out into something more than personal. It becomes a repository of what the American critic Helen Vendler—whose inspired analysis of Keats's technical development of the sonnet form shows her brilliantly exploring its workings like some sibylline car mechanic—calls "potential sharing." This is a literary artifact about literary sharing in whose exhilaration we are all invited to participate. From the start, we want to know about these far-off countries and where the geographical metaphor is taking us. Keats confidently expects to carry us with him.

He begins as a tourist, looking around at the kingdoms of classical Greek mythology, although there's something more resonant and, in early-nineteenth-century terms, potentially radical, than that idea immediately suggests. It's a dig at class privilege. Keats wasn't well-heeled enough to make a real-life Grand Tour of Greece and the Levant, unlike the aristocratic Lord Byron, whose *Childe Harold's Pilgrimage* was inspired by his travels. Moreover, Keats, the armchair imagist, equates poetry with political power, five years before Shelley wrote his "A Defence of Poetry," in which he made his now famous claim that poets were the "unacknowledged legislators of the World":

> Much have I traveled in the realms of gold,
> And many goodly states and kingdoms seen;
> Round many western islands have I been
> Which bards in fealty to Apollo hold.

> Oft of one wide expanse had I been told
> That deep-browed Homer ruled as his demesne . . .

By interconnecting poetry and polity, Keats is asserting that literature's realm is no decorative aesthete's retreat but a place of power.

In the draft Keats sent to his friend Clarke, which the latter read at his breakfast table in Clerkenwell, the next line was an admission of insecurity:

> But could I never judge what men could mean
> Till I heard Chapman speak out loud and bold.

Yet in the version that was later published in 1817 in his first collection, *Poems,* Keats changed this to:

> Yet did I never breathe its pure serene
> Till I heard Chapman speak out loud and bold.

It's possible to work out exactly why he made this change, ditching his admission that he couldn't understand what men could mean to refer to breathing the "pure serene" of Homer via Chapman's words.

The first part of the sonnet employs quite highfalutin language until we get to the downright Anglo-Saxon monosyllables of "Till I heard Chapman speak out loud and bold": the archaic "goodly"; the Homeric epithet "deep-browed" for Homer himself; more archaism in "demesne" which, as the rhyme in both versions shows us, Keats must have pronounced "de-meen." (It's a version of "domain," a medieval legal term to do with land ownership, retaining the silent "s" from old French.) By substituting "Yet did I never breathe its pure serene" for "But could I never judge what men could mean," Keats was able to play up the contrast further by leaving the monosyllabic, Anglo-Saxon directness to the close of the octave.

"Serene" as a noun was a rare and highly literary word meaning a clear blue sky, its only other usage being as a specialized term employed by meteorologists. As John Kandl has argued recently, Keats may in fact have brazenly stolen it from Pope's Homer, which includes the line "When not a breath—disturbs the deep serene." In contrast to the detached, objective perspective in Pope's line, Keats boldly presents himself as physically breathing in the air in the first person. Playing on the fact that the word "inspiration" comes from the Latin for "breath," he's almost satirically repurposing Pope's precious vocabulary to assert how he, Keats, a medical student who has never learned Greek, is grasping—and literally gasping—the right to be poetically inspired.

The brusque "loud and bold" then pulls us up into the moment. It registers a shift away from high-flown literary language to what Keats sees as the greater authenticity and directness of Chapman's less polished voice. At the same time, it also registers a shift from the visual ("seen") to the auditory ("heard"). As such, it's a reflection of the fact that, in actual life, Keats and his friends were accustomed to take possession of other writers' poetry by reading it out loud to one another in their own voices, just as he and Clarke did when they read Chapman's Homer together in Warner Street.

In the sestet, rather than contemplating, debating or concluding the proposition of the quatrain, as would be the norm, Keats instead goes on to push the spatial metaphor further, alluding to new discoveries in astronomy, and then to the first sighting of the Pacific Ocean by the sixteenth-century European Hernán Cortés, about which he had read at school in William Robertson's *The History of America* (1777):

> Then felt I like some watcher of the skies
> When a new planet swims into his ken;
> Or like stout Cortez when with eagle eyes
> He stared at the Pacific—and all his men
> Looked at each other with a wild surmise—
> Silent, upon a peak in Darien.

Since Tennyson pickily pointed it out in the nineteenth century, it's been a crux of Keats criticism that it was not in fact Cortés, the conqueror of Mexico, but his contemporary, Balboa, who, in 1513, led the first party across Panama, where Darien is situated, to cast the first European eyes on the Pacific. Did Keats just make a mistake? Not really. It might even make sense that he refers to Cortés, the second European explorer to see the Pacific, not the first, since Chapman had offered his second view of Homer after Pope's version.

Indeed, even Keats's reference to "some watcher of the skies" is too generalized to refer specifically, as is often assumed, to the astronomer Herschel himself, who was the first to spot Uranus. It could be any "watcher" on the lookout for a newly discovered planet, even perhaps through the Clarke's Academy telescope (though the latter is unlikely to have been powerful enough). Literalistic nitpicking isn't the point. Democratic openness is.

Just as interesting is what Keats does here with the sonnet's iambic pentameters. He flexes the rhythm to represent a moment of astonished acceleration in the syncopated, hypermetric line "He stared at the Pacific—and all his men," which contains a break and a hurried beat too many. The final line, "Silent, upon a peak in Darien," has the right number of syllables, but works against the metrical rhythm as the English word "silent" is naturally emphasized on the first, not the second, syllable. The upshot is that the sonnet does not feel "finished." It is as if we're brought up short to contemplate an endlessly unfolding expanse that is continuing to unfurl beyond the poem's end. The original manuscript in Keats's handwriting that survives in the Harvard archive reveals a confident twirl on the "D" of Darien and stretches the word out as if beyond its natural limit.

Today's postcolonial consciousness alerts us to the fact that Cortés was a conqueror with blood on his hands. Would Keats have seen him like that? It's notable that this poem, about Chapman's imaginative colonization of Keats's poetic consciousness, offers an alternative to exploitative political power. The "states" and "kingdoms" he has explored are not those of historical Greece and Troy, but open states of mind. The "realms of gold" represent not rapacious plunder but the world of imaginative creativity itself, held in fealty to Apollo, the god of poetry and the sun—and, significantly, also of healing and medicine—whose light gilds what it touches. At the end of this sonnet, Keats offers a healing alternative to Cortés's history of despoliation in the image of the Pacific, literally pacifying or peaceful. This is an idealized, optimistic vision of poetry's dominion, pinning in words Keats's own reading moment of discovery.

———

DURING THE WEEK, Keats was still working all hours at the hospital. Only his weekends and some evenings were his own. The Saturday after he wrote the Chapman sonnet,

November 2, 1816, he went again to Hampstead to visit Leigh Hunt, who was by now dislodging Charles Cowden Clarke as a potential patron and mentor. Once in Hunt's circle, Keats would also meet other ambitious artistic aspirants, such as the painter Benjamin Robert Haydon, who went on to make Keats's life mask that December; the poet John Hamilton Reynolds (unread today), who became a close friend; and the now iconic Percy Bysshe Shelley. Keats held the latter—an upper-class anarchist, whose tall, etiolated frame contrasted with Keats's own compact, five-foot stature—at a nervous distance.

Keats, or Clarke, must have subsequently shown or given Hunt a manuscript of "Chapman's Homer," for the following Sunday morning *The Examiner* announced it was planning to publish "The SONNET ON CHAPMAN'S HOMER by J.K." This "noble sonnet," as Hunt later called it, had convinced the editor that here was a truly exciting new poetic voice. He went on to publish it in full in *The Examiner* on December 1 as part of an article on "Young Poets," in which he informed readers (in the editorial first-person plural) how recently seen manuscripts by Keats had "fairly surprised us with the truth of their ambition, and ardent grappling with Nature."

Emboldened by Hunt's enthusiastic notice, by December Keats had begun planning his first collection, *Poems,* which was finally published in March 1817. The contents included his verse letter to Charles Cowden Clarke and also "On First Looking into Chapman's Homer," which comes up as number eleven in a group of twenty-one sonnets, giving little sense that Keats himself regarded it as exceptional.

I'm sitting in the British Library with a book on the desk in front of me. It's a massy 1616 folio of Chapman's Homer.

The decorated title page is printed with an architectural doorway flanked by figures of Achilles and Hector and topped, on the pediment, with the gods Ares and Apollo. The grand design also features swagged fruits and leaves which remind me of the mini-swags on the rather more austere seventeenth-century frontage of Clarke's Academy, as it survives in a Victorian photograph taken before it was demolished in 1872.

A few minutes later, another, much smaller book is delivered to my desk: a first edition of Keats's *Poems* of 1817. It's a slim pocket volume, about as long and as wide as my (child-sized) hand. It weighs a lot less than the Chapman, though it's generously printed with wide margins, one sonnet to a page. The frontispiece is a profile head of Shakespeare, crowned with laurels and roses. The epigraph, a quotation from Spenser, offers what would have been read at the time as a Huntian political statement: "What more felicity can fall to creature, / Than to enjoy delight with liberty." Published by C. & J. Ollier of Welbeck Street, Cavendish Square, the book had a small initial print run and was not reissued in Keats's lifetime. As a result, not many copies have survived. I'm lucky that the British Library allows readers to handle this rare example. Today you can buy a seventeenth-century Chapman for around £5,000. But a first edition of Keats's *Poems* of 1817 is currently on sale at an antiquarian bookseller's in London for £47,000.

2

"A thing of beauty is a joy for ever"

A thing of beauty is a joy for ever:
Its loveliness increases; it will never
Pass into nothingness; but still will keep
A bower quiet for us, and a sleep
Full of sweet dreams, and health, and quiet breathing.
Therefore, on every morrow, are we wreathing
A flowery band to bind us to the earth,
Spite of despondence, of the inhuman dearth
Of noble natures, of the gloomy days,
Of all the unhealthy and o'er-darkened ways
Made for our searching: yes, in spite of all,
Some shape of beauty moves away the pall
From our dark spirits.

from *Endymion*

"A THING OF BEAUTY is a joy for ever" is perhaps Keats's most famous single line. Even people who never read poetry will recognize it. Julie Andrews as Mary Poppins utters it, spit-spot, when she removes a potted plant from her capacious carpetbag in the 1964 Disney film. I've lost count of the times I've walked past a poster outside Keats House printed with those words. They are also there on a website devoted to "Timeless Quotes by John Keats That Will Touch Your Heart."

During the course of the nineteenth century, as his posthumous reputation was established in the public mind, Keats became ever more defined as a disciple of pure beauty: apolitical, disembodied, almost the incarnation of the line itself. It was for this that art-for-art's-sake aesthetes of the fin de siècle, such as Oscar Wilde, came to worship him. Even by the time Charles Cowden Clarke first published his recollections in the Victorian era, this particular iambic pentameter, out of all those that Keats wrote, had already, as Clarke put it, "passed into a proverb."

The Victorian age also saw it passing into mythical anecdotage. Sir Benjamin Ward Richardson (1828–1896), a distinguished doctor, claimed to have heard about the very moment of its creation from his fellow physician Henry Stephens (1796–1864), who had known Keats as a medical student at Guy's:

> One evening, in the twilight . . . the two students sitting together, Stephens at his medical studies, Keats at his dreaming. Keats breaks out to Stephens that he has composed a new line:—
>
> A thing of beauty is a constant joy
>
> "What do you think of that, Stephens?" "It has the true ring but is wanting in some way," replies the latter, as he dips once more into his medical studies. An interval of silence, and again, the poet:—
>
> A thing of beauty is a joy for ever.

"What do you think of that, Stephens?" "That it will live for ever."

That was, however, a false memory. The legendary line was not in fact written in hugger-mugger student digs in London in 1816, but in solitude in a boardinghouse on the Isle of Wight in March 1817, where Keats had gone to find the mental space to dedicate himself uninterruptedly to a new poetic project.

In the spring of 1817, around the time he published his first collection of verse, Keats quit medicine to focus on poetry full-time. This was a momentous step for someone in his position. He was able to take it only because, having turned twenty-one the previous October, he was now in possession of enough of an inheritance to release him from being tied on to the conveyor belt of a professional career with a guaranteed future income. *Poems* was no money-spinner—it was said to have sold no more than "some dozens"—and there was no indication that Keats's next volume would make him rich. His career as a poet was thus made possible by unearned, if relatively modest, wealth. In that respect, he was socially identifying up, toward, say, Shelley, whose rebel career was predicated on his future inheritance as heir to his still living— and incandescent—baronet father.

Most of Keats's own circle was composed of young men with less inherited sense of entitlement than Shelley. Unlike the latter, they hadn't had the privilege of university, which was then reserved for an elite few. However, their early jobs were in what we would now regard as standard, middle-class graduate careers. Reynolds, for example, worked for the Amicable Insurance Company; after a brief interlude as a freelance writer, he gave it up to become articled to a solicitor and went on to pursue a bourgeois career in law. Another friend, James Rice, was also a lawyer.

After committing himself to full-time poetry, Keats considered going back to medicine on a couple of occasions, either by studying further at Edinburgh or by applying to be a ship's doctor on an East Indiaman. On July 6, 1819, he told his sister Fanny that he regarded his training as having provided him with a fallback or safety net that would always be there to "ensure me an employment & maintainance" if he really needed it. Because he died at twenty-five, we simply don't know how his life would have worked itself out: would he have gone on to yet greater literary achievements, or might he have put the Romantic craze for poetry behind him to embrace bourgeois security as a doctor?

His decision to give up medicine in 1817 seems inevitable in Sir Benjamin Ward Richardson's manufactured secondhand memory. But the real Keats was far from being a dreamer who failed to attend to his medical studies. The latest research has shown him to have been a conscientious, indeed a brilliant, student doctor, excelling at Guy's in the same way he had excelled at school. It's worth wondering whether his quarrel with his apprentice-master Hammond—which appears to have come to physical blows reminiscent of the schoolboy pugilist, since Keats later said he had raised his fist during the argument—might have been occasioned partly by frustration on Keats's part at not being given enough challenging work.

In the summer of 1816, after breaking with Hammond, Keats passed the notoriously hard apothecaries' exam the first time, unlike Henry Stephens. He was, as has been noted, at an advantage in the Latin paper—the language in which prescriptions were still written—on which many students fell down. Then, only six months after signing on at Guy's, Keats was promoted to the role of "dresser." That may sound rather lowly, but it involved much more than helping to dress superficial wounds. Indeed, this coveted position was more like that of a junior doctor today, though the different hospital departments were less separated. Keats not only assisted more experienced surgeons in complex operations, he also performed surgical procedures himself, as well as being on call, 24/7, in the equivalent of Accident and Emergency one week in four, dealing with urgent cases as they came in. Giving up a career in which he was already proving himself was no small thing.

But poetry was bigger. In the spring of 1817, he set himself a gargantuan poetic task which was, he told his brother George, to be "a test, a trial of my Powers of Imagination and chiefly of my invention which is a rare thing indeed—by which I must make 4000 Lines of one bare circumstance and fill them with Poetry." He would have, he said, "no right" to "being a Poet" until he finished it. He also set himself a deadline: to finish this magnum opus by the autumn.

"A thing of beauty is a joy for ever" is the opening clause of the result, *Endymion,* which Keats completed, just slightly over deadline, on November 28, 1817. Ironically enough, despite the first line's ubiquity, the work itself is one of Keats's least read poems, at least in its entirety. Weighing in at 4,050 lines, fifty over his projected goal, it is also his longest.

The epic length explains why it hasn't made it into the anthologies. But this "poetic romance," as Keats called it, is also difficult to digest, at turns astonishing and exasperating, though it's an important, experimental staging post in his poetic development. It's also significant because it was the work which provoked the notorious critical attacks that were later said to have killed Keats by sapping his confidence and undermining his health. As Byron put it in *Don Juan*:

> John Keats, who was killed off by one critique,
> Just as he really promised something great,
> If not intelligible, without Greek
> Contrived to talk about the gods of late,
> Much as they might have been supposed to speak.
> Poor fellow! His was an untoward fate:—
> 'Tis strange the mind, that very fiery particle,
> Should let itself be snuffed out by an Article.

The "one bare circumstance" on which the poem's story is based is the Greek myth of Endymion, a young shepherd-prince who falls in love with the Moon goddess in a dream. Keats probably took the idea from the brief entry in Lemprière's classical dictionary, with which he had been familiar since school. A bald summary of the overarching story, however, gives little flavor of the poem's omnium-gatherum scope or its fertile instability of tone. The narrative is hard to grasp on a first—or indeed on any—reading, interrupted as it is by personal contemplations, intricate side plots, a visit to the Underworld and even a political tirade against the English establishment. Indeed, the whole work seems made up of digressions. It takes four "books" of rhyming couplets before the mortal hero and his immortal beloved finally get together "in a blissful swoon."

The opening line itself is something of a conundrum. Although it's made it into nearly every book of quotations, it has always left me with an obscure sense of deflation. What is this nondescript thing of beauty, which is referenced only by the indefinite article "a"? The line sets out a proposition, expecting us to accept it as an obvious a priori given. But, in its abstraction, it doesn't seem to grapple with the sweeping generalization it appears to assert.

In his lodgings on the Isle of Wight, where he had gone to start writing the poem, Keats found on the wall in the hall a print of Shakespeare, which he moved into his own bedroom, a talisman, "ominous of good," which made him "fancy" that the bard was watching over him as a tutelary "Presider" as he set himself to work. But *Endymion*'s first line is so abstract that it almost perversely fails to do what Shakespeare, in *A Midsummer Night's Dream,* defined as the poet's imaginative task: "to give to airy nothing / A local habitation and a name."

Compared to the concrete images in "On First Looking into Chapman's Homer," this feels bleached out, flat, emotionally disconnected. Later on in *Endymion,* Keats's language becomes much more gritty, physiological and Chapman-like: "nervy knees"; "men-slugs"; "naked brain" (it's a jolt to remember that Keats had actually seen a naked brain in the anatomy room). Odd archaisms abound, such as "drave" for "drove." So do neologisms, including "serpentry," "fenny" (marshy, like the Norfolk Fens), the excruciatingly excessive compound adverb "tremulous-dazzlingly" and the strange noun "taperness" to refer to the taper-shape of a finger in "Fold / A rose leaf round thy finger's taperness."

Here too we find Keats's first use of the voluptuously hyphenated food image "manna-dew" that would later appear in "La Belle Dame sans Merci." Although *Endymion*'s first line is abstract almost to the point of nullity, the narrative later erupts into a physicality that, particularly in the erotic passages, went on to prompt one unsympathetic contemporary reviewer, in the *British Critic,* to call it "gross" and complain about Keats's "foul language." A phrase such as "slippery blisses" to depict a woman's lips makes you realize what the critic might have been alluding to. There's a suggestion of saliva here, an awareness of bodies and their fluids that can perhaps be traced to Keats's medical background.

Many of Keats's stylistic oddities—which seem so idiosyncratic out of context—can in fact be traced to the influence of Leigh Hunt and the new "school" of poetry he had attempted to launch in his article on Young Poets that featured the Chapman sonnet. Hunt's own poetry also features nouns newly turned into adjectives ("farmy fields," and indeed "pillowy fields," to describe Hampstead Heath; "piny" to describe a forest; "scattery light"; "pranksome"; "lightsome"), as well as compound words, as in "passion-plighted spots." To make free with the English language reflected Hunt's belief in political, and indeed sexual, freedom. "The Story of Rimini" had revolted conservatives with its sympathetic treatment of Dante's adulterers Paolo and Francesca. Keats's erotic euphemisms seem coy to us, but in 1816 their perceived affectation was edgier and viewed by readers as markers of Huntian license.

The first line of *Endymion,* while stylistically comparatively flat, revolves around two key Huntian concepts, beauty and joy. Poetry was, for Hunt, "the utterance of a passion for truth, beauty and power," but its ends were "pleasure . . . the keeping alive among us the enjoyment of the external and the spiritual world." "I do not write for the sake of a moral . . . I write to enjoy myself," he trumpeted.

Hunt's epicurean aesthetic identified beauty with "delight" and often appears to the more skeptical reader to have been based on a breathtaking capacity for denial. In "The Story of

Rimini," for example, Hunt blithely announces that poetry ("song") has magically transformed the bitter "sorrow" of Paolo and Francesca (they, of course, die and go to hell) into "balmy fruitage" and eternal sweetness:

> The woe was earthly, fugitive, is past;
> The song that sweetens it, may always last.

"Happy Poetry Preferred" was the somewhat self-parodic-sounding heading used in Hunt's *Examiner* review of Keats's *Poems* of 1817. It singled out for quotation a passage from Keats's poem "Sleep and Poetry" in which Keats asserts that the "great end / Of poesy" is to "be a friend / To soothe the cares of man."

The opening passage of *Endymion,* following on from the famous first line, has many Huntian features, but quite how soothing it is remains uncertain:

> A thing of beauty is a joy for ever:
> Its loveliness increases; it will never
> Pass into nothingness; but still will keep
> A bower quiet for us, and a sleep
> Full of sweet dreams, and health, and quiet breathing.
> Therefore, on every morrow, are we wreathing
> A flowery band to bind us to the earth,
> Spite of despondence, of the inhuman dearth
> Of noble natures, of the gloomy days,
> Of all the unhealthy and o'er-darkened ways
> Made for our searching: yes, in spite of all,
> Some shape of beauty moves away the pall
> From our dark spirits.

"Loveliness," for example, recalls Hunt's penchant for the word "lovely," which is repeated a dozen times in "The Story of Rimini." The idea of the "bower"—like the one Hunt re-created in his prison cell with its trellised wallpaper and pot plants—is pure Hunt. So is the "feminine"—or two-syllable—rhyme of "breathing / wreathing." Despite this, there are many other features in *Endymion*'s opening which suggest that Keats was already straining against his mentor's threadbare pleasure principle.

The Keats scholar Walter Jackson Bate once wrote, without further explanation, that the meaning of *Endymion*'s opening lines is "transparent." It's not to me. The opening seems to offer a proposition in logic that leads inexorably to the "Therefore . . . ," which opens the second sentence, in line six. Yet what we are offered as a "therefore" doesn't seem to follow on.

If a thing of beauty is a joy for ever—something in which we can have confidence because it is unchanging, abstract and eternal—why should we be weaving a flowery band to bind us to the earth, where flowers die? And what does it mean to do so "on every morrow," when we all know that tomorrow never comes? This is indeed a conceptual bandage, one that exposes the denial at the heart of the Huntian philosophy of "delight" even as it channels it. It's worth remembering that Keats had hands-on experience of applying ligatures around actual wounds, with only limited hope, in the days before antibiotics, that sepsis, and consequent death, would not occur.

When Keats conjures an escapist Huntian bower of beauty "Full of sweet dreams, and health, and quiet breathing," all I can think of is the fact that Keats had intimate knowledge of disturbed sleep, ill health and labored breathing, having tended his mother when she was dying from tuberculosis. By the time he wrote this, his brother Tom may already have been showing telltale symptoms of the same disease, which would go on to kill him too before it killed Keats himself. Moreover, during the period that Keats was working at Guy's Hospital, *The London Medical Repository* recorded that the most common ailments in the capital included pulmonary conditions such as asthma, pneumonia and whooping cough.

Keats later wrote that "axioms in philosophy are not axioms until they are proved upon our pulses." Physical suffering was, for him, no poetic trope but something that he—who had literally taken patients' pulses—had witnessed hands-on. He wanted art to be a "balm." But how—or if—it could make sense of the "fever, and the fret" with which humans have to contend was his perennial question. Was art escapist denial or needful catharsis? Did it gesture toward something beyond, or was it all a dream? Should it incorporate ugliness, sorrow and pain, or tune them out?

Keats spent his poetic career worrying away at the challenge of how art should respond to the sordid, quotidian reality of individual human suffering, and whether it could assuage it. The opening lines of *Endymion* are so much knottier than Hunt's easygoing couplets because they are shot through with doubt. The famous first line alludes to "joy." On November 22, 1817, six days before he wrote the last line, Keats confessed to his friend Benjamin Bailey, "I scarcely remember counting upon any Happiness."

In the same letter, he also admitted, "I have never yet been able to perceive how anything can be known for truth by consequitive [*sic*] reasoning." This makes the seemingly consequential "Therefore" which starts *Endymion*'s second sentence look glib. A month later, on December 22, 1817, Keats first came up with his now famous concept of "negative capability" in a letter to his brothers: the state in which "a man is capable of being in uncertainties, Mysteries, doubts, without any irritable reaching after fact & reason." Such ability to sustain doubt and ambiguity was in fact already there in embryo in the opening of *Endymion*. The lines aren't as transparent as Walter Jackson Bate asserted in the twentieth century, nor are they incomprehensible, as the *Quarterly Review* would soon opine in Keats's own lifetime. They show Keats grappling— and possibly half-consciously satirizing Hunt's glibness.

Endymion's overarching theme of a mortal aspiring to unite with a divinity looks like a metaphor for the actual hungering after the ideal, a typically Romantic topos, already treated by Shelley in *Alastor* (1816). Keats was fascinated by the problem of the relationship between the real and the ideal, physical actuality and the world of the imagination. But he came to believe that creativity was less about seeking an answer than about being open to questions.

Some critics have tried to read a clear-cut, preplanned Neoplatonic allegory into *Endymion,* but the truth is that its trajectory is all over the place—as indeed was Keats himself when he wrote it. Having already lived at so many addresses— Craven Street, the Swan and Hoop, Clarke's Academy, his grandmother's homes at Ponders End and then Edmonton, Hammond's surgery, Dean Street—in March 1817 he had moved yet again, with his brothers, this time to Well Walk in Hampstead, not far from Leigh Hunt's place. Within a month, he was off again to the Isle of Wight to begin *Endymion.*

The seven or eight months he spent working on his magnum opus would see him zigzagging across the country, unable to settle: from the Isle of Wight to Margate, which was a hundred and fifty miles away on the east coast, where he still couldn't settle, visiting several other places in the locale including Canterbury, Hastings and Bo-Peep (now St. Leonards-on-Sea). Then back to Hampstead. Then to Oxford, where he stayed with a new friend, Benjamin Bailey, who was a student at Magdalen Hall reading for the Church and hoping to secure an entry-level job in the Anglican hierarchy as a curate. Then back to Hampstead again, and finally on to Burford Bridge near Dorking in Surrey, where he completed Book Four on November 28, before returning once again to Well Walk.

His geographical restlessness was matched by his changeable moods. He had succeeded in overcoming his nerves at Guy's when performing surgical procedures. But he felt overwhelmingly nervous—blocked and panicky—when it came to beginning his poetic test piece. Having always lived with others, it was a jolt to find himself alone for the first time in an Isle of Wight boardinghouse. With no immediate outside pressure to make him focus, he felt not "over capable" in his "upper Stories" and was neither eating nor sleeping properly. He overcame his block by setting himself a smaller task—writing a sonnet to the sea—but he managed less than ten days in the boardinghouse before moving on to Margate, where Tom joined him.

Two days after arriving in Margate, he told Leigh Hunt he had got over being "down in the Mouth," but had been questioning his new, self-chosen identity as a full-time poet. "I have asked myself so often why I should be a Poet more than other Men,—seeing how great a thing it is,—how great things are to be gained by it," he confessed, acknowledging his desire for literary "Fame." His aggrandizement of poetry as a vocation was very much defined by the unusual cultural capital attached to it in the Romantic era in which he lived. Yet his own ambition was unique and made him feel overwhelmed at times: "the Cliff of Poesy towers above me."

By now, his mood was swinging to one of omnipotent elation. The self-imposed poetic "test" seemed to be a David and Goliath contest that Keats was easily winning. When Tom read out loud to him from Pope's Homer, the lines "seem[ed] like Mice to mine." The mood swings would, however, continue throughout the composition of *Endymion,* leading Keats to feel that his "horrid Morbidity of Temperament" was his "greatest Enemy and stumbling block."

Keats's labile state seems written into *Endymion*'s unstable, nervy landscape in which the real and the ideal abrade. Although the scenario is set up as that of mythic Greece, where nymphs waft through literary-fantastical groves, Keats splices his pastoral scenes with actual depictions of the real countryside he has encountered, from the Isle of Wight to Surrey's Box Hill. Greek divinities rub shoulders with a Miltonic reference to the biblical "Lucifer." Toward the end, an "Indian maid" appears, an orientalist fantasy out of Thomas Moore's bestselling 1817 literary fantasia, *Lalla Rookh.*

The tone is equally unstable. One minute, the Moon goddess is depicted like a flighty Regency flirt in rouge, teasing Endymion with "lips and eyes, / blush-tinted cheeks, half-smiles and faintest sighs," her "scarf . . . fluttering." The next, we are deep in epic tragedy:

> But this is human life: the war, the deeds,
> The disappointment, the anxiety,

Imagination's struggles, far and nigh,
All human.

On a wider cultural level, this instability of tone reflects the uncertain tenor of the times. During the Regency period, questions of taste and cultural authority were as much in flux as were politics and society as a whole. The tonal instability also reflects Keats's own insecure place in the world, now that he had jettisoned the safe option of a medical career for the as-yet-undefined "great thing" of poetry. Yet carefully calibrated storytelling, or overarching allegory, wasn't Keats's first aim. The "test" he set himself was more one of stamina and quantity than of artistic wholeness. On his own terms, he passed it, as he had always passed exams.

He explained to his brother that he hoped readers would view *Endymion* as a sort of literary potpourri in which they could wander at random, picking up whatever images attracted them. In August 1820, he told Shelley that his mind was like a "pack of scattered cards" when he was writing it—a gaming image that conjures up the gamble he was taking. (As middle-class trippers playing at being high-society Regency bucks, George and Tom Keats lost money playing rouge et noir in a Paris casino on a jaunt in September 1817.) Would readers fall in love with the poem as the Moon goddess does with its hero? Or would Keats end up like Chatterton, to whose memory he eventually decided to dedicate it, who had chosen suicide once his poetic ambitions had come to naught?

By now, however, Keats had what turned out to be a new source of stability in his life in the shape of a new publisher, Taylor & Hessey. Its editorial director, John Taylor, who was in his mid-thirties, showed a commitment to and a concern for Keats and his work beyond the short term. So did Taylor's friend and adviser Richard Woodhouse, a literary-minded lawyer. Both men firmly believed in Keats's genius, and that his poetry would last.

For Taylor & Hessey, it wasn't a problem from a publishing perspective that Keats had chosen, for his second book, to write a 4,000-line poetic romance. Narrative verse had been commercial since Walter Scott's bestselling *The Lady of the Lake* in 1810. But the point is that Taylor & Hessey did not need Keats to be commercial. Their list included a raft of popular tracts that provided a steady income stream. As a result, they were able to take a risk with a new poet and support his artistic development, regardless of his earning potential.

After Taylor received the manuscript of *Endymion* from Keats, he was, he confessed to his brother, slightly disappointed that the finished work did not please him as much as he had hoped. However, he never wavered in his support. The surviving fair copy, made in early 1818 for the printer, shows Taylor's detailed corrections and also, importantly, Keats's own attention to detail when it came to the minutiae of punctuation and wording. However, Taylor was clearly concerned about how to present his new poet to the public, including to the critics. When Keats penned a preface, Taylor made him rewrite it.

This canceled, first-draft preface shows Keats—who had once declared that his own lines made mice of Pope's—wearing his insecurities on his sleeve, putting on a pose that Taylor feared sounded "affected" in its Huntian informality of style. Looking back at how nervous he was on the Isle of Wight, before flexing his muscles to begin *Endymion,* we can see that Keats was patently sincere in overtly admitting in the canceled preface that before he began *Endymion* he had "no inward feel of being able to finish" and that he regarded it as "an endeavor" rather than "a thing accomplish'd." But he wrapped the admission in a swaggeringly arch, meta-register: "A preface however should be down in so many words; and such a one that, by an eye glance over the type, the Reader may catch an idea of an Author's modesty, and non opinion of himself."

He went on to say, with pseudo-Byronic nonchalance, that he should perhaps have kept *Endymion* back for a year or two, knowing it to be faulty. His poet friend Reynolds worried that such supposed protestations of humility would backfire. In his reply, Keats himself admitted that his words contained an "undersong of disrespect to the Public" by suggesting he was averse to going the extra mile for the sake of pleasing readers.

Keats's style in the canceled preface was breezily collo-quial, the tone bullishly underdog and aggressive-defensive. He joked, for example, that he would erect an umbrella to protect himself from a "London drizzle or a scotch Mist"—a reference to the critical cold shower he might potentially receive from the *Quarterly Review* in London or from either the *Edinburgh Review* or *Blackwood's Edinburgh Magazine*. The rewritten preface, the one that was printed in *Endymion* when it was published as a book in April 1818, was shorter and less pugilistic. But its quieter expressions of modesty did nothing to shield Keats from the critical obloquy of either the *Quarterly* or *Blackwood's*.

Periodical culture in 1818 was a seething piranha pool in which poetry and politics were joined at the hip. Keats's joke about being rained on by the critics shows how aware he was that he was releasing *Endymion* into a hostile microclimate, but he may not have anticipated quite how hostile it was, as he also announced, in the draft preface, that he hoped to begin a "conversation" with his critics.

Since October 1817, the Tory-supporting *Blackwood's Magazine* had been running a campaign against the liberal Leigh Hunt and his new "school" of poetry, which he had launched with his article on Young Poets featuring Keats's Chapman sonnet in 1816. The anonymous *Blackwood's* author, who signed himself "Z," satirically christened it the "Cockney school," and fingered Hunt as a man of "extravagant pretensions" and "exquisitely bad taste." We now regard Keats as identified with the elevated concepts of "beauty and truth," but in his lifetime, Cockney poetry was attacked as ersatz, the equivalent of sporting an artificial flower in a buttonhole. (It must be admitted that Hunt's more sentimental poetry is not wholly devoid of kitsch.)

"Cockney" had originated in the Middle Ages as a term meaning an effete city-dweller. By the beginning of the twentieth century, it came to be used in a much more limited, and distinctly less precious, sense to refer to gritty working-class Londoners born within the sound of Bow bells—the church bells of St. Mary-le-Bow in Cheapside. Following the Second World War, many identifying as cockney in that sense moved out of London proper to Essex. Their cockney accent has since become increasingly diluted into so-called Estuary English.

In Keats's era, however, the individuals targeted as "Cockney" by *Blackwood's* were hardly working-class. They weren't street traders with fruit stalls, or stevedores on the docks. *Blackwood's* used "Cockney" as a pejorative and politically motivated term, suggesting upstart, urban, undereducated, pseudy—and politically liberal—vulgarity. The upper classes, though they might spend the "season" in London, owned country houses as their main residences. Those, like Keats or Leigh Hunt, whose sole residence was in London rentals occupied a socially ambiguous space, but they were middle-class. One ought to remember that Hunt's father was a lawyer and that Keats supported his poetic career on a small trust fund. Yet, interestingly enough, Keats himself would in fact have qualified as a traditional cockney under the Bow bells stipulation if he was born at the Swan and Hoop, since it's less than half a mile from Cheapside, as indeed was Craven Street, the other possible site of his birth.

Blackwood's noticed and targeted Keats as a scion of "the Cockney school of versification, morality and politics" because he was known as Hunt's protégé. This was ironic, as by the time *Endymion* was published, Keats had in fact begun to disengage from Hunt, with whom he had become increasingly disillusioned. Although he'd shown him the first book in draft for comment, Keats felt betrayed when he found out that Hunt had been mocking him to Reynolds behind his back, saying that the 4,000-line poem would have ended up at a swollen 7,000 had it not been for his, Hunt's, intervention. However, Keats was uncomfortable because he knew that he had, in his own exasperated words, "the Reputation of Hunt's elevé [*sic*]."

It took until August for *Blackwood's* to land its punch. When it did, it was below the belt. The review was published under the pseudonymous initial "Z," like the previous attacks in *Blackwood's* on Hunt and the so-called Cockney school. Considering not only *Endymion,* but Keats's earlier 1817 volume of *Poems,* Z attacked his "loose, nerveless versification"; called *Endymion* a farrago of "imperturbable drivelling idiocy"; and concluded that the author, whom it patronizingly called Johnny, must be not just an uneducated ignoramus, who knew Homer only from Chapman, but a leering lech whose affections were "not confined to objects purely ethereal," given his penchant for "amorous scenes."

More to the point, it targeted Keats as a political subversive who had learned to "lisp sedition" at Hunt's knee. Quoting Keats's sonnet celebrating Hunt's release from prison, which had been printed in *Poems,* Z reminded readers, in a moment of manufactured solemnity, that "the cause of Hunt's confinement was a series of libels against his sovereign." However, Z also—and this was potentially more wounding—got personal. He regaled his readers with some choice gossipy facts about "Mr. John Keats" that were designed to skewer him on class grounds as a pretentious wannabe.

The article had begun by lamenting that, due to the current craze for it, poetry had ceased to be an elite form. There might be the odd talented outsider, such as the peasant Robert Burns, or Joanna Baillie, who was (heaven forefend) a woman. But the success of these lone individuals of genius had turned the heads of a generation, including farm servants and governesses, to aspire beyond their ability and status. So advanced was the infection rate from this new epidemic of "metromania" that "our very footmen compose tragedies."

Shaking his head with mock concern, Z embarked on an extended medical metaphor to describe the poetic "malady," from which the author under review was said to be suffering in a particularly virulent form ("the symptoms are terrible"). He went on to reveal some choice personal information: that Keats was a "young man" who, "we understand, . . . was bound apprentice some years ago to a worthy apothecary in town." If only, Z lamented, this latest upstart poet had stuck to his proper place in society, he might have used his abilities more wisely and proved a respectable citizen. Rather than entering into the conversation Keats had hoped to start, the article set out to humiliate him in the most ad hominem way possible. "[S]o back to the shop Mr. John, back to 'plasters, pills, and ointment boxes &c,'" it ended.

Blackwood's was Tory, but to regard it as a representative of the fuddy-duddy elderly establishment would be wrong. Founded only the previous year, it was a new periodical which wanted to draw as much attention to itself as possible, often by causing offense. Z made a lot of Keats's youth: he was a "flimsy stripling," a "bantling," a "boy of pretty abilities" gone wrong. Yet the man behind the pseudonym, John Gibson Lockhart, was in fact only a year Keats's senior. His attack was more like that of some alt-right Young Turk today, keen to cause controversy by unleashing as much bile as possible on a "Lefty," although the political landscape then was very different. *Blackwood's* cleverly developed its anarchic voice not to challenge but to support the mainstream political establishment.

In Keats's time, the political "Left" (if you want, anachronistically, to call it that) had no legitimate voice, and certainly could not have been attacked in the way, say, that the *Spectator* today might attack the so-called liberal establishment. What Regency radicals were calling for in terms of democratic reform seems conservative from our perspective, as they did not even include women in their demands to extend the franchise. And yet those who advocated reform ran the risk of being silenced by the courts—or in the kangaroo court of the press—when they questioned the political, religious or social status quo, whether by attacking monarchical privilege, Church of England dogma or indeed the institution of marriage.

In later life, following the Reform Act, Reynolds and Keats's mutual friend Charles Wentworth Dilke recalled the atmosphere of political prejudice that had dominated their youth, and noted how ideas once attacked as radical had since come to be accepted as commonsensical modernity: "Twenty years ago, reformers were hunted down in society as vulgar unwashed mechanicals, and any man who desired to live quietly and pleasantly, was obliged to be silent if he entertained opinions that now pass current all England over."

Back in 1818, when *Endymion* was published, Keats had not been silent but had spilled out his imaginings without self-consciousness. His opponent Z—who, unlike Keats himself, was hidden behind a pseudonym—spoke in the hyped-up language of a bare-knuckle boxer on the ropes, but he was in fact defending the status quo from a position of entitlement. Book Three of *Endymion* began with a clear egalitarian and anti-authoritarian rallying cry:

> There are who lord it o'er their fellow-men
> With most prevailing tinsel . . .

This is what Z called lisping sedition. It was easier to mock Keats than to engage with him ideologically.

Nor was Z, as his words implied, speaking from the well-defended high ground of the aristocratic classes. Lockhart's father was a clergyman of modest means; no way did he employ a footman. The only thing John Gibson Lockhart had over Keats on his CV was his university education in the humanities. He had attended three, Glasgow, Oxford and Edinburgh, before giving up the law for literature—which made him not that dissimilar from Keats's own middle-class lawyer friends Reynolds and Rice.

In reality, the caste division between Keats and Z was nothing near so great as the ideological differences. In fact, the only reason Lockhart knew about Keats's early career in medicine was because their social circles overlapped. Lockhart had met Keats's Oxford friend Benjamin Bailey at a dinner party given by a bishop in Scotland, and, like the keen young journalist he was, had taken the opportunity to draw the information out of him. Today, the worlds of poetry publishing and tabloid scoops seem miles apart, unless the poet in question were, perhaps, the poet laureate and the story involved some sex scandal. In 1818, poetry as a genre was so politically explosive that the work of even a promising but barely known young practitioner became a tinderbox.

Less gratuitously offensive, from a personal perspective, and thus perhaps even more potentially damning, was the review of *Endymion* that appeared in September in the more august *Quarterly Review,* a genuinely establishment Tory periodical. The unsigned notice was thought at the time to have been written by the paper's sexagenarian editor, William Gifford, but it was actually the work of its chief critic, John Wilson Croker, who was in his thirties. The reviewer detected signs of "powers of language, rays of fancy, and gleams of genius" in Keats, but damned him as a "copyist of Hunt," though "more unintelligible . . . twice as diffuse, and ten times more tiresome and absurd than his prototype." Croker at least analyzed the "diction and versification" to show how Keats's couplets diverged from the model set by Pope, if only to throw up his hands in horror. However, he rather undid his own claims as a critic by openly admitting to the *Quarterly's* readers that, despite a "superhuman" effort, he had not read beyond Book One of Keats's work.

The humiliations heaped on Keats by these negative reviews certainly stung, but the idea that they caused his death does not stand up to scrutiny. Keats also received some good reviews for *Endymion,* some of which were, admittedly, written by his friends. The attacks certainly didn't stop him from writing. Indeed, he was yet to write his best poetry. It was in the context of the assaults of *Blackwood's* and the *Quarterly* that Keats confidently told his brother that he thought he would be "among the English Poets" after his death. He was right. In the context of his oeuvre, *Endymion* was a failed experiment, but it has indeed outlived him, its first line taking on a life of its own as it has replicated through culture.

Lockhart considered it obscenely arrogant of "city sparks" like "Johnny Keats" "to look upon yourselves as so many future Shakespeares and Miltons." Keats was proved right. His work is now indeed in the canon alongside that of Shakespeare and Milton.

Lockhart went on to establish himself at the heart of nineteenth-century literary culture by marrying the daughter of the revered Sir Walter Scott. He died in 1854 at the age of sixty. His literary achievements—including penning a somewhat scurrilous biography of his famous father-in-law, in which he exposed some embarrassing issues to do with the latter's finances—are mainly forgotten. Today he's best remembered for one bitchy review, written when he was twenty-four.

3

Isabella; or, The Pot of Basil

I.

Fair Isabel, poor simple Isabel!
  Lorenzo, a young palmer in Love's eye!
They could not in the self-same mansion dwell
  Without some stir of heart, some malady;
They could not sit at meals but feel how well
  It soothed each to be the other by;
They could not, sure, beneath the same roof sleep
But to each other dream, and nightly weep.

II.

With every morn their love grew tenderer,
  With every eve deeper and tenderer still;
He might not in house, field, or garden stir,
  But her full shape would all his seeing fill;
And his continual voice was pleasanter
  To her, than noise of trees or hidden rill;
Her lute-string gave an echo of his name,
She spoilt her half-done broidery with the same.

III.

He knew whose gentle hand was at the latch
    Before the door had given her to his eyes;
And from her chamber-window he would catch
    Her beauty farther than the falcon spies;
And constant as her vespers would he watch,
    Because her face was turned to the same skies;
And with sick longing all the night outwear,
To hear her morning-step upon the stair.

IV.

A whole long month of May in this sad plight
    Made their cheeks paler by the break of June:
"To-morrow will I bow to my delight,
    To-morrow will I ask my lady's boon."
"O may I never see another night,
    Lorenzo, if thy lips breathe not love's tune."
So spake they to their pillows; but, alas,
Honeyless days and days did he let pass—

V.

Until sweet Isabella's untouched cheek
    Fell sick within the rose's just domain,
Fell thin as a young mother's, who doth seek
    By every lull to cool her infant's pain:
"How ill she is," said he, "I may not speak,
    And yet I will, and tell my love all plain:
If looks speak love-laws, I will drink her tears,
And at the least 'twill startle off her cares."

VI.

So said he one fair morning, and all day
    His heart beat awfully against his side;
And to his heart he inwardly did pray
    For power to speak; but still the ruddy tide
Stifled his voice, and pulsed resolve away—
    Fevered his high conceit of such a bride,
Yet brought him to the meekness of a child:
Alas! when passion is both meek and wild!

VII.

So once more he had waked and anguishèd
    A dreary night of love and misery,
If Isabel's quick eye had not been wed
    To every symbol on his forehead high.
She saw it waxing very pale and dead,
    And straight all flushed; so, lispèd tenderly,
"Lorenzo!"—here she ceased her timid quest,
But in her tone and look he read the rest.

VIII.

"O Isabella, I can half-perceive
    That I may speak my grief into thine ear.
If thou didst ever anything believe,
    Believe how I love thee, believe how near
My soul is to its doom: I would not grieve
    Thy hand by unwelcome pressing, would not fear
Thine eyes by gazing; but I cannot live
Another night, and not my passion shrive.

IX.

"Love! thou art leading me from wintry cold,
    Lady! thou leadest me to summer clime,
And I must taste the blossoms that unfold
    In its ripe warmth this gracious morning time."
So said, his erewhile timid lips grew bold,
    And poesied with hers in dewy rhyme:
Great bliss was with them, and great happiness
Grew, like a lusty flower, in June's caress.

X.

Parting they seemed to tread upon the air,
    Twin roses by the zephyr blown apart
Only to meet again more close, and share
    The inward fragrance of each other's heart.
She, to her chamber gone, a ditty fair
    Sang, of delicious love and honeyed dart;
He with light steps went up a western hill,
And bade the sun farewell, and joyed his fill.

XI.

All close they met again, before the dusk
    Had taken from the stars its pleasant veil,
All close they met, all eves, before the dusk
    Had taken from the stars its pleasant veil,
Close in a bower of hyacinth and musk,
    Unknown of any, free from whispering tale.
Ah! better had it been for ever so,
Than idle ears should pleasure in their woe.

XII.

Were they unhappy then?—It cannot be—
    Too many tears for lovers have been shed,
Too many sighs give we to them in fee,
    Too much of pity after they are dead,
Too many doleful stories do we see,
    Whose matter in bright gold were best be read;
Except in such a page where Theseus' spouse
Over the pathless waves towards him bows.

XIII.

But, for the general award of love,
    The little sweet doth kill much bitterness;
Though Dido silent is in under-grove,
    And Isabella's was a great distress,
Though young Lorenzo in warm Indian clove
    Was not embalmed, this truth is not the less—
Even bees, the little almsmen of spring-bowers,
Know there is richest juice in poison-flowers.

XIV.

With her two brothers this fair lady dwelt,
    Enrichèd from ancestral merchandise,
And for them many a weary hand did swelt
    In torchèd mines and noisy factories,
And many once proud-quivered loins did melt
    In blood from stinging whip—with hollow eyes
Many all day in dazzling river stood,
To take the rich-ored driftings of the flood.

XV.

For them the Ceylon diver held his breath,   ·
  And went all naked to the hungry shark;
For them his ears gushed blood; for them in death
  The seal on the cold ice with piteous bark
Lay full of darts; for them alone did seethe
  A thousand men in troubles wide and dark:
Half-ignorant, they turned an easy wheel,
That set sharp racks at work, to pinch and peel.

XVI.

Why were they proud? Because their marble founts
  Gushed with more pride than do a wretch's tears?—
Why were they proud? Because fair orange-mounts
  Were of more soft ascent than lazar stairs?—
Why were they proud? Because red-lined accounts
  Were richer than the songs of Grecian years?—
Why were they proud? again we ask aloud,
Why in the name of Glory were they proud?

XVII.

Yet were these Florentines as self-retired
  In hungry pride and gainful cowardice,
As two close Hebrews in that land inspired,
  Paled in and vineyarded from beggar-spies—
The hawks of ship-mast forests—the untired
  And panniered mules for ducats and old lies—
Quick cat's-paws on the generous stray-away—
Great wits in Spanish, Tuscan, and Malay.

XVIII.

How was it these same ledger-men could spy
    Fair Isabella in her downy nest?
How could they find out in Lorenzo's eye
    A straying from his toil? Hot Egypt's pest
Into their vision covetous and sly!
    How could these money-bags see east and west?—
Yet so they did—and every dealer fair
Must see behind, as doth the hunted hare.

XIX.

O eloquent and famed Boccaccio!
    Of thee we now should ask forgiving boon,
And of thy spicy myrtles as they blow,
    And of thy roses amorous of the moon,
And of thy lilies, that do paler grow
    Now they can no more hear thy gittern's tune,
For venturing syllables that ill beseem
The quiet glooms of such a piteous theme.

XX.

Grant thou a pardon here, and then the tale
    Shall move on soberly, as it is meet;
There is no other crime, no mad assail
    To make old prose in modern rhyme more sweet:
But it is done—succeed the verse or fail—
    To honour thee, and thy gone spirit greet,
To stead thee as a verse in English tongue,
An echo of thee in the north-wind sung.

XXI.

These brethren having found by many signs
  What love Lorenzo for their sister had,
And how she loved him too, each unconfines
  His bitter thoughts to other, well nigh mad
That he, the servant of their trade designs,
  Should in their sister's love be blithe and glad,
When 'twas their plan to coax her by degrees
To some high noble and his olive-trees.

XXII.

And many a jealous conference had they,
  And many times they bit their lips alone,
Before they fixed upon a surest way
  To make the youngster for his crime atone;
And at the last, these men of cruel clay
  Cut Mercy with a sharp knife to the bone,
For they resolvèd in some forest dim
To kill Lorenzo, and there bury him.

XXIII.

So on a pleasant morning, as he leant
  Into the sun-rise, o'er the balustrade
Of the garden-terrace, towards him they bent
  Their footing through the dews; and to him said,
"You seem there in the quiet of content,
  Lorenzo, and we are most loth to invade
Calm speculation; but if you are wise,
Bestride your steed while cold is in the skies.

XXIV.

"To-day we purpose, ay, this hour we mount
    To spur three leagues towards the Apennine;
Come down, we pray thee, ere the hot sun count
    His dewy rosary on the eglantine."
Lorenzo, courteously as he was wont,
    Bowed a fair greeting to these serpents' whine;
And went in haste, to get in readiness,
With belt, and spur, and bracing huntsman's dress.

XXV.

And as he to the court-yard passed along,
    Each third step did he pause, and listened oft
If he could hear his lady's matin-song,
    Or the light whisper of her footstep soft;
And as he thus over his passion hung,
    He heard a laugh full musical aloft;
When, looking up, he saw her features bright
Smile through an in-door lattice, all delight.

XXVI.

"Love, Isabel!" said he, "I was in pain
    Lest I should miss to bid thee a good morrow:
Ah! what if I should lose thee, when so fain
    I am to stifle all the heavy sorrow
Of a poor three hours' absence? but we'll gain
    Out of the amorous dark what day doth borrow.
Good bye! I'll soon be back." "Good bye!" said she—
And as he went she chanted merrily.

XXVII.

So the two brothers and their murdered man
    Rode past fair Florence, to where Arno's stream
Gurgles through straitened banks, and still doth fan
    Itself with dancing bulrush, and the bream
Keeps head against the freshets. Sick and wan
    The brothers' faces in the ford did seem,
Lorenzo's flush with love.—They passed the water
Into a forest quiet for the slaughter.

XXVIII.

There was Lorenzo slain and buried in,
    There in that forest did his great love cease.
Ah! when a soul doth thus its freedom win,
    It aches in loneliness—is ill at peace
As the break-covert blood-hounds of such sin.
    They dipped their swords in the water, and did tease
Their horses homeward, with convulsèd spur,
Each richer by his being a murderer.

XXIX.

They told their sister how, with sudden speed,
    Lorenzo had ta'en ship for foreign lands,
Because of some great urgency and need
    In their affairs, requiring trusty hands.
Poor girl! put on thy stifling widow's weed,
    And 'scape at once from Hope's accursèd bands;
Today thou wilt not see him, nor tomorrow,
And the next day will be a day of sorrow.

XXX.

She weeps alone for pleasures not to be;
    Sorely she wept until the night came on,
And then, instead of love, O misery!
    She brooded o'er the luxury alone:
His image in the dusk she seemed to see,
    And to the silence made a gentle moan,
Spreading her perfect arms upon the air,
And on her couch low murmuring "Where? O where?"

XXXI.

But Selfishness, Love's cousin, held not long
    Its fiery vigil in her single breast.
She fretted for the golden hour, and hung
    Upon the time with feverish unrest—
Not long—for soon into her heart a throng
    Of higher occupants, a richer zest,
Came tragic—passion not to be subdued,
And sorrow for her love in travels rude.

XXXII.

In the mid days of autumn, on their eves
    The breath of Winter comes from far away,
And the sick west continually bereaves
    Of some gold tinge, and plays a roundelay
Of death among the bushes and the leaves,
    To make all bare before he dares to stray
From his north cavern. So sweet Isabel
By gradual decay from beauty fell,

XXXIII.

Because Lorenzo came not. Oftentimes
    She asked her brothers, with an eye all pale,
Striving to be itself, what dungeon climes
    Could keep him off so long? They spake a tale
Time after time, to quiet her. Their crimes
    Came on them, like a smoke from Hinnom's vale;
And every night in dreams they groaned aloud,
To see their sister in her snowy shroud.

XXXIV.

And she had died in drowsy ignorance,
    But for a thing more deadly dark than all.
It came like a fierce potion, drunk by chance,
    Which saves a sick man from the feathered pall
For some few gasping moments; like a lance,
    Waking an Indian from his cloudy hall
With cruel pierce, and bringing him again
Sense of the gnawing fire at heart and brain.

XXXV.

It was a vision.—In the drowsy gloom,
    The dull of midnight, at her couch's foot
Lorenzo stood, and wept: the forest tomb
    Had marred his glossy hair which once could shoot
Lustre into the sun, and put cold doom
    Upon his lips, and taken the soft lute
From his lorn voice, and past his loamèd ears
Had made a miry channel for his tears.

XXXVI.

Strange sound it was, when the pale shadow spake;
　For there was striving, in its piteous tongue,
To speak as when on earth it was awake,
　And Isabella on its music hung.
Languor there was in it, and tremulous shake,
　As in a palsied Druid's harp unstrung;
And through it moaned a ghostly under-song,
Like hoarse night-gusts sepulchral briars among.

XXXVII.

Its eyes, though wild, were still all dewy bright
　With love, and kept all phantom fear aloof
From the poor girl by magic of their light,
　The while it did unthread the horrid woof
Of the late darkened time—the murderous spite
　Of pride and avarice, the dark pine roof
In the forest, and the sodden turfèd dell,
Where, without any word, from stabs he fell.

XXXVIII.

Saying moreover, "Isabel, my sweet!
　Red whortle-berries droop above my head,
And a large flint-stone weighs upon my feet;
　Around me beeches and high chestnuts shed
Their leaves and prickly nuts; a sheep-fold bleat
　Comes from beyond the river to my bed:
Go, shed one tear upon my heather-bloom,
And it shall comfort me within the tomb.

XXXIX.

"I am a shadow now, alas! alas!
    Upon the skirts of human-nature dwelling
Alone. I chant alone the holy mass,
    While little sounds of life are round me knelling,
And glossy bees at noon do fieldward pass,
    And many a chapel bell the hour is telling,
Paining me through: those sounds grow strange to me,
And thou art distant in humanity.

XL.

"I know what was, I feel full well what is,
    And I should rage, if spirits could go mad;
Though I forget the taste of earthly bliss,
    That paleness warms my grave, as though I had
A seraph chosen from the bright abyss
    To be my spouse: thy paleness makes me glad;
Thy beauty grows upon me, and I feel
A greater love through all my essence steal."

XLI.

The Spirit mourn'd "Adieu!"—dissolved, and left
    The atom darkness in a slow turmoil;
As when of healthful midnight sleep bereft,
    Thinking on rugged hours and fruitless toil,
We put our eyes into a pillowy cleft,
    And see the spangly gloom froth up and boil:
It made sad Isabella's eyelids ache,
And in the dawn she started up awake—

XLII.

"Ha! ha!" said she, "I knew not this hard life,
   I thought the worst was simple misery;
I thought some Fate with pleasure or with strife
   Portioned us—happy days, or else to die;
But there is crime—a brother's bloody knife!
   Sweet Spirit, thou hast schooled my infancy:
I'll visit thee for this, and kiss thine eyes,
And greet thee morn and even in the skies."

XLIII.

When the full morning came, she had devised
   How she might secret to the forest hie;
How she might find the clay, so dearly prized,
   And sing to it one latest lullaby;
How her short absence might be unsurmised,
   While she the inmost of the dream would try.
Resolved, she took with her an agèd nurse,
And went into that dismal forest-hearse.

XLIV.

See, as they creep along the river side,
   How she doth whisper to that agèd dame,
And, after looking round the champaign wide,
   Shows her a knife.—"What feverous hectic flame
Burns in thee, child?—What good can thee betide,
   That thou shouldst smile again?" The evening came,
And they had found Lorenzo's earthy bed—
The flint was there, the berries at his head.

XLV.

Who hath not loitered in a green church-yard,
    And let his spirit, like a demon-mole,
Work through the clayey soil and gravel hard,
    To see skull, coffined bones, and funeral stole;
Pitying each form that hungry Death hath marred
    And filling it once more with human soul?
Ah! this is holiday to what was felt
When Isabella by Lorenzo knelt.

XLVI.

She gazed into the fresh-thrown mold, as though
    One glance did fully all its secrets tell;
Clearly she saw, as other eyes would know
    Pale limbs at bottom of a crystal well;
Upon the murderous spot she seemed to grow,
    Like to a native lily of the dell—
Then with her knife, all sudden, she began
To dig more fervently than misers can.

XLVII.

Soon she turned up a soilèd glove, whereon
    Her silk had played in purple phantasies,
She kissed it with a lip more chill than stone,
    And put it in her bosom, where it dries
And freezes utterly unto the bone
    Those dainties made to still an infant's cries:
Then 'gan she work again; nor stayed her care,
But to throw back at times her veiling hair.

XLVIII.

That old nurse stood beside her wondering,
   Until her heart felt pity to the core
At sight of such a dismal laboring,
   And so she kneelèd, with her locks all hoar,
And put her lean hands to the horrid thing.
   Three hours they labored at this travail sore—
At last they felt the kernel of the grave,
And Isabella did not stamp and rave.

XLIX.

Ah! wherefore all this wormy circumstance?
   Why linger at the yawning tomb so long?
O for the gentleness of old Romance,
   The simple plaining of a minstrel's song!
Fair reader, at the old tale take a glance,
   For here, in truth, it doth not well belong
To speak—O turn thee to the very tale,
And taste the music of that vision pale.

L.

With duller steel than the Persèan sword
   They cut away no formless monster's head,
But one, whose gentleness did well accord
   With death, as life. The ancient harps have said,
Love never dies, but lives, immortal Lord:
   If Love impersonate was ever dead,
Pale Isabella kissed it, and low moaned.
'Twas love—cold, dead indeed, but not dethroned.

LI.

In anxious secrecy they took it home,
　　And then the prize was all for Isabel.
She calmed its wild hair with a golden comb,
　　And all around each eye's sepulchral cell
Pointed each fringèd lash; the smearèd loam
　　With tears, as chilly as a dripping well,
She drenched away—and still she combed, and kept
Sighing all day—and still she kissed, and wept.

LII.

Then in a silken scarf—sweet with the dews
　　Of precious flowers plucked in Araby,
And divine liquids come with odorous ooze
　　Through the cold serpent pipe refreshfully—
She wrapped it up; and for its tomb did choose
　　A garden-pot, wherein she laid it by,
And covered it with mold, and o'er it set
Sweet basil, which her tears kept ever wet.

LIII.

And she forgot the stars, the moon, and sun,
　　And she forgot the blue above the trees,
And she forgot the dells where waters run,
　　And she forgot the chilly autumn breeze;
She had no knowledge when the day was done,
　　And the new morn she saw not, but in peace
Hung over her sweet basil evermore,
And moistened it with tears unto the core.

LIV.

And so she ever fed it with thin tears,
   Whence thick, and green, and beautiful it grew,
So that it smelt more balmy than its peers
   Of basil-tufts in Florence; for it drew
Nurture besides, and life, from human fears,
   From the fast moldering head there shut from view:
So that the jewel, safely casketed,
Came forth, and in perfumèd leafits spread.

LV.

O Melancholy, linger here awhile!
   O Music, Music, breathe despondingly!
O Echo, Echo, from some sombre isle,
   Unknown, Lethean, sigh to us—O sigh!
Spirits in grief, lift up your heads, and smile.
   Lift up your heads, sweet Spirits, heavily,
And make a pale light in your cypress glooms,
Tinting with silver wan your marble tombs.

LVI.

Moan hither, all ye syllables of woe,
   From the deep throat of sad Melpomene!
Through bronzèd lyre in tragic order go,
   And touch the strings into a mystery;
Sound mournfully upon the winds and low;
   For simple Isabel is soon to be
Among the dead. She withers, like a palm
Cut by an Indian for its juicy balm.

LVII.

O leave the palm to wither by itself;
    Let not quick Winter chill its dying hour!—
It may not be—those Baälites of pelf,
    Her brethren, noted the continual shower
From her dead eyes; and many a curious elf,
    Among her kindred, wondered that such dower
Of youth and beauty should be thrown aside
By one marked out to be a Noble's bride.

LVIII.

And, furthermore, her brethren wondered much
    Why she sat drooping by the basil green,
And why it flourished, as by magic touch.
    Greatly they wondered what the thing might mean:
They could not surely give belief, that such
    A very nothing would have power to wean
Her from her own fair youth, and pleasures gay,
And even remembrance of her love's delay.

LIX.

Therefore they watched a time when they might sift
    This hidden whim; and long they watched in vain:
For seldom did she go to chapel-shrift,
    And seldom felt she any hunger-pain;
And when she left, she hurried back, as swift
    As bird on wing to breast its eggs again;
And, patient as a hen-bird, sat her there
Beside her basil, weeping through her hair.

LX.

Yet they contrived to steal the basil-pot,
    And to examine it in secret place.
The thing was vile with green and livid spot,
    And yet they knew it was Lorenzo's face:
The guerdon of their murder they had got,
    And so left Florence in a moment's space,
Never to turn again. Away they went,
With blood upon their heads, to banishment.

LXI.

O Melancholy, turn thine eyes away!
    O Music, Music, breathe despondingly!
O Echo, Echo, on some other day,
    From isles Lethean, sigh to us—O sigh!
Spirits of grief, sing not your "Well-a-way!"
    For Isabel, sweet Isabel, will die—
Will die a death too lone and incomplete,
Now they have ta'en away her basil sweet.

LXII.

Piteous she looked on dead and senseless things,
    Asking for her lost basil amorously;
And with melodious chuckle in the strings
    Of her lorn voice, she oftentimes would cry
After the pilgrim in his wanderings,
    To ask him where her basil was; and why
'Twas hid from her: "For cruel 'tis," said she,
"To steal my basil-pot away from me."

LXIII.

And so she pined, and so she died forlorn,
　　Imploring for her basil to the last.
No heart was there in Florence but did mourn
　　In pity of her love, so overcast.
And a sad ditty of this story born
　　From mouth to mouth through all the country passed:
Still is the burthen sung—"O cruelty,
To steal my basil-pot away from me!"

Isabella; or, The Pot of Basil was written between the beginning of March and April 27, 1818, just after Keats had finished revising *Endymion* but before the latter had been reviewed. Rather than referencing any eternal, abstract "thing of beauty," this poem shows Keats putting the mortal body at the forefront in stomach-churning fashion. It features a heroine who digs up the corpse of her murdered lover and then cuts off the head, which she secretly buries under a pot plant to which she becomes insanely attached. When her brothers, who are responsible for the murder, discover what's in the basil pot, they take it away. Bereft, she dies.

The macabre narrative has an almost absurdist ring when baldly summarized: too sick for high tragedy, too outlandish for realism. Pre-Raphaelite painters later made dreamy images, inspired by Keats's poem, of Isabella as a long-haired beauty delicately embracing her basil pot. But paintings such as those produced by William Holman Hunt (1868), Arthur Trevethin Nowell (1904) and John William Waterhouse (1907) edit out the grotesquerie of Keats's original. In the revised preface to *Endymion,* written around the same time as *Isabella,* Keats opined that childhood was healthy, mature adulthood was healthy, but that there was a "mawkish" space between, which he, as a young man, occupied himself.

Here, he seems to be parading his attraction to sick imagery as an artistic choice, although the work that resulted was later called his "finest thing" by the Romantic critic Charles Lamb. The ease with which Lamb absorbed the poem's queasiness was not, perhaps, unrelated to the fact that murder and madness were quotidian experiences for him; in 1796, his sister Mary had stabbed their mother to death during a mental breakdown. But he was right to admire the poem's artistry. Written in stanzas rather than couplets, *Isabella* is much shorter and tighter than *Endymion,* and has a narrative momentum the latter lacks.

The idea came from one of the tales in Boccaccio's fourteenth-century *Decameron,* which Keats read in a seventeenth-century English translation. Like Chaucer's *The Canterbury Tales,* which slightly postdates it, *The Decameron* is a mixed bag of stories told by a group of disparate characters. Chaucer's storytellers are staying at an inn en route to a religious pilgrimage site, but those in *The Decameron* have left Florence to escape the plague. They are entertaining each other while holed up in lockdown, quarantining in the countryside. At the time he wrote *Isabella,* Keats, as ever on the move, was staying by the seaside at Teignmouth in Devon with his brother Tom. Tom was by then spitting blood, showing signs of the tuberculosis that would kill him by the end of the year. Sea air was thought to be beneficial for lung conditions. In its own way, escaping the city had prophylactic connotations for them too.

The sea, then, might have been a consoling presence, but it inspired a dark mood in Keats. On March 25, he penned a verse letter to his fellow young poet John Hamilton Reynolds, to whom he had become close since Hunt promoted them together as new voices in his *Examiner* article of 1816. He confessed that he should have felt at home and at ease by the seaside, but instead sensed himself being pulled into a proto-Darwinian dystopia:

> —but I saw
> Too far into the sea, where every maw
> The greater on the less feeds evermore.—
> But I saw too distinct into the core
> Of an eternal fierce destruction,
> And so from happiness I far was gone.

Keats had previously felt held back by his morbidity of temperament. Now he was channeling it directly into his poetry.

Keats never published those lines in his lifetime, but the fact that he exposed his own dark fears was a statement of his trust in Reynolds, and his desire to cement their intimacy. Keats's own decision to leave off medicine was probably prompted by the fact that Reynolds himself had quit his job in insurance to become a full-time freelance writer. Only a year older than Keats, Reynolds was, at that time, a precocious performer, with three books of poetry in print and another on the way. His debut, *Safie,* published in 1814 when he was nineteen, had been praised by Byron, no less. And yet Reynolds was generous, always aware that Keats's talent was the more original. By November 1817, he had given up his short-lived freelance career to train in law, while Keats continued devoting himself full-time to the "great thing" of poetry, not yet contemplating, even for a moment, a return to a steady medical career.

Keats's choice of Boccaccio as a source was of a piece with Leigh Hunt's taste for Italian medievalism, as shown in the latter's Dante-inspired "The Story of Rimini." *Isabella* was in fact initially conceived by Keats as part of a proposed joint project with Reynolds to produce a whole book of Boccaccio stories in verse, but it never got off the ground. Keats's poem and a couple of unmemorable fragments later published by Reynolds are the sole, disconnected results.

Although the choice of source refracts Hunt's continuing influence, *Isabella* reads like an ironic rebuke to Huntian optimism. "The Story of Rimini" contained the facile metaphor:

> E'en tales like this, founded on real woe,
> From bitter seed to balmy fruitage grow.

In making a basil plant flourish literally out of a severed head, it's as if Keats took this image and pushed it to a gruesome near-satirical extreme. Certainly, *Isabella* is not a work that lends itself to the headline "Happy Poetry Preferred."

To see what makes Keats's *Isabella* so unique, it is worth comparing it with a contemporaneous poetic treatment of the same Boccaccio tale: *A Sicilian Story*, published in 1820 by the pseudonymous "Barry Cornwall" (real name Bryan Waller Procter), under the Ollier imprint that Keats had ditched for Taylor & Hessey after the publication of his first book. Keats and Reynolds were clearly not the only poets to be drawn to Boccaccio at the time. It's even possible that Cornwall had heard something through literary London's grapevine about their proposed, and then abandoned, plan for a whole Boccaccio book and had decided to compete.

Eight years older than Keats, Cornwall is an intriguing figure, a solicitor who turned to full-time poetry for a few years
in the heady Romantic period before returning to the law.
As a verse narrative in couplets, his *Sicilian Story* is slavishly
imitative of Hunt's "The Story of Rimini" in many respects.
But he was an odd amalgam: a self-styled "Cockney" poet
who neutralized the edgier elements of cockneydom to seek
success with a popular commercial audience. He became particularly successful with women readers, largely because of his
canny use of erotic euphemisms, which allowed ladies to revel
in his coyly charged verses without shame.

Cornwall's aim was to please his readers, not to alarm
them. His smooth telling of the "pot of basil" story goes out
of its way to avoid discomfort by presenting it as a sentimental tale of star-crossed love and female constancy. He even
bows to respectability by making the lovers secretly married,
thus legitimizing their amorous union, as is not the case
either in Boccaccio's or in Keats's version. In stark contrast
to the Cornwall, Keats's rendition of the story has a definite undersong of resistance to pleasing the reader. He later
expressed the opinion, on August 23, 1819, that to seek "the
favour of the public" was "a cloying treacle to the wings of
independence."

However, Keats was not wholly disengaged from taking the
temperature of the current literary marketplace at the time he
first drafted *Isabella* in the spring of 1818. The stanzaic verse
form he chose—ottava rima—had been developed by Boccaccio, who used it in some of his minor poetry, although not
in the prose *Decameron*. However, it was also of the moment,
as it had just been employed by Byron in *Beppo,* a seriocomic
satire on Venetian amours that had just been published. By
now Byron was in exile following the scandal of his marriage

breakup, and his once "sweetly sad" poetic voice was becoming increasingly sardonic. That tone is also present in the opening stanza of Keats's poem:

> Fair Isabel, poor simple Isabel!
>   Lorenzo, a young palmer [i.e., pilgrim] in Love's eye!
> They could not in the self-same mansion dwell
>   Without some stir of heart, some malady;
> They could not sit at meals but feel how well
>   It soothed each to be the other by;
> They could not, sure, beneath the same roof sleep
> But to each other dream, and nightly weep.

The first line—"Fair Isabel, poor simple Isabel!"—employs its exclamation mark in a much more ironic mode than that found in the early sonnets beginning "Byron, how sweetly sad thy melody!" or "O Chatterton! how very sad thy fate!" As we will discover later on, Isabella is not poor in a material sense: it is, on the contrary, because her family is rich that her brothers disdain her lowly lover Lorenzo, who's their "servant." They plot to do away with him because they are planning to betroth her to a "high noble" landowner and, through that alliance, cement their power and pride. Nor is her simplicity mere innocence: by the end of the poem, we will discover that she becomes "simple," in the sense of having lost her wits, because she has been driven to the nadir of mental illness by trauma.

You can tell at the start that Keats is not identifying with the emotions of his characters. He's hovering above in a state of what seems irony. In his lines, high-flown devotion to romantic love as to a quasi-religious ideal rubs comically up against the prosaism of sitting at meals. In contrast, Barry

Cornwall makes Lorenzo glamorously high-born, to avoid the element of class conflict, while inviting his readers to give themselves up to the pleasure of swooshing around unquestioningly in the heroine's romantic feelings.

But what really distinguishes Cornwall's version from Keats's is that the former dispenses with the central plot device of the severed head. As he explained to his readers in a footnote, Cornwall regarded the idea as too "ghastly." As a result, he changed the body part that the heroine preserves from a head to a "heart," a word whose metaphorical usage as a shorthand for romantic passion went a long way to disguising its physicality as a bodily organ. When Cornwall's Isabel finds the corpse lying on the ground, he not only glosses over the scene in a mere three lines, but he literally has her washing the offending item:

> And then she wept. At last—but wherefore ask
> How, tremblingly, she did her bloody task?
> She took the heart and washed it in the wave . . .

Even after being potted under the basil, this remarkable heart does not molder; "unlike the common dead," it remains "unperished."

Keats, on the other hand, makes much more of the physicality of death, of what he calls the "wormy circumstance." He takes us to a graveyard and makes us imagine the rotting bodies underfoot:

> Who hath not loitered in a green church-yard,
>   And let his spirit, like a demon-mole,
> Work through the clayey soil and gravel hard,
>   To see skull, coffined bones, and funeral stole;

> Pitying each form that hungry Death hath marred
> And filling it once more with human soul?

Where Cornwall's heroine merely stumbles on the corpse, in Keats's version it has been buried in the earth. It takes Isabella, assisted by her nurse, a grueling "three hours" of physical "laboring" to exhume it, their only digging tool the "knife" that's later used to cut off the head. When Isabella's brothers finally discover the secret of the basil pot, in which she has concealed the head, the latter is found to be in a state of gruesome decomposition:

> The thing was vile with green and livid spot.

———

Isabella was a poem about which Keats felt ambivalent, although he cared enough about it to rework it in draft. Only after some debate did he ultimately agree to include it in what became his third and final book, published in 1820 as *Lamia, Isabella, The Eve of St. Agnes, and Other Poems.* For all his belief that his poetry would live on after his death, and his claims not to care about pleasing the public, he had become sensitized to mockery following the *Blackwood's* jibes. As a result, he wavered over *Isabella*'s inclusion, telling Richard Woodhouse that he feared that this particular poem was too "smokeable" to be printed in his lifetime. In the slang of the time, that meant too likely to be laughed at as ridiculous and overblown.

The plot of this Gothic extravaganza indeed seems far-fetched. Yet, Keats added mysteriously, "There are very few would look to the reality." What precisely he meant by that is enigmatic, but it's an acknowledgment that aspects of the grisly tale he had told had real-life as well as literary roots. Certainly, his medical training had acquainted him with dead bodies, both whole and cut up on the anatomist's table.

Putrefaction was a physical reality to a medical student. So was exhumation. Isabella and her nurse are amateur body-snatchers, but anatomists relied on the professionals. Prior to the 1832 Anatomy Act, the only cadavers that could be legally used for dissection purposes were those of executed murderers. But the growth of medical education and research meant that demand outstripped supply, leading to an illegal trade in corpses.

The legendary surgeon who oversaw Keats's training at Guy's, Astley Cooper (1768–1841), had personally dug up bodies in his youth under cover of night to feed his passion for anatomical science. He later ran a clandestine network of body-snatchers. To Keats, Cooper was not a distant figure but rather a hands-on mentor, who, as recent research has shown, took him under his wing, helping him to find lodgings after he left his apprenticeship with a suburban apothecary to train at a teaching hospital in the capital.

By the time he took Keats on, Cooper was already a charismatic leader in his field. His medical notes reveal his extraordinary capacity to find beauty in the human body in states that most people would find repulsive. In *Isabella,* Keats, too, finds poetic beauty in the "vile." At Guy's, operations and dissections had the quasi-aesthetic quality of a stage play, performed as they were in an anatomical theater with raked seating for the student audience. In *Isabella,* Keats creates a theatrical Gothic scene in which he—and by implication the reader—is a fascinated but detached observer of the severed head, and of the heroine's subsequent decline into insanity.

During the course of his long career, Astley Cooper performed many experimental operations that paved the way for modern techniques, enabled, it must be said, by the absence of today's ethical standards of informed consent. Cooper describes how on one occasion he applied a ligature to a man's dilated aorta—a crude forerunner of the recently developed PEARS (personalized external aortic root support) procedure, in which I have to admit an interest, as it was successfully performed in 2019 on my husband by the brilliant surgeon Conal Austin of Guy's and St. Thomas' Hospital, where Keats was trained two centuries ago. As a result, my husband can now expect to live a normal, healthy life span. That Cooper's patient, who was not anesthetized, survived as long as forty hours after the surgeon had probed his innards with an unsterilized fingernail was, in its own way, amazing.

Keats wasn't present at that particular operation, but he would have been there at others. As a "dresser," he played an active role, assisting the leading surgeon. This would have involved intimate contact with physical pain and suffering on a level experienced by few poets: applying tourniquets, disposing of amputated limbs and holding down conscious, moaning patients during surgery at a time before anesthesia when the only sedatives available were alcohol and opium. According to his former schoolfellow Richard Horne, Keats as a trainee doctor took "great pleasure in alleviating suffering, but it was a dreadful profession on account of having to witness so much."

Keats's temperament was certainly highly sensitized, naturally unboundaried, though his drive and focus provided a clamp during his surgical training. After redefining himself as a poet, he let himself go. Instead of focusing his energies and ambition on cutting off his emotional response, he went on to express how much he valued and cultivated his ability to enter into other selves. He was so empathetic, he told his friend Benjamin Bailey on November 22, 1817, that he could imagine himself into the body of a sparrow: "if a Sparrow come before my Window I take part in its existence and pick about the Gravel." Later, he told his publisher's adviser Richard Woodhouse that he could revel in empathizing with the subjective experience of being a billiard ball: "he has affirmed that he can conceive . . . that it may have a sense of delight from its own roundness, smoothness . . . volubility & the rapidity of its motion," Woodhouse reported to Taylor in October 1818.

Astley Cooper, in contrast, had such an extreme ability to compartmentalize and objectify that it's hard to imagine him looking at a cadaver and "filling it once more with human soul" as Keats imagines in *Isabella; or, The Pot of Basil,* in which the poet's detachment and empathy fight seemingly to the death. Keats found it much harder to switch off his awareness of bodies—whether of live patients or of corpses—as people. He later confessed that his sensitivity, even in normal social situations, meant that he had to "smother" his feelings under an "everlasting restraint," which was relieved only when he was composing poetry.

Years later, his friend Charles Armitage Brown averred that Keats was afraid his hands-on involvement with patients would lead to a loss of composure that might render him "unfit to perform a surgical operation." However, newly unearthed evidence, dating from the time when he was actually working as a dresser, indicates, on the contrary, that Keats succeeded in suppressing his emotions and going about his work with consummate professionalism.

It reveals the sangfroid and success with which in March 1816 Keats, then aged twenty, had treated a traumatized woman, Jane Hull, who was brought into Guy's Hospital as an emergency case, with a gunshot wound to her head and neck. *Isabella; or, The Pot of Basil* features a family murder; what is, in the context of Boccaccio's medieval Italy, effectively an honor killing. The real-life case of Jane Hull—which might have ended up being one of murder had Keats not cleanly extracted the pistol ball—was also a family affair, this time a crime passionnel committed by a jealous husband. The incident reveals that Keats had indeed encountered murderousness in the context of everyday "reality."

Jane Hull had been standing at the bar of the Prince Regent pub drinking a cordial when her husband Samuel, a breeches maker, came in and shot her point-blank with a pistol, aiming at her head. In the pockets of the assailant were found two letters informing him of his wife's infidelity. Piercing the lobe of the ear, the bullet had glanced off the skull and embedded itself in the neck. The subsequent court report, printed in the *Morning Chronicle,* noted the evidence of "Mr. Keats, one of the surgeons belonging to Guy's hospital," who had extracted the pistol ball, which he produced in evidence. This must have been the future poet John Keats, as no other surgeon called Keats was on the Guy's roster at the time. His medical expertise meant that Mrs. Hull survived, though she subsequently declined to press charges. The emotional fallout between her and her husband is unrecorded.

When Keats later told Richard Woodhouse that there were very few who would look to the reality behind *Isabella,* he must have had in mind his medical experience, which featured not only dead body parts but unrecorded histories of psychological damage. However, it is also possible that elements of his own family background seeped at a twisted tangent into the grisly poem.

There are no direct plot parallels between the story of the Keatses and that of Isabella, her forbidden lover and her homicidal brothers. However, similarities of theme have been noted, most recently by Nicholas Roe. It's as if Keats is picking up dismembered anxieties about his own parents' narrative, and half-weaving them into Boccaccio's warped tale in a "disjointed" manner, to use a word Keats applied to his own life around this time. As Roe pointed out in 2012, Lorenzo's status as a lowly employee or "servant" parallels that of Keats's father Thomas, who began as a humble ostler in his future father-in-law's employ. In addition, the fact that Lorenzo meets his end while out riding echoes Thomas's death in an unexplained fall from his horse.

In the real-life case of Jane Hull, Keats had seen a case of attempted murder in everyday experience. Might he have suspected that his own father's death had involved foul play? Although the tragedy was accepted as a mishap at the time, such a fall was so out of character for Thomas, given his expert horsemanship, that it might have begged a question as to whether he was pushed or, more likely, given he was riding, pulled from his mount.

At two centuries' distance, it's impossible to determine what actually happened on that April night in 1804. Accidents on horseback, many of them random and meaningless, were as common as car accidents today. But we can glimpse how Keats might have processed the tragedy in his own mind. His letters reveal that he saw it as part of his nature to harbor suspicions. Writing to Bailey on June 10, 1818, he admitted that he had "suspected every Body" all his life, while implying that early emotional trauma—the "loss of [his] parents and even . . . earlier Misfortunes"—was the cause. "I am a little given to bode ill like the raven; it is my misfortune not my fault," he later told Fanny Brawne on July 15, 1819, reiterating that "the general tenor of the circumstances of my life" had "rendered every event suspicious." Leigh Hunt, too, recalled that Keats suffered from "irritable morbidity" that drove "his suspicions to excess."

Unlike the fictional Isabella, whose passion for a low-born employee renders her brothers murderous, Keats's mother Frances's untoward marriage was ultimately accepted by her parents, the Jenningses, who went on to allow their former ostler Thomas to take over the family business. In that respect, the analogy with Boccaccio's tale doesn't work. However, another murder plot from literature, which was on Keats's mind at the time, fits rather more snugly than Boccaccio's story: that of Shakespeare's *Hamlet*. On May 3, 1818, less than a week after he had completed *Isabella,* Keats told Reynolds that he'd had an epiphany: that it was only by connecting the "fine things" we read in literature to our own private stories that we can "feel them to the full." Now that he has realized this, he says, he will "relish Hamlet more than . . . ever."

In the play, Prince Hamlet's mother, Gertrude, has been unfaithful to his father, the king. As soon as he dies, she marries her lover Claudius with indecent haste. Hamlet suspects that Claudius has murdered his father to usurp both his bed and his kingship. In 2012, biographer Nicholas Roe speculated that Keats's father Thomas might have been murdered by unknown "jealous rivals" in the livery trade. It seems more likely to me that Keats, in his more paranoid moments, might have suspected his mother's second husband of Claudius-like designs.

Like Gertrude, Frances Keats certainly remarried within an indecently short time of being widowed, whereupon her new husband, William Rawlings, installed himself as the proprietor of the livery stables. He changed the name from the Keates Livery Stables, as they'd been since Keats's father Thomas took over, to the Rawlings Livery Stables—which could easily have looked like a flagrant act of usurpation to Keats himself.

Several biographers have surmised that Frances was already involved with Rawlings even before Thomas Keats died. Keats's *Hamlet* reference suggests that he suspected as much himself. The Keats siblings' legal guardian Richard Abbey later painted a portrait of Keats's mother Frances as a dissolute woman, implying she may have had serial affairs, and also stating that, after she split from Rawlings, she lived in sin with yet another man, "a Jew at Enfield, named Abraham." Certainly, Keats did not remember his mother as a constant presence, even before the nuclear family was blown apart following his father's death when he was eight, after which Frances ran off with Rawlings and ceased to play any maternal role in his life.

Keats told Joseph Severn "that his great misfortune had been that from his infancy he had no mother," suggesting that Frances had never been fully there for him. Perhaps she had not taken easily to the daily grind of parenting and, from an early date, had sought distraction elsewhere. In the poem, Isabella's insane fidelity to one lover—and his severed head—represents the extreme flip side of the restless Frances, who moved from man to man, rather as her poet son later moved from place to place and, though he had a gift for friendship, refocused from friend to friend. When, in the poem, Isabella is pining for Lorenzo, Keats depicts her cheek growing thin "as a young mother's, who doth seek / By every lull to cool her infant's pain"—an ideal image of the self-sacrificing mother love that Keats believed he had never experienced even in infancy.

Little is known about Keats's mother's second husband, who was significantly younger than she was. Aged only twenty at the time they married, he was a junior bank clerk at Smith, Payne & Smith, the equivalent of a management trainee. The firm was an ancestor company of the modern NatWest (now part of the Royal Bank of Scotland), an old-established merchant bank even then, with offices near to the Mansion House in the City. To get that position, Rawlings must have had more formal education, and perhaps more of a patina of "class," than the former ostler Thomas, though he clearly lacked the latter's steady ambition.

According to Richard Abbey, Rawlings was in line, had he been patient, to earn a more than handsome upper-middle-class salary of £700 per annum at the bank. However, Keats's sister Fanny recalled in later life that Rawlings was "not too flush of cash" with "no property whatever." His decision to marry Frances and join the livery business—in which, unlike her first husband, he had no proven aptitude—suggests he was as much of a gambler as she was. He may have simply intended to sell the business on. It is quite possible that Rawlings seduced Frances for her money but he seems, however, an unlikely murderer, more delinquent than Machiavellian, hardly a Claudius. If Keats suspected him, he was perhaps projecting his own unconscious murderous feelings onto the man who had taken his mother away.

In *Isabella,* Keats lambasts the trade of money-getting, personified in the merchant brothers, whom he denotes "ledger-men." It's likely that this is indeed, as Nicholas Roe has suggested, a buried, cynical allusion to Rawlings the bank clerk. Yet, in an aside that sticks in the modern throat, Keats also compares the brothers' "gainful cowardice" with that of "close Hebrews." From today's perspective, Keats has a good record when it comes, for example, to expressing antislavery views, but he is, distressingly, not prejudice-free.

Anti-Semitic attitudes are also visible in Keats's letters, though this has, unsurprisingly, tended to be ignored by commentators. When church silver was stolen from the chapel of St. Paul at Stansted in Hampshire, for example, he assumed Jews were the culprits. (The chapel had been paid for by the philanthropist Lewis Way, who was determined to convert Jews to Christianity because he believed that it would bring about the Second Coming.)

The butt of a tasteless practical joke Keats once played was also Jewish. The escapade involved a new tenant to whom his friend Charles Armitage Brown had sublet his house for the summer: "Mr. Benjamin a Jew," as Keats called him. The joke involved a fabricated letter Keats wrote addressed to Brown, signed "Nathan Benjamin." ("By a fortunate hit I hit upon his right hethen name—his right Pronomen," Keats gleefully announced.) It stated a complaint about the water supply, in which Mr. Benjamin supposedly demanded financial recompense from Brown his landlord for the kidney stone he had suffered in consequence. The upshot was bemusement and embarrassment on the part of the real Nathan Benjamin when Brown wrote him an insulting note refusing to offer him remuneration. Brown roared with laughter when he finally discovered the joke.

Casual anti-Semitism was, unhappily, endemic in English society in this period. However, Keats's negative attitude to Jews might also have had a personal edge. We'll never know, but it's certainly possible that memories of that "Jew at Enfield," with whom his runaway mother had consorted after leaving Rawlings, were playing somewhere at the back of Keats's mind, giving a personal fillip to his prejudices.

Unlike the petty bank clerk Rawlings, Isabella's wealthy merchant brothers have inherited a vast international business empire. In the poem, Keats uses this as the occasion for an extended tirade against commerce, which George Bernard Shaw considered to be the most powerful indictment of capitalism in English literature. Keats depicts a global economy driven by the dystopian dynamic "where every maw / The greater on the less feeds evermore," as he had put it in his verse epistle to Reynolds. Cocooned in their Florentine mansion, the merchant brothers blind themselves to the far-flung and unethical sources of their wealth, and to the suffering that entails.

Keats the medic delineates the human cost of the merchant brothers' drive for wealth in physiological detail. "For them" the Ceylon pearl diver "held his breath" until "his ears gushed blood," while other workers stand all day in rivers, dazzled by the sun, to pan for gold. In an allusion to industrial machinery, the brothers—"these money-bags," as Keats calls them—turn an "easy wheel" that sets "sharp racks" in motion, causing a thousand men to "seethe," a prediction of political unrest.

The evil brothers' "red-lined accounts" are, in addition, steeped in the blood of slavery and the slave trade, where "many once proud-quivered loins did melt / In blood from stinging whip." For those on what we might now call the Left, like Keats, Abolitionist sympathies were the norm. Although the slave trade had been officially banned by the British in 1807, it remained a live issue in 1818. The institution of slavery itself was, moreover, still legal in British-controlled territories abroad, though not within the British Isles.

Indeed, the trade itself continued as a powerful force in global commerce, since other countries had not signed up to the ban. Long past the date of Keats's death in 1821, many British financial institutions, such as banks and insurance companies, remained tied at a remove to the international slave economy, whose tentacles stretched far and wide. According to University College, London's recent research project on Legacies of Slave Ownership, Smith, Payne & Smith, the bank for which Rawlings worked, had a particular history of lending to slave owners and itself owned a Jamaican slave plantation in the 1790s.

Rawlings may have worked for a compromised bank, but it's unlikely that Keats, who lived on inherited wealth based on his grandmother's investment portfolio, fully investigated the sources of his own cash. Indeed, most Britons at this period would have found it hard, even had they made a concerted effort, to make sure that their investments were ethically pure. The British economy was so entangled with the global slave trade that in 1824 a new Act of Parliament had to be brought in to bolster the Abolition Act. It was designed to target indirect financial involvement, such as insuring slaving ships or doing business with slave traders at a remove, but it was only marginally effective.

The attack on global commerce mounted by Keats in *Isabella* is vigorous and clear. Keats's personal attitude toward his own petty finances in real life was, in contrast, marked by confusion, anxiety and denial. His habit of avoidance is plain in his admission "I have all my life thought very little of these matters," made in August 1819, at a time when his own "cash-recourses" had come to a full stop. Money and inheritance were toxic issues in the Keats family, associated with discord and lawsuits. His grandfather John Jennings was well-off when he died in 1805, leaving stocks and annuities amounting to £12,000 plus other interests, but his will was poorly drafted. Following his death, Keats's mother Frances, along with her new husband Rawlings, immediately brought an action against his estate, claiming that she was owed more than the derisory legacy of £50 per annum which she received.

Subsequent litigation—including a later action by the widow of Keats's maternal uncle—became baroque and so sclerotic that the failure of the Chancery court to produce a result until well into the 1820s has led some to suppose that Dickens had the Keatses in mind when he created the interminable case of Jarndyce and Jarndyce in *Bleak House,* published in 1852. That novel, inter alia, also includes a cruel caricature of a superannuated Leigh Hunt in the character of Harold Skimpole, who reads the newspapers in bed and is fond of making fancy sketches in pencil but is useless with money, an impoverished parasite relegated to sponging off his friends.

In the case of the Keatses, the legal detail, first picked over by Robert Gittings in *The Keats Inheritance* (1964), is mind-boggling. Keats himself was not interested in the intricacies. The way in which money and family feuding intertwine in *Isabella* offers a melodramatic counterpart, painted in clear-cut, vivid colors, to the muddy morass of the Keats family's financial squabbles.

Against a backdrop of strife, in which his mother had contested her father's will, Keats also had a difficult relationship to negotiate with Richard Abbey, the man his grandmother Alice Jennings appointed as legal guardian for him and his three younger siblings, George, Tom and Fanny, after she was widowed, to ensure their interests would be looked after in the event of her own death. Until they each came of age,

Abbey was to hold their inheritances in trust. It was Abbey, for example, who transferred the funds to pay for Keats's medical training. A tea broker by trade, he had presumably been chosen by Alice for his reliability and business acumen.

Abbey was cautious, bourgeois and lacking in warmth. None of the Keats siblings found his guardianship easy, though he did his duty. He allowed John to break his apprenticeship bond with the apothecary Hammond, despite the financial loss that entailed. He apprenticed George as a junior in the countinghouse (finance department) of his company when the latter was thirteen. He and his wife also had Fanny, the youngest, to live with them when she wasn't at boarding school. But he did not earn their love.

The Keats siblings, who had never experienced much family stability, proved too unreliable for Abbey's taste. After moving to Guy's Hospital, with Abbey's agreement, John threw up his medical training, in which so much money had been invested; George left the countinghouse following some argument; Fanny came to regard her berth with the Abbeys as prisonlike. In 1819, frustrated by John's foray into the financial desert of poetry writing, the business-minded Abbey tried to persuade him to take a job with a firm of hatters. Keats rejected the idea point-blank, regarding it as absurd, although it was not necessarily as crazy as a family friend today encouraging a recent graduate to take a business traineeship with a fashion retailer. In a letter to his sister, Keats jokily expressed the suspicion that the money-minded Abbey must have had a stake in the hat-making firm. Money was an issue that made Keats scared and cynical.

The Abbeys, for their part, regarded the Keats children as congenitally feckless, perhaps influenced by inside knowledge of their mother's sad story. Tom died at nineteen, but

Keats's other siblings proved as adventurous as he was. In 1818, George used his inheritance to marry and immigrate to America, hoping to make his fortune. Fanny went on, in later life, to marry a Spaniard and escape her home country to live in Europe.

Once in America, George, perhaps naïvely, invested his funds in a scheme to fund a Mississippi steamboat, initiated by a man he had met by chance: John James Audubon, a flamboyant self-mythologist now remembered as an ornithological illustrator of genius, although he has recently been exposed as a slaveholder. It turned out that Audubon was better at drawing birds than he was at business, unless—which remains a distinct possibility—he was an out-and-out con man. Audubon was in fact insolvent and had no stake in the steamboat project. George was fleeced.

Leaving his wife and child in America, George came back to London, briefly, in 1820, to raise more funds from Abbey, leading to later accusations that he had defrauded his own brother John of money due to him from the legacy left by their brother Tom, who had died in December 1818. Those allegations were rehearsed after Keats's death by his friend Charles Brown, but Keats seems to have willingly lent some of his portion to George. Whatever the truth of the matter, it underlines two things. First, it demonstrates Keats's lack of interest in the practicalities of his own finances. Such matters "seemed not to belong to me," he confessed to Fanny Brawne. Second, it symbolizes the fact that conflict over money was part and parcel of the Keats legacy. George went on to run a sawmill in Kentucky, where, disturbingly, despite his progressive roots in London, he had no qualms about exploiting the labor of rented slaves. He eventually made his fortune but then lost it again.

Keats had, despite the fact that his father had been a mere ostler, grown up with a sense of financial entitlement. Although socially underconfident, he preferred to identify upward, toward the upper-class Shelley, rather than downward, toward the peasant poet Robert Burns. His frequent stays at holiday destinations, such as the Isle of Wight, were predicated on his assumption that he could pay for leisure on unearned income: in his case, the leisure to work hard at writing poetry. He liked fine claret and was generous in lending money to friends—until his funds ran out. By the time he left for Rome to die he was broke. He sold all the copyrights for his work to Taylor & Hessey, yet was still reliant on gifts to fund his final journey to Italy. Ironically, Gittings's investigations into the tortuous tangle of the Keats family finances suggested that there was an extra pot of money owed to him from his grandmother's estate that he could have accessed through the courts had he been aware of it.

Keats's decision to leave medicine for full-time poetry in 1817 was made after he turned twenty-one and came into his inheritance. Even then, he was immediately obliged to take loans from others, despite the fact that he was handing them out to profligate self-proclaimed painter of genius Benjamin Robert Haydon. Taylor & Hessey proved generous, though the publisher's advance had not yet been established as a contractual norm in the industry.

On May 16, 1817, while at Margate, during the writing of *Endymion,* Keats wrote to thank his publishers in lordly, comedic, carelessly unpunctuated tones for their "liberality in the Shape of a manufactu[r]ed rag value £20"—as if being in debt was a badge of artistic pride. He would proceed, he said, in the manner of a literary knight of romance, to conquer "the Dun," the debt collector, for which the said knight would need no "Sword. Shield Cuirass Cuisses Herbadgeon spear Casque, Greves Pauldrons Spurs Chevron or any other scaly commodity: but he need only take the Bank Note of Faith and Cash of Salvation."

Turning his financial naïveté into a sexual joke, on June 10 he added that he must endeavor to lose his "Maidenhead with respect to money" because the "Duns" were at him. Please could he have some more as, though he'd laid by "25 good Notes . . . to write with" he was afraid that he could only keep the "Duns" at bay a fortnight. Without John Taylor's patience, belief and liberality, Keats would not have published *Endymion* or his 1820 collection. Posterity has a reason to be glad.

The central image in *Isabella* is of a beautiful, flourishing basil plant rooted in the repulsive decay of death. Unlike the abstract "thing of beauty" in *Endymion,* its beauty is revealed to be dependent on ugliness. For Keats, the realization that poetry was not just about escaping reality but embracing it—that its "balm" was not to be found in denial but in fevered acceptance—was a crucial insight. He also came, perhaps, to the conclusion that his desire to make art, like his "Morbidity of Temperament," was rooted in his own history of trauma, and that the purpose of that art was to represent paradox and contradiction as the truth about the human state. There's certainly something about Isabella's pathological attachment to the basil pot, her inability to give it up, that resonates with Keats's overwhelming need—and it was a need, not a rationally calculated decision—to work and work and work at the craft of writing poetry.

4

"The Eve of St. Agnes"

I.

St. Agnes' Eve—Ah, bitter chill it was!
The owl, for all his feathers, was a-cold;
The hare limped trembling through the frozen grass,
And silent was the flock in woolly fold:
Numb were the Beadsman's fingers, while he told
His rosary, and while his frosted breath,
Like pious incense from a censer old,
Seemed taking flight for heaven, without a death,
Past the sweet Virgin's picture, while his prayer he saith.

II.

His prayer he saith, this patient, holy man;
Then takes his lamp, and riseth from his knees,
And back returneth, meagre, barefoot, wan,
Along the chapel aisle by slow degrees:
The sculptured dead, on each side, seem to freeze,
Emprisoned in black, purgatorial rails;
Knights, ladies, praying in dumb orat'ries,

He passeth by; and his weak spirit fails
To think how they may ache in icy hoods and mails.

III.

Northward he turneth through a little door,
And scarce three steps, ere Music's golden tongue
Flattered to tears this agèd man and poor;
But no—already had his deathbell rung:
The joys of all his life were said and sung:
His was harsh penance on St. Agnes' Eve.
Another way he went, and soon among
Rough ashes sat he for his soul's reprieve,
And all night kept awake, for sinners' sake to grieve.

IV.

That ancient Beadsman heard the prelude soft;
And so it chanced, for many a door was wide,
From hurry to and fro. Soon, up aloft,
The silver, snarling trumpets 'gan to chide:
The level chambers, ready with their pride,
Were glowing to receive a thousand guests:
The carvèd angels, ever eager-eyed,
Star'd, where upon their heads the cornice rests,
With hair blown back, and wings put cross-wise on their
breasts.

V.

At length burst in the argent revelry,
With plume, tiara, and all rich array,
Numerous as shadows haunting faerily
The brain, new stuff'd, in youth, with triumphs gay

Of old romance. These let us wish away,
And turn, sole-thoughted, to one Lady there,
Whose heart had brooded, all that wintry day,
On love, and winged St. Agnes' saintly care,
As she had heard old dames full many times declare.

VI.

They told her how, upon St. Agnes' Eve,
Young virgins might have visions of delight,
And soft adorings from their loves receive
Upon the honeyed middle of the night,
If ceremonies due they did aright;
As, supperless to bed they must retire,
And couch supine their beauties, lily white;
Nor look behind, nor sideways, but require
Of Heaven with upward eyes for all that they desire.

VII.

Full of this whim was thoughtful Madeline:
The music, yearning like a God in pain,
She scarcely heard: her maiden eyes divine,
Fixed on the floor, saw many a sweeping train
Pass by—she heeded not at all: in vain
Came many a tip-toe, amorous cavalier,
And back retired—not cooled by high disdain,
But she saw not: her heart was otherwhere.
She sighed for Agnes' dreams, the sweetest of the year.

VIII.

She danced along with vague, regardless eyes,
Anxious her lips, her breathing quick and short:

The hallowed hour was near at hand: she sighs
Amid the timbrels, and the thronged resort
Of whisperers in anger, or in sport;
'Mid looks of love, defiance, hate, and scorn,
Hoodwinked with faery fancy—all amort,
Save to St. Agnes and her lambs unshorn,
And all the bliss to be before to-morrow morn.

IX.

So, purposing each moment to retire,
She lingered still. Meantime, across the moors,
Had come young Porphyro, with heart on fire
For Madeline. Beside the portal doors,
Buttressed from moonlight, stands he, and implores
All saints to give him sight of Madeline
But for one moment in the tedious hours,
That he might gaze and worship all unseen;
Perchance speak, kneel, touch, kiss—in sooth such things
have been.

X.

He ventures in—let no buzzed whisper tell,
All eyes be muffled, or a hundred swords
Will storm his heart, Love's fev'rous citadel:
For him, those chambers held barbarian hordes,
Hyena foemen, and hot-blooded lords,
Whose very dogs would execrations howl
Against his lineage: not one breast affords
Him any mercy, in that mansion foul,
Save one old beldame, weak in body and in soul.

XI.

Ah, happy chance! the agèd creature came,
Shuffling along with ivory-headed wand,
To where he stood, hid from the torch's flame,
Behind a broad half-pillar, far beyond
The sound of merriment and chorus bland:
He startled her; but soon she knew his face,
And grasped his fingers in her palsied hand,
Saying, "Mercy, Porphyro! hie thee from this place:
They are all here to-night, the whole blood-thirsty race!

XII.

"Get hence! get hence! there's dwarfish Hildebrand—
He had a fever late, and in the fit
He cursèd thee and thine, both house and land:
Then there's that old Lord Maurice, not a whit
More tame for his grey hairs—Alas me! flit!
Flit like a ghost away."—"Ah, gossip dear,
We're safe enough; here in this arm-chair sit,
And tell me how—" "Good Saints! not here, not here;
Follow me, child, or else these stones will be thy bier."

XIII.

He followed through a lowly archèd way,
Brushing the cobwebs with his lofty plume,
And as she muttered, "Well-a—well-a-day!"
He found him in a little moonlight room,
Pale, latticed, chill, and silent as a tomb.
"Now tell me where is Madeline," said he,
"O tell me, Angela, by the holy loom
Which none but secret sisterhood may see,
When they St. Agnes' wool are weaving piously."

XIV.

"St. Agnes! Ah! it is St. Agnes' Eve—
Yet men will murder upon holy days:
Thou must hold water in a witch's sieve,
And be liege-lord of all the Elves and Fays,
To venture so: it fills me with amaze
To see thee, Porphyro!—St. Agnes' Eve!
God's help! my lady fair the conjuror plays
This very night. Good angels her deceive!
But let me laugh awhile, I've mickle time to grieve."

XV.

Feebly she laugheth in the languid moon,
While Porphyro upon her face doth look,
Like puzzled urchin on an agèd crone
Who keepeth closed a wondrous riddle-book,
As spectacled she sits in chimney nook.
But soon his eyes grew brilliant, when she told
His lady's purpose; and he scarce could brook
Tears, at the thought of those enchantments cold,
And Madeline asleep in lap of legends old.

XVI.

Sudden a thought came like a full-blown rose,
Flushing his brow, and in his painèd heart
Made purple riot; then doth he propose
A stratagem, that makes the beldame start:
"A cruel man and impious thou art:
Sweet lady, let her pray, and sleep, and dream
Alone with her good angels, far apart
From wicked men like thee. Go, go!—I deem
Thou canst not surely be the same that thou didst seem."

XVII.

"I will not harm her, by all saints I swear,"
Quoth Porphyro: "O may I ne'er find grace
When my weak voice shall whisper its last prayer,
If one of her soft ringlets I displace,
Or look with ruffian passion in her face:
Good Angela, believe me by these tears,
Or I will, even in a moment's space,
Awake, with horrid shout, my foemen's ears,
And beard them, though they be more fanged than wolves
    and bears."

XVIII.

"Ah! why wilt thou affright a feeble soul?
A poor, weak, palsy-stricken, churchyard thing,
Whose passing-bell may ere the midnight toll;
Whose prayers for thee, each morn and evening,
Were never missed."—Thus plaining, doth she bring
A gentler speech from burning Porphyro,
So woeful, and of such deep sorrowing,
That Angela gives promise she will do
Whatever he shall wish, betide her weal or woe.

XIX.

Which was, to lead him, in close secrecy,
Even to Madeline's chamber, and there hide
Him in a closet, of such privacy
That he might see her beauty unespied,
And win perhaps that night a peerless bride,
While legioned faeries paced the coverlet,
And pale enchantment held her sleepy-eyed.

Never on such a night have lovers met,
Since Merlin paid his Demon all the monstrous debt.

XX.

"It shall be as thou wishest," said the Dame:
"All cates and dainties shall be storèd there
Quickly on this feast-night; by the tambour frame
Her own lute thou wilt see. No time to spare,
For I am slow and feeble, and scarce dare
On such a catering trust my dizzy head.
Wait here, my child, with patience; kneel in prayer
The while. Ah! thou must needs the lady wed,
Or may I never leave my grave among the dead."

XXI.

So saying, she hobbled off with busy fear.
The lover's endless minutes slowly passed;
The dame returned, and whispered in his ear
To follow her; with agèd eyes aghast
From fright of dim espial. Safe at last,
Through many a dusky gallery, they gain
The maiden's chamber, silken, hushed, and chaste;
Where Porphyro took covert, pleased amain.
His poor guide hurried back with agues in her brain.

XXII.

Her faltering hand upon the balustrade,
Old Angela was feeling for the stair,
When Madeline, St. Agnes' charmèd maid,
Rose, like a missioned spirit, unaware:
With silver taper's light, and pious care,

She turned, and down the agèd gossip led
To a safe level matting. Now prepare,
Young Porphyro, for gazing on that bed—
She comes, she comes again, like ring-dove frayed and fled.

XXIII.

Out went the taper as she hurried in;
Its little smoke, in pallid moonshine, died:
She closed the door, she panted, all akin
To spirits of the air, and visions wide—
No uttered syllable, or, woe betide!
But to her heart, her heart was voluble,
Paining with eloquence her balmy side;
As though a tongueless nightingale should swell
Her throat in vain, and die, heart-stiflèd, in her dell.

XXIV.

A casement high and triple-arched there was,
All garlanded with carven imag'ries
Of fruits, and flowers, and bunches of knot-grass,
And diamonded with panes of quaint device,
Innumerable of stains and splendid dyes,
As are the tiger-moth's deep-damasked wings;
And in the midst, 'mong thousand heraldries,
And twilight saints, and dim emblazonings,
A shielded scutcheon blushed with blood of queens and
kings.

XXV.

Full on this casement shone the wintry moon,
And threw warm gules on Madeline's fair breast,
As down she knelt for heaven's grace and boon;

Rose-bloom fell on her hands, together pressed,
And on her silver cross soft amethyst,
And on her hair a glory, like a saint:
She seemed a splendid angel, newly dressed,
Save wings, for Heaven—Porphyro grew faint;
She knelt, so pure a thing, so free from mortal taint.

XXVI.

Anon his heart revives: her vespers done,
Of all its wreathèd pearls her hair she frees;
Unclasps her warmèd jewels one by one;
Loosens her fragrant bodice; by degrees
Her rich attire creeps rustling to her knees:
Half-hidden, like a mermaid in sea-weed,
Pensive awhile she dreams awake, and sees,
In fancy, fair St. Agnes in her bed,
But dares not look behind, or all the charm is fled.

XXVII.

Soon, trembling in her soft and chilly nest,
In sort of wakeful swoon, perplexed she lay,
Until the poppied warmth of sleep oppressed
Her soothèd limbs, and soul fatigued away—
Flown, like a thought, until the morrow-day;
Blissfully havened both from joy and pain;
Clasped like a missal where swart Paynims pray;
Blinded alike from sunshine and from rain,
As though a rose should shut, and be a bud again.

XXVIII.

Stolen to this paradise, and so entranced,
Porphyro gazed upon her empty dress,

And listened to her breathing, if it chanced
To wake into a slumbrous tenderness;
Which when he heard, that minute did he bless,
And breathed himself: then from the closet crept,
Noiseless as fear in a wide wilderness,
And over the hushed carpet, silent, stepped,
And 'tween the curtains peeped, where, lo!—how fast she
slept.

XXIX.

Then by the bed-side, where the faded moon
Made a dim, silver twilight, soft he set
A table, and, half anguished, threw thereon
A cloth of woven crimson, gold, and jet—
O for some drowsy Morphean amulet!
The boisterous, midnight, festive clarion,
The kettle-drum, and far-heard clarinet,
Affray his ears, though but in dying tone;
The hall door shuts again, and all the noise is gone.

XXX.

And still she slept an azure-lidded sleep,
In blanchèd linen, smooth, and lavendered,
While he from forth the closet brought a heap
Of candied apple, quince, and plum, and gourd,
With jellies soother than the creamy curd,
And lucent syrups, tinct with cinnamon;
Manna and dates, in argosy transferred
From Fez; and spicèd dainties, every one,
From silken Samarkand to cedared Lebanon.

XXXI.

These delicates he heaped with glowing hand
On golden dishes and in baskets bright
Of wreathèd silver; sumptuous they stand
In the retirèd quiet of the night,
Filling the chilly room with perfume light.
"And now, my love, my seraph fair, awake!
Thou art my heaven, and I thine eremite:
Open thine eyes, for meek St. Agnes' sake,
Or I shall drowse beside thee, so my soul doth ache."

XXXII.

Thus whispering, his warm, unnervèd arm
Sank in her pillow. Shaded was her dream
By the dusk curtains—'twas a midnight charm
Impossible to melt as icèd stream:
The lustrous salvers in the moonlight gleam;
Broad golden fringe upon the carpet lies.
It seemed he never, never could redeem
From such a steadfast spell his lady's eyes;
So mused awhile, entoiled in woofèd phantasies.

XXXIII.

Awakening up, he took her hollow lute,
Tumultuous, and, in chords that tenderest be,
He played an ancient ditty, long since mute,
In Provence called, "La belle dame sans mercy,"
Close to her ear touching the melody—
Wherewith disturbed, she uttered a soft moan:
He ceased—she panted quick—and suddenly
Her blue affrayèd eyes wide open shone.
Upon his knees he sank, pale as smooth-sculptured stone.

XXXIV.

Her eyes were open, but she still beheld,
Now wide awake, the vision of her sleep—
There was a painful change, that nigh expelled
The blisses of her dream so pure and deep.
At which fair Madeline began to weep,
And moan forth witless words with many a sigh,
While still her gaze on Porphyro would keep;
Who knelt, with joinèd hands and piteous eye,
Fearing to move or speak, she looked so dreamingly.

XXXV.

"Ah, Porphyro!" said she, "but even now
Thy voice was at sweet tremble in mine ear,
Made tuneable with every sweetest vow;
And those sad eyes were spiritual and clear:
How changed thou art! how pallid, chill, and drear!
Give me that voice again, my Porphyro,
Those looks immortal, those complainings dear!
O leave me not in this eternal woe,
For if thy diest, my Love, I know not where to go."

XXXVI.

Beyond a mortal man impassioned far
At these voluptuous accents, he arose,
Ethereal, flushed, and like a throbbing star
Seen mid the sapphire heaven's deep repose;
Into her dream he melted, as the rose
Blendeth its odour with the violet—
Solution sweet. Meantime the frost-wind blows
Like Love's alarum pattering the sharp sleet
Against the window-panes; St. Agnes' moon hath set.

XXXVII.

'Tis dark: quick pattereth the flaw-blown sleet.
"This is no dream, my bride, my Madeline!"
'Tis dark: the icèd gusts still rave and beat.
"No dream, alas! alas! and woe is mine!
Porphyro will leave me here to fade and pine.—
Cruel! what traitor could thee hither bring?
I curse not, for my heart is lost in thine,
Though thou forsakest a deceivèd thing—
A dove forlorn and lost with sick unprunèd wing."

XXXVIII.

"My Madeline! sweet dreamer! lovely bride!
Say, may I be for aye thy vassal blessed?
Thy beauty's shield, heart-shaped and vermeil dyed?
Ah, silver shrine, here will I take my rest
After so many hours of toil and quest,
A famished pilgrim—saved by miracle.
Though I have found, I will not rob thy nest
Saving of thy sweet self; if thou think'st well
To trust, fair Madeline, to no rude infidel.

XXXIX.

"Hark! 'tis an elfin-storm from faery land,
Of haggard seeming, but a boon indeed:
Arise—arise! the morning is at hand.
The bloated wassaillers will never heed—
Let us away, my love, with happy speed—
There are no ears to hear, or eyes to see,
Drowned all in Rhenish and the sleepy mead;
Awake! arise! my love, and fearless be,
For o'er the southern moors I have a home for thee."

XL.

She hurried at his words, beset with fears,
For there were sleeping dragons all around,
At glaring watch, perhaps, with ready spears—
Down the wide stairs a darkling way they found.
In all the house was heard no human sound.
A chain-drooped lamp was flickering by each door;
The arras, rich with horseman, hawk, and hound,
Fluttered in the besieging wind's uproar;
And the long carpets rose along the gusty floor.

XLI.

They glide, like phantoms, into the wide hall;
Like phantoms, to the iron porch, they glide;
Where lay the Porter, in uneasy sprawl,
With a huge empty flaggon by his side:
The wakeful bloodhound rose, and shook his hide,
But his sagacious eye an inmate owns.
By one, and one, the bolts full easy slide—
The chains lie silent on the footworn stones—
The key turns, and the door upon its hinges groans.

XLII.

And they are gone—ay, ages long ago
These lovers fled away into the storm.
That night the Baron dreamt of many a woe,
And all his warrior-guests, with shade and form
Of witch, and demon, and large coffin-worm,
Were long be-nightmared. Angela the old
Died palsy-twitched, with meagre face deform;
The Beadsman, after thousand aves told,
For aye unsought for slept among his ashes cold.

KEATS'S ROMANTICISM IS often associated with romantic love, embodied in his tragically unfulfilled relationship with Fanny Brawne, which was cut short by his early death. She indeed inspired his only experience of an all-consuming attachment. Yet he did not get to know her until late 1818, well after he established his voice as a poet, and his feelings for her did not crystallize into full-blown obsession for several months after that—despite the fact that he later told her, in retrospect, that it had been love at first sight. In fact, his attitudes toward women, love and sex were complex, contradictory and not always idealistically romantic.

Endymion ends in a sort of transubstantiated erotic cloud, as the human hero consummates his love for a goddess. In *Isabella; or, The Pot of Basil,* the heroine, on the contrary, focuses her passion on a decaying severed head. As a young man who died unmarried at the age of twenty-five, what sort of sexual experience had Keats had, and how did his conflicted feelings around women and desire play out in his work? "I am certain I have not a right feeling towards Women," Keats told Benjamin Bailey on July 18, 1818.

"The Eve of St. Agnes," written in January 1819, is Keats's most explicitly erotic poem, to the extent that, when he came to publish it in his 1820 collection, Taylor & Hessey wanted him to tone it down. It has sometimes been read as a romantic fantasy connected with Fanny Brawne, but its theme, according to Richard Woodhouse, was in fact suggested to him by another woman: the only named woman, in fact, apart from Fanny Brawne, with whom Keats is known to have had a sexually charged relationship, or at least, in this case, a series of encounters. Her name was Mrs. Jones. Keats confessed that he had "warmed with her . . . and kissed her." She is a slippery character.

Like *Isabella; or, The Pot of Basil,* "The Eve of St. Agnes" is set in the Middle Ages and written in stanzas, this time in the Spenserian stanzas that had been employed by the eponymous poet in *The Faerie Queene* in the Elizabethan age, and also, more recently, fashionably revived by Byron in his bestselling *Childe Harold's Pilgrimage.* However, the plot isn't based on a particular literary source in the way the other is on Boccaccio's *Decameron.* Instead, it's inspired by an old folk legend: that on the night of St. Agnes Eve, January 20, young virgins can, if they follow the right rituals, see visions of a future husband or lover in their dreams. The poem's heroine, Madeline, goes to bed in her ancestral castle hoping for just such a visitation. She is rewarded by more than a mere dream: by the arrival of flesh-and-blood Porphyro, who enters her room while her kinsmen are feasting in the hall downstairs, secretly watches her undress, gets into her bed and deflowers her as she dreams, before the couple finally elope together into the storm.

The poem itself is a verbal feast, its images appealing to all the senses, from the muffled sound of the kettledrums in the hall, to the sight of colored light refracted through stained glass, to the feel of tactile rustling silks, to the taste of spicy cinnamon. However, it ends on a note of starved desolation rather than sated triumph, after the lovers flee away. We hear nothing of their after-story, which remains a blank. They simply disappear. Those left behind in the castle are, meanwhile, be-nightmared by witches, demons and coffin worms. Madeline's old nurse, with whom Porphyro has colluded to gain entry, dies palsy-twitched. In the final line, an old priest, saying his "aves" on his rosary ad infinitum, ends dying ignored "among his ashes cold."

During the course of its reception history, "The Eve of

St. Agnes" has inspired some contradictory interpretations. In the twentieth century, it was fashionable among academic critics to view it as a spiritual allegory, until Jack Stillinger pointed out the worrying possibility that it portrays Porphyro as a Peeping Tom and sexual predator. Keats even uses the word "peeped" of Porphyro, and describes him hiding in Madeline's bedroom like a hunter in a "covert." The scenario certainly feels uncomfortable today. Even in 1819, it discombobulated Richard Woodhouse and John Taylor of his publishers Taylor & Hessey, who thought the poem went against "Decency & Discretion" and was thus "unfit for ladies."

That latter phrase appears to reek of antiquated double gender standards. But you don't need to be a nineteenth-century prude to share Taylor's anxiety that the story has the potential to offer an affront to "the Suffrages of Women." Although Madeline is presented as "moaning" and "panting" with enthusiasm at Porphyro's tender touch, the fact remains that she is asleep or half-asleep at the time, which precludes her consent. As soon as she's fully awake, and realizes what has happened, she cries, "alas! alas! and woe is mine!" Keats even makes an explicit rape analogy by comparing her to a "tongueless nightingale"—an allusion to the classical myth of Philomel, who was turned into a nightingale by the gods after Tereus raped her and cut out her tongue. His riposte to Woodhouse's objection was swaggeringly macho. He told him that "he should despise a man who would be such an eunuch . . . as to leave a . . . maid, with that character about her, in such a situation." Yet in reality Keats was more insecure than predatory.

The sexual activity in the poem is, of course, presented under a veil of imagery, with the result that some readers today are reluctant to conclude that sex takes place at all.

But the evidence shows that Keats had no doubt that he wanted contemporary readers to know what his metaphors meant. He told Woodhouse that if there was any "opening for doubt what took place, it was his fault for not writing clearly and comprehensibly." Indeed, he added some lines to make the action more explicit, though they did not make it into the published version. Woodhouse himself, the poem's first reader, found its underlying scenario unambiguous. He complained to Keats that "Porphyro presses breast to breast, and acts all the acts of a bona fide husband, while she fancies she is only playing the part of a Wife in a dream." There is also a clue in the heroine's name: Madeline. A "magdalen"—from Mary Magdalen in Scripture—was a term used for a fallen woman. In London, Guy's Hospital was close to the Magdalen Hospital, a refuge home for former prostitutes.

In his letters to male friends, Keats was relaxed about using sexual slang words (all metaphors too). In the idiom of the day, a penis was a "nail" or "yard," or sometimes "chair," the French word for flesh, while semen was "cordial," and words for the vagina included "puddle," "vallis lucis," "haven," "cony," "mater omnium," "haven" and "bower." There's no anatomical crudeness in "The Eve of St. Agnes," but in fact few readers at the time would have missed the sensual import when, say, Porphyro plays a "ditty" on Madeline's "hollow lute." Or when he lays out a feast that elides sexual appetite with food, including "lucent syrups, tinct with cinnamon" and those glutinous "jellies soother than the creamy curd." (It's the cinnamon and the quince, according to the recent Keats scholar Richard Marggraf Turley, that were two key ingredients in the syrup recommended for patients in the latter stage of gonorrhea, as described in William Houlston's medical textbook of 1794, *Pharmacopoeia Chirurgica.*) Or the way in which Porphyro's passion climaxes euphemistically in the liquid materiality of "solution sweet." Physical and spiritual language coexist in uneasy tension throughout the poem, yet Keats's contemporaries were arguably more, not less, alert to erotic subtexts than we are, as there was less scope for literal explicitness in public discourse.

Biographers have long since concluded that Keats believed he had contracted syphilis (rather than gonorrhea) from some unrecorded sexual encounter, probably with a prostitute. On October 8, 1817, shortly after completing Book Three of *Endymion,* he told Benjamin Bailey, the trainee curate who had recently hosted him in Oxford, "The little Mercury I have taken has corrected the Poison and improved my Health— though I feel from my employment that I shall never again be secure in Robustness." Mercury was the standard treatment for syphilis; the Poison appears to be a euphemism for the clap.

Unsurprisingly, Keats left no record of his casual sexual contacts. However, he was rather pleased to find the "Women being a little profligate" when he arrived on the Isle of Wight to write *Endymion.* His male friends, moreover, were sexually active, and clearly took similar risks. In a letter to his lawyer friend James Rice, Keats mentions how he'd seen some barmaids of their acquaintance, one of whom asked whether Rice preserved "a secret she gave you on the nail"—which sounds as though he thought Rice too was at risk of having contracted the Poison.

When Joseph Severn, then an art student, fathered an illegitimate child in September 1819 (without the knowledge of his parents, with whom he was living at the time), Keats passed on the gossip to George and Georgiana in a tone of masculine joshing that made no allowances for his sister-in-law's feminine sensibilities:

> Severn has had a little Baby—all his own let us hope—he told Brown he had given up painting and had tur[n]'d modeller. I hope sincerely tis not a party concern; that no Mr—— or ***** is the real *Pinxit* and Severn the poor *Sculpsit* to this work of art.

Clearly, Keats believed that the woman in question had been sleeping with other men in their friendship group at the same time.

Severn went on to marry respectably, have several more—legitimate—children and become a pillar of the establishment. In contrast, Charles Armitage Brown, who by 1819 had become Keats's closest friend, was unusual: he brought his working-class mistress, Abigail O'Donoghue, to live with him at Wentworth Place as his housekeeper. Their son Carlino was born in 1820. He later claimed that his parents had secretly married in Ireland in 1819, but no record of the wedding has ever been found. More likely, Carlino—who grew up to emigrate to New Zealand, where he became a politician and preferred to be called Charles—was embarrassed by his illegitimacy.

Sexual mores were more fluid in the Regency period than they later became for the Victorians. Severn's youthful indiscretion, and even Brown's bohemian domestic setup, were small fry compared to the operatic scale on which Byron and Shelley pursued free love. Byron had to leave the country in 1814 following his scandalous marriage breakup, amid rumors of his incestuous affair with his half sister and his penchant for anal sex (the rumors were true). Shelley left his young wife Harriet to run off to the Continent with Mary Godwin, whom he later married, and her stepsister Claire. The latter went on to have a child by Byron and possibly one by Shelley too.

In 1816, Shelley's abandoned wife Harriet committed suicide by drowning herself in the Serpentine in Hyde Park. She was twenty-one and pregnant by another man. That month, Keats, also twenty-one, was still a dresser at Guy's, on duty at the hospital twenty-four hours a day one week in four. It would be interesting to know whether any of the patients he treated while he was on duty were attempted suicides by drowning. The hospital was close to the river Thames.

Leigh Hunt, too, was as liberal in his sexual attitudes as he was in his politics. His suburban household in Hampstead was an emotional tinderbox, though he bounced above it on a typical wave of denial. He was married to Marianne, with whom, by the time Keats met him, he already had four children (the number eventually rose to ten), but he was also in the habit of making advances to his live-in sister-in-law, Elizabeth Kent. According to Benjamin Robert Haydon, this involved dawdling over her bosom, leaning against her thigh and playing with her petticoats, though without bothering to go to "the effort of furious gratification." The stress led to Elizabeth attempting to drown herself in a pond on Hampstead Heath, in unsuccessful imitation of Harriet Shelley, in February 1817. Brief encounters with barmaids—whatever the health hazards—were commonplace by comparison.

Keats's literary treatment of erotic themes goes back to one of his earliest surviving poems, "Fill for me a brimming bowl," written in 1814 when he was eighteen. In it, he recorded the apparently drunken longing he had felt for the "Paradise" breasts of a random woman he had seen only from afar while on a trip to Vauxhall Gardens. Vauxhall was Regency London's premier pay-to-enter pleasure dome, where ticket-holders could enjoy walking among the arcades and fountains, listening to music by lantern light, dancing and people-watching. Respectable ladies rubbed shoulders with ladies of the night, and no one knew quite who was who. In the poem, Keats says he wants to forget the "lewd desiring" this unknown woman with the perfect breasts engendered at a distance. But he clearly didn't, as he wrote it down. (Lockhart later jibingly compared Keats's lush classical allusions to the ersatz decor found at Vauxhall.)

The verse letter addressed to Charles Cowden Clarke, written in October 1816 when Keats was working as a dresser at Guy's, makes a slightly embarrassed reference to breasts in a self-conscious allusion to Spenser's *Epithalamion*. The term refers to the Greek for a bridal chamber and the genre was often used by the Elizabethans as an excuse for literary erotics. Spenser's original includes the line "Her brest like to a bowle of creame uncrudded" (an echo of which is perhaps detectable in "The Eve of St. Agnes" line "soother than the creamy curd," written more than two hundred years later). Keats admiringly hymns his Elizabethan poetic hero, with a stolidness that trips over into the coy, with the line "Fondled the maidens with the breasts of cream." In doing so, he implicitly admits that he's not yet in Spenser's league either sexually or poetically.

The ideal woman and the real were constantly rubbing up against one another in Keats's imagination, fed by his confused relationship with his mother, and perhaps also by the necessary objectification of patients' bodies at the hospital. It's a jolt to remember that, at Guy's, Keats would have come into daily contact with more unclothed female forms, in far from idealized states, than the average poet. His mentor Astley Cooper wrote a treatise on breasts based on unromantic, yet fascinated, close observation: "The breasts are slung upon the chest, supported by the fibrous tissues . . ."

Cooper went on to complain that painters and sculptors tended to regularize the mammaries unnaturally, whereas in life any individual woman's two breasts are not likely to be exactly identical in shape, size or positioning. In "The Eve of St. Agnes," Keats skillfully leaves the exact appearance of Madeline's "fair breast" to the reader's imagination. But when "warm gules" are thrown upon it, by moonlight passing through a stained-glass window that's "blushed with blood," we know that he is heating up the atmosphere. In the next stanza, she "Loosens her fragrant bodice" and disrobes: "by degrees / Her rich attire creeps rustling to her knees." At no point do we actually see her naked body; her "empty dress" tells us all we need to know when Porphyro gazes on it in aroused entrancement.

Voyeurism, a predatory hero, nonconsensual sex and a male poet's fantasy that that's what women want: "The Eve of St. Agnes" certainly looks like aggressive masculine posturing. Yet it's riven with ambiguities that suggest that this male fantasy arises as much from vulnerability as from confidence, channeling Keats's anxious awareness of his "not right" feelings around women. Bird images imply that Madeline, the "tongueless nightingale," is Porphyro's quarry, a "ring-dove frayed and fled." But she's also depicted as "Hoodwinked with faery fancy." It's not innocent doves that are hoodwinked but falcons, birds of prey whose handlers place a hood over their eyes and remove it when they release them for the kill. Even in her passivity, this female character is a suppressed aggressor.

Indeed, the entire encounter between the protagonists is presented in a way that places the very idea of ambiguity or double meaning at the fore. As Woodhouse put it, everything is left to "inference," inviting the reader to decode what's going on under the rich language. According to Woodhouse, Keats "had a fancy for trying his hand to play with his reader." Indeed, the poem's tonal dissonances—are we meant to find it comic or tragic? arousing or amusing? disturbing or diverting?—make it hard as a reader to position oneself within its shifting moods.

Intriguingly, Isabella Jones, the woman who came up with the idea for the poem in the first instance, was herself an ambiguous figure whose mixed messages Keats found hard to read. She has remained something of a mystery to posterity, but was equally so to Keats himself. "She has always been an enigma to me," he told his brother George. However, what we know of their relationship suggests that the swagger with which Keats later defended "The Eve of St. Agnes" to Woodhouse was not rooted in sexual confidence. Rather, the poem's ambiguities refract something of the uncertainty provoked in Keats by his confusing encounters with the slippery Mrs. Jones. In their real-life dealings, Keats, always respectful of her, was certainly no predator. Indeed, it may have been the other way around.

Despite the efforts of succeeding Keats biographers, Isabella Jones has largely slipped their net. Her historical footprint was so sparse in 1924 that Amy Lowell doubted whether she had ever existed at all. In 1936, Edmund Blunden added some strands of flesh onto her ghost in his biography of John Taylor, Keats's publisher, including the fugitive sound of her epistolary voice. A letter she wrote to Taylor, with whom she was clearly well acquainted, shows her to have been a sophisticated woman of the world with an arch, flirtatious turn of phrase—"You once favoured me with the most amusing and delightful letter I ever read (Love epistles excepted)"—but it tells us nothing about when or where she was born or who her immediate family were. Further research by Robert Gittings in the 1950s revealed a little more about her upper-class social connections—clearly, she was no barmaid—but the name Jones is too anonymous to admit of easy tracing. However, she was (even more clearly) no "maid," as she went by the title Mrs. Her suggestion that Keats should write a poem about a virgin's Agnes Eve dream was perhaps as arch as her epistolary style.

Most of what we know about Keats's relations with Isabella Jones comes from a long and vivid letter he wrote to George and Georgiana, who were by then in America, between October 14 and 31, 1818. Writing on October 24, he refers to her as "that same Lady . . . whom I saw at Hastings." That must have been in May–June 1817, during the writing of *Endymion,* after Keats left the Isle of Wight (and its profligate women) to wander around Margate and the southeast coast. The fact that Keats uses the word "saw"—rather than "met"—implies that this was not the first time they'd been introduced. John Taylor seems the obvious conduit. Keats then refers to another meeting with her in London, "when we were going to the English Opera," though whether this was a chance encounter on a theater trip with George and Georgiana or a pre-organized rendezvous is unclear.

Then, shortly before he put pen to paper on October 24, Keats bumped into Mrs. Jones once more in central London, in "a street that goes from Bedford Row to Lamb's Conduit Street," now called Rugby Street. The eighteenth-century red-brick terraced houses that looked down on their encounter are still there. Keats describes how he'd walked past her, suddenly recognizing her and turning back. He was, he recorded, relieved that she had not taken offense because he had had to backtrack to greet her.

One has to wonder, did she not see him? Or did she make a split-second decision to let him pass? Was it up to a gentleman to greet a lady first according to the etiquette of the day? What if he'd already "warmed with her and kissed her" in the past, as he later explained he had? We can't know the answers to these questions, but neither perhaps could Keats, who was left feeling rather gauche. His description of how this latest encounter ensued brings out the ambiguities of the situation and gives a unique historical insight, early-nineteenth-century style, into the uncertain ways in which young people connect, disconnect and circle one another when sex is the unspoken possibility.

By October 1818, Keats was living with an increased level of anxiety. Since writing *Isabella; or, The Pot of Basil* earlier that year, he'd seen George and Georgiana sail for America, leaving him in sole charge of ailing Tom, who was by now seriously ill and would be dead by the end of the year. The pain of witnessing Tom's decline was agonizing—Keats felt his younger brother's identity pressing on his unbearably. He'd escaped it over the summer, by setting off, with his new best friend Charles Brown, on an eight-week walking tour that took in the Lake District, the Highlands of Scotland, and Northern Ireland. But in August, Keats was forced prematurely by his own ill health to return to Well Walk—where Tom was being cared for by their landlords, Mr. and Mrs. Bentley. In Scotland, Keats had developed a bad chill and a raging sore throat, which suggests that his own immune system was already compromised. He arrived home, sick, to find Tom much worse.

August and September 1818 also saw him reeling from the assaults of *Blackwood's* and the *Quarterly,* just at a time when he himself was ill and was being forced to come to terms with the fact that Tom's consumption was terminal. It's astonishing to think that, through all this, Keats continued writing, beginning a new epic, *Hyperion,* a dark Miltonic tale of fallen gods in which he embraced the nervy sinews of human pain.

I have limited the scope of this book to nine poems, but it's as well to remember that there are a hundred and fifty-nine individual works in the Penguin edition of *John Keats: The Complete Poems,* all written between 1814 and 1820, most of them after 1816. Among those not covered here are lengthy works, such as *Hyperion* itself, which was left unfinished at Keats's death, though he published it in 1820 as "a fragment"; *Lamia,* a brilliantly serpentine narrative of more than 700 lines, featuring a magical snake-woman and set in mythological Greece like the earlier *Endymion,* though a lot more sophisticated, which was also published in the 1820 volume; and the forgettable pseudo-Shakespearean five-act tragedy *Otho the Great,* which wasn't published in his lifetime.

Some of the poems are undistinguished. A few lines are downright bad. Witness the following couplet, from the otherwise important "Sleep and Poetry," written in 1817:

What is more gentle than a wind in summer?
What is more soothing than the pretty hummer [i.e., a bee]?

Benjamin Britten later set this couplet to swaying, staccato music that punches far above the weight of the text. As a corpus, however, Keats's poetry offers such individual highs that the lows not merely do not count, but seem like essential experimental stepping-stones.

The sheer quantity points to his frenetic productivity:

proof that he meant what he said in his now famous sonnet "When I have fears that I may cease to be / Before my
pen has gleaned my teeming brain." That urgent expression
of his desire to write as much as he could before he died was,
perhaps surprisingly, written in January 1818, long before he
knew that he himself was dying; it was not published until
1848. When he started on *Endymion,* he was intending to
work to a disciplined schedule, but his creativity, prolific as it
was, came in fits and starts.

By the time Keats bumped into Mrs. Jones at the end of
October 1818, Tom—who had only five more weeks to live—
was in a desperate state. The encounter perhaps promised a
welcome distraction. With apparently little preamble, Keats
then accompanied Mrs. Jones on what turned out to be a
long walk to Islington, where she eventually called in on a
friend who kept a boarding school. Whether he knew exactly
where they were going when they set off is unclear from his
letter. Afterward, he told George and Georgiana, he "pressed
to attend her home." Her lodgings proved to be located—
Keats gives the precise address—at 34 Gloucester Street,
Queen Square, although there's some uncertainty as he glosses
the address with "not exactly so." The fact was, she wasn't the
actual householder, as Keats appears to have assumed, but was
renting a few rooms at the property.

Her sitting room, which impressed Keats as "tasty," was
furnished in the height of boho-bourgeois fashion. He item-
izes its contents as if searching for clues in an attempt to
"place" her. As well as unspecified books and pictures, there
was a "bronze statue of Buonaparte." After Waterloo, having
a figurine of Napoleon in your room was a bit like displaying
a bust of Lenin in the 1960s: a sort of radical chic. The radical journalist William Hazlitt, whom Keats admired, had a

smaller, cheaper-sounding Napoleon statuette, which he gave as a weird love token to his landlady's daughter, with whom he was sexually obsessed. Keats himself, more modestly, had a Napoleon snuff box (he referred to it in a letter to Reynolds's sisters on September 5, 1817).

Mrs. Jones also had what Keats called an "aeolian Harp," a symbol of lyric poetry, like the image of the lyre that later featured on Keats's own grave in Rome. It can't have actually been an "Aeolian" lyre, or wind harp, which is hung in a tree and makes music when the breeze blows through it, and which Shelley used as a symbol for the poet's responsiveness to nature. There would be no point in having one in one's sitting room. More likely, Isabella Jones had a harp-lute or harp-guitar, newfangled instruments designed for drawing room use by fashionable ladies. Then, there were a couple of caged birds, a parrot and a linnet, which offered their own mixed message: linnets are known for the natural beauty of their song, while parrots are frauds that emptily ape.

In his letter, Keats confides that as soon as he and Mrs. Jones had made it to her rooms, he lunged at her. "As I had warmed with her before and kissed her—I thought it would be living backwards not to do so again." That phrase "warmed with" has proved troublesome to biographers. But whether "warmed" is a Keatsian neologism or a long-lost slang term, it's hard to interpret it, as some have done, as referring to mere verbal conversation. It's such a visceral word; it seems evidence of a prior physical encounter that involved more than kissing, though how much more we can never know.

Yet Mrs. Jones, previously open, "contrived to disappoint" Keats. He put her sexual rebuff down to her "better taste," saying she only "shrunk from it" because she perceived he saw it as a "thing of course"—that he was taking her acceptance of his overtures for granted. The man who later wrote that only a eunuch would have failed to fornicate with the fictional Madeline gives Mrs. Jones the benefit of the doubt at every stage, following her lead in sexual manners, and worrying that he might have offended her in the past without realizing it.

At every stage, his depiction of the encounter is a mélange of anxiety and contradiction mixed up with wounded pride. He ends on a complete volte-face, claiming, somewhat unconvincingly, that he actually regards Isabella Jones in the same platonic light as his own sister-in-law: that he has "no libidinous thought about her," and that, apart from Georgiana, she is the only other woman "à peu près de mon age"—he'd perhaps caught a whiff of fashionable Frenchification from Mrs. Jones's conversation—whom he "would be content to know for their mind and friendship alone." Maybe he's even quoting what he said to Mrs. Jones to save face, after pulling back from trying to kiss her.

The idea that his feelings for her are purely platonic sits uneasily with his account of their history. This woman had clearly aroused his amorous expectations by warming with him in the past. She takes him on a wild-goose chase to Islington and then goes on to manipulate him into thinking that it's he who is pressing to attend her home. And then she puts him on the back foot by making him question his own taste rather than her mixed messages.

Before he leaves, Mrs. Jones makes a play of showing she is in control by putting Keats decisively in her debt: she sends him away with a gift of grouse for Tom's dinner and asks for his address so she can send him more game. She was true to her word, given that, in a later letter, Keats tells George and Georgiana about a further carnivorous gift from her. Unlike Shelley, who was a vegetarian, Keats liked meat. While he was hiking in Scotland, the meager diet of "Oat-cakes" made him "despair." Exhausted by climbing Ben Nevis, he "long[ed]for some famous Beauty to . . . approach me . . . & give me—a dozen or two capital roast beef sandwiches." He later (on February 19, 1819) described his "palate-passion" as including game. "I must plead guilty to the breast of a Partridge, the back of a hare, the backbone of a grouse, the wing and side of a Pheasant and a Woodcock *passim.*"

The grouse Mrs. Jones gives him in lordly fashion is eloquent, as if she regards Keats himself as some sort of prey. It also suggests a hint of class patronage since it implies she had access to a landed estate. His acceptance of her largesse marks him out as a vassal. Seen through the lens of this encounter, "The Eve of St. Agnes" posits a role reversal in which the woman, Madeline, becomes prey to Porphyro, not a giver of game, but game in herself. It shows Keats trying doggedly to assert his masculine sexuality in response to confusing signals from the woman who inspired it. In "trying his hand to play with his reader," he was perhaps reacting to Isabella Jones, who had toyed with him but was the more adept player when it came to games of hearts.

"The Eve of St. Agnes" may bear the invisible traces of a failed seduction, but its contradictions and complexities are also linked to Keats's conflicted literary attitudes toward women as writers and readers. *Endymion* had aroused the scorn of *Blackwood's* and the *Quarterly,* but Mrs. Jones, in contrast, was a fan, declaring it a "favourite"; she wasn't the only woman who liked it. However, Keats was ambivalent about attracting female literary admirers. He was not entirely bowled over by the compliment when Woodhouse told him in December 1818 that *Endymion* had delighted his cousin, Miss Frogley of Hounslow, and also "one of the Misses Porter (of romance celebrity)," who wanted to meet him (Jane and Anna Maria Porter wrote commercial romantic novels with a Gothic twist). His reply was buttoned up and seesawing all over the place:

> My dear Woodhouse,
>   *I am greatly* obliged to you. I must needs feel flattered by making an impression on a set of Ladies—I should be content to do so in meretricious romance verse if they alone and not Men were to judge. I should very much like to know those Ladies—tho' look here Woodhouse— I have a new leaf to turn over—I must work—I must read—I must write—I am unable to afford time for new acquaintances.

Later, when Woodhouse objected that "The Eve of St. Agnes" was "unfit for ladies," Keats rejoined that he didn't want ladies to read him anyway—a somewhat self-defeating remark at a time when women made up a large and significant section of the reading public. Keats frequently denied that he cared about reviews or sales or readers (unless the latter were the future generations who would appreciate him after his death). He declared to Taylor on August 23, 1819, "I equally dislike the favour of the public with the love of a woman." However, he was not in reality quite so certain on either count (by August 23, 1819, he would in fact be passionately in love with Fanny Brawne, and had even penned a love letter to her the week before). Back around the time he wrote "The Eve of St. Agnes," in early 1819, he may, however, have been hoping to write something that would, finally, sell.

It is notable that he chose to write "The Eve of St. Agnes" in the Spenserian stanza form made popular by Byron. He told George and Georgiana in February 1819 that he'd heard how much the latter's publisher John Murray had made as a result: "What think you of £25,000? He sold 4000 coppies of Lord Byron." Keats never sold 4,000 copies in his lifetime, but he was not wholly immune to the idea of appealing to the popular market, though his comments about doing so are so contradictory. Lamenting that *Endymion* had not succeeded, he said he was determined to "try the public again."

Referring to "The Eve of St. Agnes," among other titles, he told George and Georgiana he was doing a "fine mother Radcliff" in his medievalist and exotic choice of names. Ann Radcliffe was one of the most successful female authors of the day. Her Gothic romances were devoured by the fictional heroine of Jane Austen's *Northanger Abbey* and countless real-life female readers besides. Keats's satirical reference to her as "mother Radcliff" betrays some scorn toward this older woman who had conquered the market—and yet he was, at the same time, admitting to channeling her influence. In "The Eve of St. Agnes," that goes much further than the characters' names. Radcliffe's contribution to the Gothic genre is known as the "explained supernatural"—the introduction of unexplained, seemingly ghostly happenings which are revealed in the end, after three volumes of twists and turns, as having commonsense empirical explanations. "The Eve of St. Agnes" adopts exactly this plan, but concertinas the anticipation by giving flesh-and-blood reality to Madeline's supposedly supernatural dream visitation within thirty stanzas.

Keats's attitude to female literary taste was as insecure and uncertain as Mrs. Jones had made him feel. And yet he was less of a chauvinist than many of his contemporaries. Back in the 1790s, political radicalism had incorporated the feminism of Mary Wollstonecraft. Yet by Keats's era, most men on what we'd now call the Left tended to be as misogynistic as their right-wing counterparts at *Blackwood's*. Keats's desire to know Mrs. Jones, even after being rebuffed, for her mind and friendship alone makes him sound positively enlightened compared to the views of William Hazlitt.

The latter had such an "utter aversion" to "*bluestockings*"—women who liked books and could talk about them—that he did not "care a fig for any woman that even knows what an author means," as he put it in his essay *Of Great and Little Things* (1821). Keats, by contrast, hoped he would be of service to Mrs. Jones as a conversational partner in future discussions about "knowledge and taste." Despite her physical rebuff, his relationship with her must have gone on to develop in more depth than is recorded in his letters. After he died, she was considered so important in his life that she was given one or more of the books that he had owned and had asked to be divided among his friends in the event of his death.

So who was Mrs. Jones? In the search for her identity, one recent suggestion is that she was the widow of a naval officer who had died a hero on Nelson's *Victory* in 1805, since records exist of an "Isabella Jones" of that description. However, that lady would have been thirty-eight at the time, certainly not "à peu près" to Keats in age, as he was twenty-one when he first met his Mrs. Jones, and about to turn twenty-four when he came across her in the street and visited her rooms. His sister-in-law Georgiana, with whom he couples her, was even younger.

Mrs. Jones could of course have lied about her age, which would probably have been in character. However, if her late husband had been a respected public figure, it seems likely that we would know about it from other sources. It's always assumed that Mrs. Jones must have been a widow, but that's only an assumption. She was certainly unencumbered by a husband or children, but she could have been separated. In a pinch, it's even possible that she was unmarried and using the title Mrs. as a respectable shield, as many genteel "fallen" women did. It's hard not to conclude that, in its very anonymity, the name Jones itself looks a little suspicious.

Isabella Jones was one of the Regency era's women on the edge, females of that fluid period who fell between caste categories and tried to create independent identities in undefined spaces. Scholars have identified her as being socially connected with a family of Irish grandees, including Donat O'Callaghan, who must have been in his seventies when he knew her. An extant letter from her to John Taylor, written from Tunbridge Wells in May 1819, was franked by another member of the O'Callaghan clan, James, who was then the Westminster MP for a rotten borough in Cornwall. A further member of the O'Callaghan clan was in Tunbridge at the time: the Dowager Lady Lismore. By marriage the O'Callaghans were related to elevated Whig circles via the Ponsonbys (via another marriage, the latter family included Henrietta, sister of Georgiana, Duchess of Devonshire).

In *The Mask of Keats,* first published in 1956, Robert Gittings wondered how Isabella Jones could afford her luxury pad in Bloomsbury and speculated that the O'Callaghans were somehow funding her. But how she lived, who her family were, and how her life panned out after her encounters with Keats remain as mysterious today as she was to him at the time. In 1807 the poet Robert Southey complained that increasing social and geographical mobility were making it so difficult to "place" people that "there never was any age or country so favorable to the success of imposture as this very age and this very England." Mrs. Jones is certainly hard to place. Speculation that she might have been an actress or singer, published by Jonathan Bate since I first wrote this book, deserves further investigation. That would certainly fit with her anomalous social position.

Keats's depiction of their encounter vibrates with social uncertainty. During their walk to visit her friend in Islington, they passed, as he put it, "some times through shabby, sometimes through decent Street[s]," as if he is transferring his own uncertainty about Mrs. Jones's respectability to their road route. The fact that her friend kept a boarding school sounds prim, until you remember that keeping a school was the only way (apart from writing books for the market like the Misses Porter) in which a downwardly mobile educated woman, possibly with a past, could make her living. Not only could the trade provide an income; it could also offer a respectable image.

Mrs. Jones herself certainly wanted to erect a smoke screen. Keats was bamboozled by her obsession with secrecy, telling George, "she has been in a Room with you and with Reynolds and wishes we should be acquainted without any of our common acquaintance knowing it." The unspoken, the secret, the coded: these are relevant to "The Eve of St. Agnes," whose florid metaphors for sex leave everything, as Woodhouse said, to "inference."

Although seemingly a woman of independence, who lived alone in Bloomsbury, Mrs. Jones clearly did not feel as free as the Bloomsbury Group did a hundred years later to pursue her dalliances openly. She may have had tangential high-society connections, but that doesn't tell us how she knew them. Given the lack of hard fact, it's worth considering that it might be just as possible that she was the unspoken mistress of the elderly Donat O'Callaghan as that she was a "respectable" widow who had been taken under his family's wing. (Even that sort of respectable lady could be a bit questionable, such as Mrs. Clay in Jane Austen's *Persuasion*.)

A minor poem by Keats written in 1818, "Hush, hush, tread softly! hush hush my dear," features a courting couple creeping around to evade a "jealous old bald-pate," and a lot of coy sexual symbolism. Written in the first person, it refers to "my Isabel's eyes, and her lips pulped with bloom." The unnamed speaker is her young lover. He imagines that, while the old man sleeps, Isabel's latch will be lifted and her dreamy shut rose will awake full blown with warmth, leaving him "aching all through." Certainly, this "Isabel" is cheating on an elderly man. A—possibly transactional—existing relationship with a possessive older lover might explain why Mrs. Jones was so keen to keep her dalliance with the young Keats under wraps.

The name Madeline in "The Eve of St. Agnes" refers to the fact that the virgin heroine becomes, in the course of the poem, a Magdalen or fallen woman. We don't know what Mrs. Jones thought of Keats's effort, written at her own suggestion, but we do know that she was also a great admirer of Barry Cornwall, whose poetry was known for the empathy it showed with women pursuing forbidden love. She told Taylor that one of her favorite Cornwall poems was called "The Magdalen." Published in 1820, the same year that "The Eve of St. Agnes" was published, it describes what Keats's poem leaves out: the end of the story. His Madeline runs away with Porphyro, who has promised to make her his "bride" and thus cancel out the stain of her deflowering. But we never know what happens to them, or whether he fulfilled his promise. All we get at the end is what Woodhouse considered a "pettish" mood swing into the grotesque, with the witches and the coffin worms, the geriatric nurse twitching with palsy and the ancient beadsman saying his rosary into nothingness.

Unlike Keats, Barry Cornwall was more than happy to appeal directly to the sympathies of the female readers who made up his core audience, without the interference of emotional dissonance. His "The Magdalen" fills in the blank left by Keats at the end of "The Eve of St. Agnes" by showing the aftermath of a seduction and acknowledging that it's the woman who always pays. He shows a young woman who has crawled back home to die after being abandoned by her seducer once the dizzy heights of love have proved a mirage:

> In her home
> (Which she did once desert) I saw her last;
> Propped up by pillows, swelling round her like
> Soft heaps of snow . . .
> . . . O'er her temple one blue vein
> Ran like a tendril: one through her shadowy hand
> Branched like the fibre of a leaf—away.

The lines are skilled but flat. You have only to compare this with "The Eve of St. Agnes" to see how bleached out it is, particularly the way Cornwall uses pedestrian similes in contrast to Keats's marvelously clotted metaphors. In the Cornwall, the pillows swell like heaps of snow to indicate the coldness that has succeeded to the heat of passion. But when Keats's Madeline gets between the cold sheets of her bed, prior to being warmed up by Porphyro, she's "trembling in her soft and chilly nest," which combines so much in one image.

On the most literal level, she's shivering because she's cold. But she's also trembling with anticipation because she's hoping to see her future husband in a dream. At the same time, there's dramatic irony in her trembling because it indicates to the reader what she doesn't know: that she might really have something to be scared of or excited about; that she's going to lose her virginity and, true to her name Madeline, become a Magdalen. The nest is a cozy idea; to make it "chilly" is almost an oxymoron. But it cross-references to the other bird images in the poem that she's associated with—the "tongue-less nightingale" and the "ring-dove frayed and fled"—which figure innocence endangered.

Despite the Romantic antics of Byron and Shelley, women who had sex out of wedlock remained pariahs in polite society, and not all Regency girls had a Mr. Darcy in the wings, like Lydia Bennett in *Pride and Prejudice,* to force a shotgun wedding. Cornwall's poetry appealed to women because his facile sympathy acknowledged and aestheticized their plight at living in a world of double standards. We don't know why Isabella Jones was particularly taken with "The Magdalen," but it must have resonated with her for some reason.

Whatever her story was, she clearly had one, though we can't know it any more than Keats could. The very fact that generations of biographers have failed to find it out suggests that she took care to cover her tracks owing to some backstory that we can't know. It is unlikely, given the male-dominated society in which she lived, that she was actually as independent as she presented. In her own power play with Keats, she put him on the back foot. Possibly, she was passing on her own backstage disempowerment to the young poet whose work she admired but whom she perceived as a male ingenue when it came to the politics of sex.

On one level "The Eve of St. Agnes" is indeed a "meretricious romance," to use the phrase Keats himself used: teasing, titillating, playing with the reader by using the calculated literary techniques of Gothic, which had earned vast success for "mother" Radcliffe, to sustain interest and build anticipation. But although Keats had one eye to the market when he wrote it, he was too entrenched in his idealistic belief in his own artistic authenticity to make it easy for the reader. His headmaster at the dissenting Academy would not have approved of the sexual theme in "The Eve of St. Agnes," but he had instilled an important principle in Keats: stick to your individual response, regardless of the mainstream. That response, in Keats's hands, proved to have little to do with the Enlightenment rationalism that dissenters embraced and tried to square with Christianity. For him, it increasingly meant opening yourself to the contradictory human impulses inside you.

"The Eve of St. Agnes" registers those contradictory impulses but transmutes them alchemically into a bravura literary performance, in which Keats employs techniques of reader manipulation but doesn't in the end care what the reader thinks, though he came up with defensive-aggressive ripostes when challenged by Woodhouse. By the end, he perhaps fears that he himself is writing into space: that he's the lonely "Beadsman" whose "thousand aves" will forever be ignored. The final image of the old priest repetitively saying his prayers is, ultimately, perhaps an anxious joke at the poet's own expense, since the priest is endlessly recycling "Ave Maria," the old Catholic prayer to the Virgin, in a poem whose narrative centers on the loss of virginity.

If Mrs. Jones was a woman on the edge, Keats too was a young man on the edge: not so desperate that he had to write for his next meal; not concerned, as a woman might have been, about his sexual reputation; but a fringe figure whose very insecurities—social, sexual, financial, educational, health-wise—fed his creativity. He was too naïve—and at the same time too much pullulating with the complexity of trying to make sense of his own naïveté, and of life in general—to make himself write simplistically or manipulatively enough for the market. The result was a Shakespearean level of verbal fecundity.

5

"La Belle Dame sans Merci.
A Ballad"

I.

O what can ail thee, knight-at-arms,
  Alone and palely loitering?
The sedge has withered from the lake,
  And no birds sing.

II.

O what can ail thee, knight-at-arms,
  So haggard and so woe-begone?
The squirrel's granary is full,
  And the harvest's done.

III.

I see a lily on thy brow,
  With anguish moist and fever-dew,
And on thy cheeks a fading rose
  Fast withereth too.

IV.

I met a lady in the meads,
Full beautiful—a faery's child,
Her hair was long, her foot was light,
And her eyes were wild.

V.

I made a garland for her head,
And bracelets too, and fragrant zone;
She looked at me as she did love,
And made sweet moan.

VI.

I set her on my pacing steed,
And nothing else saw all day long,
For sidelong would she bend, and sing
A faery's song.

VII.

She found me roots of relish sweet,
And honey wild, and manna-dew,
And sure in language strange she said—
"I love thee true."

VIII.

She took me to her elfin grot,
And there she wept and sighed full sore,
And there I shut her wild wild eyes
With kisses four.

IX.

And there she lullèd me asleep,
    And there I dreamed—Ah! woe betide!—
The latest dream I ever dreamt
    On the cold hill side.

X.

I saw pale kings and princes too,
    Pale warriors, death-pale were they all;
They cried—"La Belle Dame sans Merci
    Thee hath in thrall!"

XI.

I saw their starved lips in the gloam
    With horrid warning gapèd wide,
And I awoke and found me here,
    On the cold hill's side.

XII.

And this is why I sojourn here
    Alone and palely loitering,
Though the sedge is withered from the lake,
    And no birds sing.

WHEN KEATS WAS about five, he stopped his mother from going out by shutting the door and threatening her so "furiously" with "a naked sword" that happened to be in the house that she burst into tears and had to be rescued by a passerby who witnessed the tableau through the window. This is the second of the only two surviving anecdotes about Keats as a pre-school child, the other being about his early delight in making rhymes. It survives because Keats's brother Tom, who heard it from a former servant, repeated it to Benjamin Robert Haydon, who noted it in his diary on April 7, 1817.

There is a lot for a biographer to wonder about in this curious vignette of life in the Keats family circa 1800. It seems to confirm that Keats feared abandonment by his mother long before she actually ran off with Rawlings. Her hysterical response—crying, rooted to the spot—suggests she found the demands of parenting three boys under five overwhelming. Certainly, she was unable to assert authority, either through coaxing or through crossness, over the eldest when he was "in one of his moods."

What was an unsheathed sword doing lying around the house anyway? Was the house rather a mess? To leave such an item within the reach of three children under five seems a little risky. Was it meant to be hanging on a wall, some Jennings heirloom maybe, or was it perhaps the property of Keats's mother's brother, who was a naval officer?

Swords can be quite weighty; only with difficulty perhaps could a five-year-old manage to lift one and wave it furiously in the air. Was the tip of the sword indeed aloft, or was it hovering just above the floor? How dangerous really was this armed child? Was his mother more concerned for his safety or her own? A cavalry saber, circa 1800, is very heavy, unliftable by a five-year-old. But naval swords were lighter, and one could easily have been vigorously, if uncontrollably, brandished by the young Keats, at more risk to himself than to anyone else. This was a frantic, driven child, determined to assert his own power. It's perhaps significant that he later worried he might hurt the feelings of women without meaning to.

Keats's abandonment by his mother at eight, soon after his father's death, and her own death when he was fourteen, caused his biographer Amy Lowell such an excess of maternal solicitude for her subject that on occasion it clouded her scholarly judgment. Writing in the 1920s, at a time when Freudian psychobiography was the fashionable mode, she concluded that Keats "never got over his need for a mother." The biographer became unable to contain her emotions at the thought of the poet hiding under the desk at school when told that his mother had died: "Poor little shaver, so pitiably unable to cope with his first great sorrow!" At an earlier moment in the narrative, she imagines Keats's reaction on being sent to boarding school for the first time, even though there is no evidence at all in the historical record as to how he felt about it. "We do not need to be told," she exclaims, "that he stuffed his bed-clothes in his mouth so that no one should hear the sobs he could not control." As one later critic responded tartly, "Indeed, we do not."

It's easy to laugh at Amy Lowell's overactive biographical imagination; for all we know, Keats found the containing atmosphere of Clarke's Academy a relief when he arrived there as a child. Yet Lowell was not the first older woman to have responded to the orphaned Keats with motherly concern. When he abruptly left the Isle of Wight soon after beginning *Endymion,* his landlady could easily have been annoyed that her paying guest was cutting short his stay. Instead, she gave him the Shakespeare engraving that he had admired on her wall—and had moved into his own room, another potential source of annoyance to a landlady—as a gift to take away. He went on to keep it as a talisman, confessing to his brother George and sister-in-law Georgiana on February 14, 1819, "I am sitting opposite the Shakspeare I brought from the Isle of wight—and I never look at it but the silk tassels on [the frame] give me as much pleasure as the face of the Poet itself."

It is hard, too, not to be touched by the generous way in which Mrs. Bentley, the Keats brothers' landlady at Well Walk, was prepared to take on the care of the gravely ill Tom when Keats went off to Scotland for the summer in 1818. She and her husband could have found other lodgers. Perhaps these landladies were indeed responding to some inchoate yearning for mother love projected by the orphaned young man. Without going so far as to diagnose a Freudian complex, the biographer cannot avoid making some connection between Keats's childhood relations with his mother and his belief that he had "not a right feeling towards Women." Even in the pre-Freudian Regency, the idea that the mother was the paradigm for men's subsequent relations with women was written into the sexual slang term *"mater omnium"* (mother of all).

The few brief accounts we have of the young Keats's relations with his mother swing between the rage and disappointment of the sword-wielding five-year-old and the tender, possessive care of the fourteen-year-old mothering his own mother on her deathbed; he would not even allow anyone else to make her meals. In his letter to Benjamin Bailey of July 18, 1818, Keats wonders aloud whether his difficulties stem from his boyhood desire to idealize women as pure goddesses in need of protection, and the consequent failure of "reality" to measure up. As a result, he cannot help blaming them. "When I am among women," he confesses, "I have evil thoughts, malice[,] spleen—I cannot speak or be silent—I am full of Suspicions." That he believed he had contracted a sexually transmitted disease might have complicated matters further, but he concludes by putting his "not right . . . feeling" down to early experiences: "You must be charitable," he begs Bailey, "and put all this perversity to my being disappointed since Boyhood."

The image of the child with the sword, bent on preventing his mother from leaving him, hovers at the fringes of my mind when I read Keats's poem "La Belle Dame sans Merci," which was written on April 21, 1819, three months after "The Eve of St. Agnes." Its protagonist is a medieval "knight-at-arms" who has loved and lost a supernatural femme fatale; she feeds him, tells him she loves him, and lulls him maternally to sleep, only to abandon him to an eternity of anemic loneliness on a cold hillside.

In contrast to the lushness of "The Eve of St. Agnes," this poem feels denuded. It even looks etiolated on the page, in comparison to the fat Spenserian stanzas of the former work. The castle in which Porphyro seduced Madeline was a colorful medieval stage set crowded with stained-glass windows, intricate stone carvings and crimson cloth shot through with gold and jet. Here, we are in an outdoor wilderness.

The two poems, written three months apart, are, however, connected by a verbal echo. The title "La Belle Dame sans Merci," taken from an early-fifteenth-century French poem by Alain Chartier, is the same as the title of the Provençal "ditty" played by Porphyro on Madeline's lute in "The Eve of St. Agnes." This new "ballad," as Keats called it, thus appears to give us the actual lyrics of Porphyro's ditty, which are not given in "The Eve of St. Agnes." Porphyro's choice of song title, however, casts an intriguing light on his conquest of the sleeping Madeline, as it suggests he is actually motivated by fear of beautiful—and merciless—women. In the new poem, it is the woman who has all the sexual power. The knight, as he discovers, is one in a long line of "pale warriors" with starved lips, all victims of the predatory belle dame.

In *Endymion,* Keats tried to put as much in as he could. In this short poem, his most verbally pared down, less is undeniably more. The plain stanzaic structure is a variant of traditional ballad form, like that in which Coleridge wrote his much longer "The Rime of the Ancient Mariner" (1798). As with the latter, this lyric employs language that is sometimes archaic but unadorned on the surface to generate an aura of mystery and unfinished business. The Mariner has condemned himself to a lifetime of perdition by one unreasoned act: shooting the albatross. Keats's knight-at-arms is likewise damned to a purgatory of unfulfillment following his encounter with the belle dame. Both characters go on to tell us their stories in the first person, about the moment of madness that led to their eternal estrangement from the world.

Before the protagonist gets going on telling his tale, Keats's poem begins with a question, asked by an anonymous voice:

> O what can ail thee, knight-at-arms,
> Alone and palely loitering?

On a sheer technical level there is much to unpack here when it comes to the mastery over poetic language that he had by now achieved. The adverb "palely" recalls the adverbial and adjectival affectations found in Leigh Hunt's verse. But, by now, Keats had come a long way from his attempt to out-Hunt Hunt in *Endymion*'s preposterous "tremulous-dazzlingly." He had made the stylistic tic not just into something of his own, but into something that outlasted the cultural moment of its composition.

"Palely" is strange, but it works. How can you loiter palely? The act of hanging around—actually, it is more a passive state than an action—cannot have a color. And yet we all know what Keats means, when it comes to representing the depressive feeling in which all color seems to have been drained out of life, in which we feel we are constantly waiting for something but that there is nothing to wait for. By counterintuitively making an adverb out of a color word, Keats adds to the idea of arrested movement by undermining the sense of action implicit in the adverbial form.

Keats had actually used a contracted spelling of this odd word in *Endymion,* but as an archaic-sounding adjective, in the phrase "There is a paly flame of hope" (according to the *OED,* "paly" meaning "pale" is found in Shakespeare). By replacing the final "e" of "pale" and adding the extra "l" before the "y," he stamps on that still small voice of hope, and at the same time creates a verbal construct that is incomparably more suggestive. The doubling of the "l" literally makes you linger over "palely" if you read it out aloud, drawing out the sense of languor and postponement.

It is the sound as much as the sense that has made this first couplet of "La Belle Dame sans Merci" take up residence in readers' minds: the way the "O" at the beginning is echoed in "Alone," and pre-echoes the belle dame's intoxicating "sweet moan" whose ending has left the knight in this sad state; and the way in which "palely" echoes "ail thee." Keats is no longer just rhyming the ends of lines as in "wind in summer . . . pretty hummer." He's working them in, in unexpected ways.

The aural dimension of his use of language has long since been recognized by critics as a defining Keatsian quality. As a former medic with an intimate knowledge of human bodies, he saw the "great thing" of poetry as involving the physical senses, not just the intellect. "La Belle Dame sans Merci" rests, however, on a paradox that adds to its atmosphere of absence. We can appreciate its verbal rhythms, but it remains a song without a tune as we do not have the score, rendering us deaf to its melody. As the poem itself tells us, we are in a world of silence where "no birds sing."

Keats's apparent preference for sound over meaning—and his desire to seek the spiritual in the earthly—made him seem too much a sensualist in the eyes of some nineteenth-century critics, as, of course, did his attraction to erotic themes. "La Belle Dame sans Merci" could be read as a poem about sex, even specifically about postcoital tristesse. Regency readers were primed to look for hidden meanings at a time when explicit eroticism was rarely found in print, and modern readers have continued to do so.

I once googled the poem, and alighted by chance on a webchat between two A level students, a boy and a girl. When the boy shyly suggested that the line "I set her on my pacing steed" could have sexual connotations, the girl immediately riposted that "steed" was just a word knights used for horses. To this day, I do not know whether she was genuinely naïve or recoiling from what she perceived as an unwanted overture. Two hundred years ago, the female poetry lovers who enjoyed Barry Cornwall's light erotica—or that of the self-styled poetess and Keats enthusiast Letitia Landon, who, from 1820, wrote similarly sensual verse in a female voice— would certainly have feigned ignorance as to the implications of such imagery.

That the belle dame is a "faery's child" makes her simultaneously earthy and unearthly. Keats's frequent references to fairies can sound twee to the modern ear—"elfin grot" might induce titters today—but his were not Disneyfied creatures in pink tutus. As in the paintings of Henry Fuseli, such as *Titania and Bottom* (1790), female fairies of the period were culturally represented as more provocative than prim. Fuseli's are strange, fetishistic creatures, with aggressively gravity-defying breasts that Astley Cooper would have dismissed as unnatural.

There is perhaps a hint of the "beautiful Mrs. Jones" (as Keats's friend Reynolds called her) in the femme fatale at the center of "La Belle Dame sans Merci." The earthly pleasures the belle dame offers the knight include edibles in the shape of "roots of relish sweet, / And honey wild, and manna-dew." Mrs. Jones had also appealed to the young poet's stomach by giving him a grouse for his dinner.

Yet "La Belle Dame sans Merci" is about much more than sex. It is also a poem about alienation and death, mourning and melancholia, about the relationship of fantasy to reality and of time to eternity; it invites us to apprehend, rather than comprehend, a mystery.

It is also, in terms of sheer economy of means, arguably the best poem Keats had yet written. The archaisms are melded seamlessly into a plain vocabulary that is predominantly monosyllabic or disyllabic. The few three-syllable words tell a story on their own if pulled out of context: "knight-at-arms . . . loitering . . . woe-begone . . . granary . . . fever-dew . . . withereth . . . beautiful . . . manna-dew . . . loitering." The repeat whereby the first and final stanzas are near-identical wraps the ballad up in a seeming finality that is in fact circularity, drawing out the sense of entrapment.

———

GIVEN THAT "La Belle Dame sans Merci" has since become one of his best-known poems, it is odd to think that Keats chose not to include it in his third and last book, *Lamia, Isabella, The Eve of St. Agnes, and Other Poems,* published in July 1820. The first-known draft of it appears, out of nowhere, in the long letter he wrote to George and Georgiana in installments between February 14 and May 3, 1819, just after his account of visiting the Panorama, with its penguins. A brief parenthesis, "—Wednesday Evening—," is what allows us to know the exact date, April 21, and time of day when he wrote it down.

The version in the letter includes some orthographical errors that suggest the speed at which he was composing (the "knight at arms"—unhyphenated—is a "knight at ams," while the lily on his brow is a "lilly"). There are also some crossings-out which show us Keats improving his first thoughts in the moment. He removes a couple of specific references to "death," replacing them with the less heavy-handed indefinite article "a" in what seems like an effort to pare the poem down further:

> a
> I see ~~death's~~ lilly on thy brow
> With anguish moist and fever dew,
> a
> And on thy cheeks ~~death's~~ fading rose
> Fast Withereth too—

In *Endymion,* "a thing of beauty" is capsized into abstract nonentity by the indefinite article. Here, the "a" is a boon, adding to the indefinable atmosphere the poem creates, in which the knight cannot explain the reason for his attraction to the belle dame, or his subsequent alienation, and has to be told by her other victims that she has him in thrall.

Keats did in fact publish "La Belle Dame sans Merci" in his lifetime, though not in a book. On May 10, 1820, it was printed in a new paper recently started by Leigh Hunt, *The*

Indicator, but with a few changes. The "knight-at-arms," for example, became a "wretched wight." However, all editors have subsequently ditched those emendations as for the worse, and the version we now read is very close to the one in the letter. We need this character to be a knight-at-arms—not just a "wight," Chaucer's word simply for a man—in order to make it possible for the poem to disarm him, and us.

Keats asserted in an earlier letter that he believed he would be among the English poets after his death. Yet it is interesting to see how little sense he had of which of his poems would later stick. His only commentary on "La Belle Dame sans Merci" in the letter is flippant: "Why four kisses—you will say," he adds in his letter to George and Georgiana after writing it out; "because I wish to restrain the headlong impetuosity of my Muse—she would fain have said 'score' without hurting the rhyme—but we must temper the Imagination as the critics say with Judgment. I was obliged to choose an even number that both eyes might have fair play: and to speak truly I think two apiece quite sufficient—Suppose I have said seven; there would have been three and a half apiece—a very awkward affair—and well got out of on my side—."

Immediately afterward, he bursts into further verse, this time an instantly forgettable "Chorus of Fairies," inspired perhaps by *A Midsummer Night's Dream,* in which the elemental spirits of Fire (Salamander), Air (Zephyr), Earth (Dusketha) and Water (Breama) are each given a say. It begins:

Sal.　Happy happy glowing fire!
Zep.　Fragrant air, delicious light!
Dusk.　Let me to my glooms retire
Bream.　I to ~~my~~ greenweed rivers bright.

There is no sense of quality control here—just the in-the-moment energy of trying things out.

———

THE FEELING THAT Keats is capturing whatever is going on in his mind at the moment of writing is why his letters have come to be regarded not simply as an adjunct to his poetry, but as an oeuvre in themselves. Letters were indeed where Keats tried things out: not just new poems but "speculations." Their unfiltered quality does not make them unliterary. Indeed, there are passages where Keats's self-conscious delight in playing with language rivals that of Laurence Sterne in *Tristram Shandy*, including a riff on the imagined physical shape of letters, projected from how their tone might seem emotionally. "[S]ome kind of letters," he opined to Reynolds on May 3, 1818, "are good squares[,] others handsome ovals, and others some orbicular, others spheroid—and why should there not be another species with two rough edges like a Rat-trap?"

What has made Keats's letters irresistible, ever since the first major tranche of them was published in 1848, is the flexible way in which they move between prose and verse, between gossipy news and philosophical speculation, between the slangy and the high-flown, between the tragic and the comic, between self-analysis and concern for others. There are few longueurs for the reader in Keats's letters, even if you read them unabridged.

Although he did not consciously craft them for publication, he clearly regarded his letters as an important diaristic record of his own development, but they were also acts of intimate literary sharing. When he went off on his northern walking tour with Charles Brown, for example, he left Tom alone with the Bentleys at Well Walk, but he did not leave him behind mentally. He used letters to allow the invalid Tom to participate in what he had seen and done on his travels, and also urged him to share them with their friends in London.

Written to divert and entertain his readers, especially Tom, these "Scotch letters" are a delight. On July 1, 1818, for example, Keats depicts a display of Scottish dancing he had seen:

> they kickit & jumpit with mettle extraordinary, & whiskit,
> & fleckit, & toe'd it, & go'd it, and twirld it, & wheel'd it,
> & stampt it, & sweated it, tattooing the floor like mad.

With the rhythms replicating the beat of the dancers' feet, and even the appearance of the words on the page mimicking the jerky repetitions of the dance, this is a comical reprise of Keats's grander poetic project: to use the abstract medium of language to bring body and soul together.

Keats's letters to his sister Fanny, eight years his junior and living with the uptight Abbeys, are as generous in their spirit of sharing as his letters to Tom. For her, he wrote a nonsense rhyme "about myself" depicting his preparations for his hiking tour:

> There was a naughty boy,
> A naughty boy was he,
> He would not stop at home,
> He could not quiet be—
> He took
> In his knapsack
> A book
> Full of vowels

And a shirt
With some towels–
A slight cap
For a night-cap—
A hairbrush,
Comb ditto,
New stockings,
For old ones
Would split O!

In the second verse, Keats laughs at his own obsessional need to poetize:

There was a naughty boy
And a naughty boy was he,
For nothing would he do
But scribble poetry . . .

All Keats's letters to his three siblings demonstrate their close emotional bond, forged following the loss of their parents. Those he wrote to George and his wife Georgiana in America, at a time when it could take months for a letter to arrive there from England, are the most substantial. The one in which "La Belle Dame sans Merci" appears near the end, written in multiple installments between February 14 and May 3, 1819, covers fifty printed pages in Rollins's edition. It was once described by the famous twentieth-century critic Lionel Trilling as one of the most remarkable documents of the culture of the nineteenth century.

Although this is not exactly what Trilling meant, there may be something historically determined about the specific cultural moment in the early nineteenth century that made it possible for Keats to create his letters as he did. Their very fluidity reflects the society in flux to which he belonged, in which issues of taste, authority and literary register were up for grabs. Moreover, Keats's confident belief in the value of recording his subjective experience as an individual was also enabled by the historical forces he inherited: the Enlightenment move to put man rather than God at the center; the dissenting religious tradition that placed the emphasis on the individual conscience; increasing social mobility and democratization; the development of the private realm as a site of emotional and aesthetic value.

Had Shakespeare's letters survived, it is very unlikely that they would have been written in such an informal, expansive, personal style as Keats's. The only Renaissance prose that feels so viscerally subjective is, perhaps, to be found in Montaigne's *Essays*. Like Keats, Montaigne preferred stream-of-consciousness "half-knowledge" to formality or certainty, but the Renaissance French essayist had to create a new genre in which to express that. Victorian letters, on the other hand, even by great writers, tend to be a little more reined in than Keats's, despite the fact that intimate epistolary expression had by then become the norm. Those of Charlotte Brontë, for example, do not offer Keats's open sense of anarchic literary free play.

The letter to George and Georgiana of February to May 1819 begins newsily, but later incorporates eleven new poems ("for the most part dash'd of[f] . . . in a hurry"), an account of Keats's one meeting with Coleridge and a meaning-of-life disquisition on the "vale of Soul-making." On the way, we get, inter alia, a paean to claret, an extended dream sequence, several pages copied out from a text by the radical journalist William Hazlitt and numerous glimpses of Keats himself.

This is the letter in which he describes himself writing with his back to the fire with one foot on the carpet, wondering in which position Shakespeare's body was when he wrote "To be or not to be."

The letter's vivid fluency—which feels death-defying when you read it—is underlined by the fact that it is unparagraphed, and often spelled with idiosyncratic carelessness. On March 19, for example, Keats announces he has "smoak'd . . . a Segar." He begins, however, on February 14, as one would expect, by asking after George and Georgiana and giving them his latest. He was still, he told them, suffering from a chronic sore throat, following the attack that had forced him home from Scotland in August. One questions the wisdom of that cigar.

By the time Keats wrote this letter, he had moved to Wentworth Place, which now houses the Keats House museum. After Tom died on December 1, 1818, he had not felt able to stay at Well Walk, with its painful associations, despite the fact that their landlords the Bentleys had by then become friends. He accepted immediately when Charles Brown suggested he should move in with him. Brown's terms were £5 a month in rent and half the bill for drink. "I am still at Wentworth Place," Keats tells his brother and sister-in-law, implying that he is not sure how long he will be able to stay there. Brown's house would in fact remain his base until May 1820, though he continued to make restless out-of-town excursions.

Brown had been living in one of the two semidetached houses that made up Wentworth Place, with a shared garden, since 1816. The other was occupied by Brown's old school friend Charles Wentworth Dilke. Keats's introduction to both men had first come via John Hamilton Reynolds, his fellow Leigh Hunt protégé. Keats had lost his brothers, but he was moving in with friends he already knew, not to an anonymous rental.

In contrast to Brown's, Dilke's instincts were bourgeois. Although he continued to read Godwin's *Political Justice,* the radical bible of the revolutionary 1790s, he had a regular job in the Navy Pay Office and was already, at twenty-nine, a family man with a wife, Maria, and a son, Charley. Yet he and Brown got on. Keats can see them through the window: "Brown and Dilke are walking round their Garden hands in Pockets making observations." It's noticeable that Keats says "their Garden." None of the places where he lived was his own.

There is a sense, here, that Keats is hunkering down at Wentworth Place. He has, he says, seen "very little of Reynolds" and has not seen "C.C.C."—Charles Cowden Clarke—since "god knows when." Hunt he hears about only secondhand. The latter is, he understands, "going on very badly," in dire financial straits, a reminder that debt was the occupational hazard of the freelance writer. Keats is now much less entranced by the "Literary world," of which he knows little, save that Byron is soon to publish a satire called "Don Giovanni." The first installment of Byron's *Don Juan* was published anonymously later that year.

By now Keats had also met Fanny Brawne. She, her widowed mother and her younger siblings, Samuel and Margaret, knew the Dilkes because they had rented Brown's half of Wentworth Place while he was away with Keats in Scotland over the summer. They were still living locally in Hampstead. "Miss Brawne and I have every now and then a chat and a tiff," Keats reports, which sounds flirtatious but not deeply involved. Mrs. Jones was still in the wings, providing regular offerings of game. "She made me take home a Pheasant the other day," he writes on February 19, implying that he has recently visited her "tasty" rooms once more. Keats handed the meat over to Maria Dilke so it could be the main course at a dinner party she was planning, whose guest list, apart from Keats himself and Brown, was also to include Reynolds, who was now focusing on his new legal career.

Keats's account of his social life sounds easygoing, until he expostulates that he is "not at all contented" with something Mrs. Brawne has tactlessly told him about a conversation she had with a neighbor. A Mr. Lewis had reportedly said of him, "O, he is quite the little Poet." Keats finds this "abominable." Despite witness evidence as to his charisma and handsome face, he perennially feared that his height made him unattractive.

"I do think better of Womankind than to suppose they care whether Mister John Keats five feet hight [*sic*] likes them or not," he had told Bailey from Scotland on July 22, 1818. For all we know, Mr. Lewis's comment was a patronizing remark about a very young, insignificant fellow who was rather too overt in making his outlandish literary ambitions known in the locale. But Keats took it as a bodily slur on his stature: "you might as well say Buonaparte is quite the little Soldier—see what it is to be under six foot and not a lord." Lord Byron was just over five foot eight. Napoleon was just under five foot six. Both would have towered over Keats.

Only later, as if in an aside, does Keats inform George and Georgiana that *Endymion* "has not at all succeeded" but says he is determined to "pluck up" the spirit to "try the public again" in the course of a year, despite his "pride" and contempt for "public opinion." All the comments he made about sending his work out into the world are conflicted. Whether he is omnipotently convinced of his future fame or terrified of present rejection, he finds the self-exposure of print highly charged, in contrast to his relaxation about self-exposure in private letters.

Back in the world of domestic gossip, Keats offers regular reports on the Dilkes, providing insights to today's social historian. Helicopter parenting was clearly as prevalent among the north London middle classes during the Regency as it is today. The Dilkes' obsession with finding the right school for Charley exasperates Keats, whose own achievements had not been predicated on parental pushiness, although he had been lucky to attend Clarke's Academy. Fearing that Charley would be spoiled, he complained that "the boy has nothing in his ears all day but himself and the importance of his education."

The Dilkes eventually decided, after much deliberation, on Westminster, a prestigious public school. But they were so concerned about Charley's welfare that they did not want him to board. Perhaps they feared he would be stuffing his bedclothes into his sobbing mouth. In consequence, they decided to move to a new home next door to the school, because the commute of five and a half miles was too far for their son to walk. As a result, sometime shortly before April 12, 1819, the Dilkes moved out of Wentworth Place. This is significant for Keats, as Dilke then let his house to the widowed Mrs. Brawne, whose daughter went on to become the love of Keats's life. That she moved in as his next-door neighbor—though we don't know exactly when—would allow their relationship to develop.

Keats, meanwhile, continued to roll his eyes over the Dilkes' tremulousness over their son, which subsequently became focused on anxieties over his relations with the other boys and with the disciplinarian masters at Westminster. This was perhaps justified. In contrast to Clarke's Academy, where corporal punishment was banned, Westminster had been famous for flogging since the days of Dr. Busby, a notoriously flagellant headmaster in the seventeenth century, satirized by Pope. Charley survived the attentions of his parents and teachers. After a successful career in politics on the liberal side, he became one of the chief promoters of the Great Exhibition of 1851 and went on to die a baronet, Sir Charles Wentworth Dilke. (Somewhat less respectably, his son, the second baronet, was later involved in a notorious sex scandal allegedly involving an incestuous-sounding threesome with his brother's mother-in-law and her daughter.)

———

SO MUCH, so inconsequential, if not for the biographer. But Keats's long letter soon moves into topics more significant from the viewpoint of the literary critic. On April 15 he writes that "last Sunday" he had been walking along the lane on the eastern side of Hampstead Heath when he happened to bump into a former acquaintance from Guy's Hospital who was himself taking a walk in the company of none other than Samuel Taylor Coleridge. "I joined them, after enquiring by a look whether it would be agreeable," Keats recorded. He kept walking with them for "near two miles."

By 1819, Coleridge was a living legend, known as the sage of Highgate, where he was then lodging, located on the other side of the Heath from Hampstead. With his best poetry by then behind him, Coleridge was focusing on prose and metaphysics but suffering from opiate addiction and depression. He was living in a room on the top floor of a house in the Grove, as a paying guest of his doctor James Gillman. (The Queen Anne house, then considered unremarkable and modest, now belongs to the model Kate Moss.) Gillman succeeded in keeping Coleridge's addiction just about under

control, but what he and his wife could not stem was the tor-
rent of words that issued incessantly from the sage's mouth.
Their unfortunate son caught a whiff of this. When sent up
to seek help with his homework from the poet in the attic, he
was beaten back down the staircase by an incomprehensible
verbal Niagara.

Keats's account of his meeting with Coleridge gives a flavor
of the sage's random monologue, sparkling as it was with nug-
gets of enigmatic profundity, yet disconnected:

> In those two Miles he broached a thousand things—let me
> see if I can give you a list—Nightingales, Poetry—on Poeti-
> cal sensation—Metaphysics—Different genera and species
> of Dreams—Nightmare—a dream accompanied by a sense
> of touch—single and double touch—A dream related—
> first and second consciousness—the difference explained
> between will and Volition—so m[an]y metaphysicians from
> a want of smoking the second consciousness—Monsters—
> the Kraken—Mermaids—southey [Coleridge's old friend,
> Robert Southey, who was by then poet laureate, having
> been elevated to that honor in 1813] believes in them—
> southeys belief too much diluted—A Ghost story—Good
> morning—

Keats felt none the wiser in the moment than the Gillmans'
son, though he was rather more inclined to listen. He concludes this vignette by saying, "I heard his voice as he came
towards me—I heard it as he moved away—I had heard it
all the interval—if it may be called so. He was civil enough
to ask me to call on him at Highgate Good Night!" The next
time he picks up his pen to add to the letter, on the morning

of Friday, April 16, he shows no sign of wanting to pay that call, noting instead that he's not going out, as "It looks so much like rain."

And yet the chance meeting with Coleridge, and the sage's strange monologue, must have registered. The theme of "Nightingales" would soon resurface in "Ode to a Nightingale." The ideas of dreams and nightmares, will and volition, and indeed of what one could call "poetical sensation," are moreover written into "La Belle Dame sans Merci," whose first draft Keats wrote down in the letter less than a week later, on Wednesday, April 21. The knight-at-arms, like Coleridge's Ancient Mariner, is magnetically drawn into a situation he cannot control, in which his will or volition is unseated. He goes on to dream a dream that becomes a nightmare, in which the belle dame's former conquests line up to tell him he is doomed. All the while, the reader's "poetical sensation" is aroused by the aurality of the text, especially in its repeated "O" sounds.

Coleridge's talk-as-you-walk lecture on will and volition— and indeed his somewhat cryptic references to "single and double touch"—was a recycling of ideas he had published in 1817 in *Biographia Literaria*. The concepts Coleridge explores in that tantalizing text, influenced by German philosophy, approach Kantian levels of abstract ratiocination but rarely quite solidify into clarity. Keats, who was never trained in technical philosophy, seems to have been inspired enough by his brief brush with the sage, despite the longueurs which interspersed the insights, to think out loud—or rather on paper—about the nature of existence. That resulted—just after he had scribbled down the text of "La Belle Dame sans Merci" and that of the "Chorus of Fairies"—in one of his most quoted passages, in which he introduces the idea of the world as a "vale of Soul-making" and contemplates the nature of the human self.

———

KEATS'S REPUTATION AS a Romantic thinker rests on a handful of passages in his letters: "What the imagination seizes as Beauty must be truth"; "negative capability"; life as "a Mansion of Many Apartments"; the "vale of Soul-making"; the "camelion Poet." Yet the most striking thing about his "speculations" is the way in which he expresses resistance to philosophy as a discipline, to the idea of any totalizing theory. In December 1819, for example, Dilke (still obsessed with Charley and his education) annoyed him as a "Man who cannot feel he has a personal identity unless he has made up his Mind about every thing" but who would "never come at a truth because he is always trying at it." Keats, in contrast, opined that the "only means of strengthening one's intellect is to make up ones [*sic*] mind about nothing—to let the mind be a thoroughfare for all thoughts."

Looked at historically, Keats's rejection of reason, as a route to truth, looks like a culturally specific reaction against the Enlightenment. Like other Romantics, he preferred the faculty of the imagination, its capacity to combine rather than to sort ideas. However, he came to that conclusion not as a result of reading a textbook on the subject but through granular mental experience, which included his reading, especially Shakespeare, and his own self-questioning. "I am however young writing at random—straining at particles of light in the midst of a great darkness," as he put it on March 19, 1819.

There is, however, a tension between Keats's distaste for

making up his mind and his continued need to worry away at questions about the meaning of life, specifically about why human experience—and he was speaking from his own— should contain so much sorrow and pain. When he comes in the letter to creating an allegory of life as a "vale of Soul-making," he rejects as "a little, circumscribe[d], straightened notion" the Christian cliché of life as a vale of tears "from which we are to be redeemed by a certain arbitrary interposition of God and taken to Heaven."

Keats's letters to friends such as Benjamin Bailey, the trainee vicar, reveal a group of young men who were earnestly keen to discuss metaphysical ideas. A surviving early letter to Keats from a fellow medical student, John Spurgin, written on December 5, 1815, just after Keats had left Hammond's for Guy's Hospital, dilates at length on the alternative philosophy of the eccentric Swedish visionary Emanuel Swedenborg (1688–1772), who moved, from an early career as an Enlightenment scientist specializing in metallurgy, to mysticism. No reply from Keats is extant. He may have found Spurgin's obsession with documenting the esoteric details de trop. (Unfazed by his failure to bond with Keats, Spurgin gave up doctoring and went on to become the longest-serving chairman of the British Swedenborg Society.)

Yet Keats was still, in 1819, trying, independently, to find a formula to make sense of things in his remarks on the vale of soul-making. Human beings, he argued, were born as "intelligences," with "sparks of divinity," but perhaps the only way they could become individuated "souls," with a true sense of personal identity, was by being schooled into shape by the travails of life which flesh is heir to. Suffering is there, he concludes, not to give God a reason to take us up to heaven, but to make us who we are. The "heart must feel and suffer in a thousand diverse ways" if an individual soul is to fulfill its potential as God's "own essence."

Keats's rejection of Christian dogma, and his belief that "divinity" inheres in the human, suggest that he was far on the road to Deism—which rejected biblical revelation and the unique divinity of Christ as God's son—and perhaps beyond it into some sort of pantheism. These were, at the time, dangerous views. "Carlisle, a Bookseller . . . has been issuing Pamphlets from his shop in fleet Street Called the Deist—he was conveyed to Newgate last Thursday—he intends making his own defense," Keats reported to George and Georgiana on February 14.

In explicating at length his theory of the vale of soul-making, however, Keats is not following any pamphlet but groping for his own words. "I can scarcely express what I but dimly perceive—and yet I think I perceive it," he confesses as he tries to explain why the world is so full of "Pains and troubles." An earlier sentence in the letter, so commonplace and yet so human that it could have come out of the mouth of any housewife in Hampstead, asks the question more poignantly: "I wonder how people exist with all their worries."

Keats's ability not just to exist, but to find joy in existence, even with all his own worries, made him a "hero" in the eyes of the critic Christopher Ricks, writing in 1974. Today, we do not need to idealize Keats, who was a complicated human being, not a saint. But we can and should marvel at the unique and lasting literary works he made, including the letters in which he documented his own humanity, written at such speed and with such little awareness that they would ever be pored over by scholars.

The most crucial of Keats's "speculations," when it comes to understanding his poetry, remains the comment he made in a letter to his brothers, written in December 1817, in which he jotted down an idea prompted by a conversation he had just had with Dilke after which "several things dovetailed in my mind":

> & at once it struck me, what quality went to form a Man of Achievement especially in Literature & which Shakespeare posessed [*sic*] so enormously—I mean *Negative Capability*, that is when a man is capable of being in uncertainties, Mysteries, doubts, without any irritable reaching after fact & reason.

Keats never again repeated the phrase "negative capability," although it has since become a watchword in Romantic literary studies and beyond. Its heuristic value to later minds has, however, been incalculable, its resonance reaching across the centuries. Indeed, it has recently been the focus of an academic project exploring how we should define creativity, run by professional philosophers at Oxford and Cambridge.

What Keats meant by it remains, though, a little enigmatic. At one level, he was perhaps responding quite specifically to Shakespeare, whom he in fact mentioned in the same breath: to the way in which the playwright leaves his works studiously open-ended, impossible to pin down by a single interpretation, and therefore infinitely fertile. Keats would later rehearse a similar train of thought when, on October 27, 1818, he told his publisher's adviser Richard Woodhouse:

> As to the poetical Character itself, (I mean that sort of which, if I am any thing, I am a Member . . .) it is not itself—it has no self—it is every thing and nothing—It has no character—it enjoys light and shade . . . It has as much

delight in conceiving an Iago as an Imogen. What shocks
the virtuous philosop[h]er delights the camelion Poet. It
does no harm from its relish of the dark side of things any
more than from its taste for the bright one.

Keats's own language is certainly "camelionic," not least in his
letters as they move effortlessly between different registers and
styles. Yet the irony is that, far from having "no self," his voice
is so individual that it could never be anyone else's.

Seen in the context of Keats's life and work, his isolated
utterances on negative capability and the poetical character
are not quite theories. Rather, they are the key to his poetic
practice. His capacity to use literary language to embody
"light and shade" simultaneously, in flickering moments of
unresolved tension that cannot be reasoned away, was soon to
reach what posterity would later regard as his creative zenith.

On April 30, 1819, another new poem appears in his letter
to George and Georgiana: "Ode to Psyche." It was a harbinger
of the so-called Great Odes, which, since the mid-nineteenth
century, have generally been regarded as the apex of his
achievement. No attempt by any new generation of critics to
change this view has ever really stuck, although understanding of the odes has increasingly been incorporated into the
wider context of Keats's oeuvre and of the culture in which
they were produced.

Keats did not know it, but he was about to write the most
significant poetry of his life. His mood was buoyant. He
ended his letter to George and Georgiana in a place far different from the cold hillside and withered sedge of "La Belle
Dame sans Merci": "this is the 3d May & every thing is in
delightful forwardness; the violets are not withered, before
the peeping of the first rose."

6

"Ode to a Nightingale"

I.

My heart aches, and a drowsy numbness pains
    My sense, as though of hemlock I had drunk,
Or emptied some dull opiate to the drains
    One minute past, and Lethe-wards had sunk:
'Tis not through envy of thy happy lot,
    But being too happy in thine happiness—
        That thou, light-wingèd Dryad of the trees,
            In some melodious plot
Of beechen green, and shadows numberless,
    Singest of summer in full-throated ease.

II.

O, for a draught of vintage! that hath been
    Cooled a long age in the deep-delvèd earth,
Tasting of Flora and the country green,
    Dance, and Provençal song, and sunburnt mirth!
O for a beaker full of the warm South,
    Full of the true, the blushful Hippocrene,
        With beaded bubbles winking at the brim,

And purple-stainèd mouth,
That I might drink, and leave the world unseen,
And with thee fade away into the forest dim—

III.

Fade far away, dissolve, and quite forget
What thou among the leaves hast never known,
The weariness, the fever, and the fret
Here, where men sit and hear each other groan;
Where palsy shakes a few, sad, last grey hairs,
Where youth grows pale, and spectre-thin, and dies;
Where but to think is to be full of sorrow
And leaden-eyed despairs;
Where Beauty cannot keep her lustrous eyes,
Or new Love pine at them beyond to-morrow.

IV.

Away! away! for I will fly to thee,
Not charioted by Bacchus and his pards,
But on the viewless wings of Poesy,
Though the dull brain perplexes and retards.
Already with thee! tender is the night,
And haply the Queen-Moon is on her throne,
Clustered around by all her starry Fays;
But here there is no light,
Save what from heaven is with the breezes blown
Through verdurous glooms and winding mossy ways.

V.

I cannot see what flowers are at my feet,
Nor what soft incense hangs upon the boughs,
But, in embalmèd darkness, guess each sweet

Wherewith the seasonable month endows
The grass, the thicket, and the fruit-tree wild—
  White hawthorn, and the pastoral eglantine;
    Fast fading violets covered up in leaves;
      And mid-May's eldest child,
  The coming musk-rose, full of dewy wine,
    The murmurous haunt of flies on summer eves.

VI.

Darkling I listen; and, for many a time
  I have been half in love with easeful Death,
Called him soft names in many a musèd rhyme,
  To take into the air my quiet breath;
Now more than ever seems it rich to die,
  To cease upon the midnight with no pain,
    While thou art pouring forth thy soul abroad
      In such an ecstasy!
  Still wouldst thou sing, and I have ears in vain—
    To thy high requiem become a sod.

VII.

Thou wast not born for death, immortal Bird!
  No hungry generations tread thee down;
The voice I hear this passing night was heard
  In ancient days by emperor and clown:
Perhaps the self-same song that found a path
  Through the sad heart of Ruth, when, sick for home,
    She stood in tears amid the alien corn;
      The same that oft-times hath
  Charmed magic casements, opening on the foam
    Of perilous seas, in faery lands forlorn.

VIII.

Forlorn! the very word is like a bell
   To toll me back from thee to my sole self!
Adieu! the fancy cannot cheat so well
   As she is famed to do, deceiving elf.
Adieu! adieu! thy plaintive anthem fades
     Past the near meadows, over the still stream,
       Up the hill-side; and now 'tis buried deep
        In the next valley-glades:
     Was it a vision, or a waking dream?
      Fled is that music—Do I wake or sleep?

KEATS'S "GREAT ODES," as critics call them, were all written in 1819. There are six if you count "Ode to Psyche," five if (like most people) you don't, the others being "Ode to a Nightingale," "Ode on a Grecian Urn," "Ode on Melancholy," "Ode on Indolence," and "To Autumn." We know that "Ode to Psyche" was written out for George and Georgiana sometime between April 21 and 30, and that "To Autumn" was composed on September 19, 1819. There are no precise dates for the others, but scholars have concluded from contextual clues that they were written in a creative burst in the late spring, with "Autumn" following after a lull. This book is going to focus on the three that have been judged the best by critics, with surprisingly little dissent, over the years: "Ode to a Nightingale," "Ode on a Grecian Urn" and "To Autumn."

The word "ode" comes from the ancient Greek for song. In classical antiquity, odes were typically celebratory, performed in honor of some god or hero, and the form represented one of the most complex and sophisticated structures in the poetic repertoire. It was first adopted as an English form by

Spenser. By the 1770s, the "modern ode" was regarded as a showstopper in which a writer could display "the boldest flights of poetical enthusiasm, and the wildest creations of the imagination," requiring "the assistance of every figure that can adorn language and raise it above its ordinary pitch." There were different options when it came to the rhyme scheme or whether to use regularly repeated stanzas, but intricacy, and the scope for original invention, were usually regarded as the key, although they weren't essential since some odes were cast in the form of simple songs.

Famous odes written in the Romantic period prior to those of Keats include Coleridge's pessimistic "Dejection: An Ode," first published in 1802, in which he expresses his own sense of paralysis; and Wordsworth's conversely optimistic "Immortality" ode, first published in 1807, which posits an idealistic notion of humanity in which we are all born "trailing clouds of glory." Keats's odes compress optimism and pessimism, light and shade, in virtuoso displays of paradox-infused poetic craft. In "Ode to a Nightingale," Keats used the self-assertive first-person voice in which to describe its opposite: a trance-like state in which he imagines his own identity dissolving as he listens to the bird's song. Here, he presents himself as a poet with no self and, at the same time, with a very strong personal voice.

Keats's "Nightingale" ode is also a technical feat. To achieve it, Keats the craftsman created his own original stanza form by taking the quatrain of a Shakespearean sonnet (rhyme scheme abab), and adding the sestet from a Petrarchan sonnet (rhyme scheme cdecde), while at the same time shortening the eighth line of each stanza to a trimeter (i.e., three metrical "feet" consisting of two syllables each), in contrast to the pentameters in which the rest is written. He then varied that by including one line with two extra syllables: "And with thee fade away into the forest dim." The line would fit the meter without "away," but he clearly wanted to draw out the slow pace contained in the idea of "fading" by adding the extra two syllables.

Keats was aiming at—and achieved—originality, but his subject was hardly original. Poems about nightingales were ten a penny in the period. Coleridge, Wordsworth and Shelley all wrote about them, as did numerous other poets of the eighteenth and early nineteenth centuries, from William Cowper and Robert Southey to Charlotte Smith and Mary Robinson. Even "mother Radcliff" had included some occasional lines to the bird in her 1791 novel *The Romance of the Forest*, beginning, "Child of melancholy song / O yet that tender strain prolong!"

George Dyer's pedestrian "Ode to the Nightingale" of 1812 uses many words and ideas similar to, or even the same as, those found in Keats's ode:

> Sweet songster! that unseen, unknown
> Dost strain thy little, heaving breast;
> Why dost thou warble still alone,
> Wakeful, when other songsters rest?
>
> Oft have I linger'd in the grove,
> Charm'd with thy soothing, melting song:
> It told—or seem'd to tell—of love,
> Nor was the night, tho' darksome, long.
>
> Yet, oh! sweet bird, why shun the light?
> Why warble still the lonesome lay?

> Those notes which smooth the brow of night,
> Might wake the genial smile of day.
>
> But tho' thou shunn'st my wistful sight,
> So melting-soft thou wont to sing,
> I deem thee not a bird of night,
> But hail thee Poet of the Spring.

How does Keats achieve so much with material that inspires so little in Dyer's hands? The answer is to be found in Keats's constant, protean play between subjective and objective, internal and external, visible and invisible spaces, and in the way in which he melts the boundaries between images.

Dyer's clichéd idea of the "melting song" was a commonplace of nightingale poems. Mary Robinson's bird also sings with "melting strains," while Ann Radcliffe's has a "liquid note." That idea of melting hovers behind Keats's use of the word "dissolve." But for him it is no longer just a commonplace metaphor for the way music flows. In Keats's ode, the idea of melting has been transposed from the bird's song to the bird itself and thence to the poet's subjective desire to dissolve:

> That I might drink, and leave the world unseen,
>   And with thee fade away into the forest dim—
>
> Fade far away, dissolve, and quite forget . . .

But more crucial to Keats's original verbal craft is the way in which he incorporates the idea of melting into the very grammar of his lines. Dyer's nightingale is literally "unseen" because the night is "darksome." But when Keats uses the word "unseen," he freights it with ambiguity, as it is not clear whether it applies to "the world" or to "I." Does Keats want to slip invisibly away, unseen by the world? Or is it that the world will no longer be seen by him after he leaves it? To expect to find an answer to those questions would, of course, be irritably reaching after fact and reason. The poem demands we access our own negative capabilities to allow both grammatical options to remain in play at once.

As Keats develops the ideas of seeing and not seeing, he contrasts the "leaden-eyed despairs" of quotidian human life with the "viewless wings of Poesy" on which he wants to fly. The word "viewless" was a poetic term meaning invisible, but here it is semantically unstable and could equally mean blind. As the stream of images flows, an allusion to blindness soon comes up in "Darkling I listen." The word "darkling" is borrowed from Milton, who used it in his epic *Paradise Lost,* which he composed after he had lost his eyesight. (Keats had taken an engraving of Haydon's picture of the blind Milton, sitting at an organ while dictating *Paradise Lost* to his daughters, to the Isle of Wight in 1817; the image summed up the idea that poetic and musical inspiration were one and the same.) The literary allusion thus links Keats's ode, beyond the moment and across time, to past poetry, just as the nightingale itself becomes an "immortal Bird" because the bird's generic call has remained the same generation after generation.

Dyer had addressed his nightingale, in a stale trope, as "Poet of the Spring." Keats, in contrast, does something much more daring with the traditional metaphorical identification between poetry and birdsong, by simultaneously internalizing and externalizing it. It is the poet himself who "will fly," like a bird, while "Poesy" is simultaneously personified as a winged goddess.

The pedantic Dyer, on the other hand, cannot leave his metaphor alone, feeling obliged to inform his readers, in a literalistic footnote:

> In these lines, . . . the two ideas concerning the nightingale were preserved; one imaginary only, that its note is plaintive; the other, the true one, that it is cheerful; justifying the application of the title, "the Poet of the Spring."

Keats, on the other hand, intermingles separate ideas—and indeed emotional registers—with such elastic ease that the reader has to share in the sensation of "uncertainties, mysteries, doubts" that underscore his dramatization of a moment of poetic creativity. There is no distinction between what is "true" and what is "imaginary only": "Was it a vision, or a waking dream?"

———

ACCORDING TO KEATS'S HOUSEMATE Charles Armitage Brown, "Ode to a Nightingale" was written one spring morning after breakfast in "two or three hours" in the garden at Wentworth Place under a plum tree in which a nightingale had built a nest. Richard Woodhouse, who transcribed the poem, dated it "May 1819" (it was also transcribed by Dilke on the blank leaves at the end of his copy of *Endymion*). By the beginning of that month, Keats had been living with Brown for around five months, sharing—in addition to the wine bills—what was a literary as well as a domestic space. He and Brown enjoyed knocking off their literary attempts side by side. Keats wrote a parodic squib in the manner of Spenser on Brown's character, alluding to the latter's slangy conversational vocabulary and appetite for wine and women.

Eight years older than Keats, Brown had been born in Lambeth, where he is said as a teenager to have protected the family home from burglars with a blunderbuss. Although he and Dilke were apparently at school together, Brown's colorful career to date had been very different from the latter's steady clerkship in the Navy Pay Office. No one could have been less bourgeois than Brown, not just in his unconventional relationship with Abigail O'Donoghue, but in his free-wheeling entrepreneurial spirit. According to Dilke, writing in 1848, by which time the pair had fallen out, "He was the most scrupulously honest man I ever knew—but he wanted nobleness to lift this honesty out of the commercial kennel."

Brown had started as a merchants' clerk at the age of fourteen, but had later run a fur-trading outfit with his brother in far-off St. Petersburg. The company made a fortune before going bankrupt. However, Charles bounced back by channeling his experiences abroad into writing the libretto for a comic operetta on a Russian theme, *Narensky; or, the Road to Yaroslaf.* Produced at Drury Lane in 1814, it became a minor hit from which Brown earned £300 and free admission to the theater for life. The score was written by the celebrated tenor John Braham, lover of Nancy Storace, who had created the role of Susanna in the first production of Mozart's *The Marriage of Figaro.*

By the time Keats was living with him, Brown had inherited enough money "to lead a life of literary leisure" on a modest scale, although he never produced a work of note. Nevertheless, the pair often sat opposite one another "authorizing," and at the time Keats found Brown's ideas intriguing, although they never came to anything.

On February 14, 1819, Keats told George and Georgiana at length about Brown's latest plot for a story, which gives one a flavor of his coarse sense of humor. It is an outlandish concoction about an old woman in a forest who is visited one night by the Devil, after which she repents of having lived a virgin all her life. A Cinderella-style transformation leads to every man she meets falling in love with her, including a procession of monks and the Devil himself. Impregnated by the latter, she lays multitudinous eggs out of which hatch all the nuisances of the world, including the editor of the *Quarterly*, William Gifford. Brown was obviously extemporizing for Keats's entertainment, but his bizarre and rough-hewn plot hints at the weird, folkloric, proto-Freudian shapes into which Romanticism went on to wrest Gothic in pursuit of commercial sensationalism in, for example, popular hits such as Weber's folk-inspired opera *Der Freischütz,* which caused audience members to faint in London in 1824, and in the *Tales* of E. T. A. Hoffmann.

In August 1819, in collaboration with Brown, who provided the plot and characters, Keats went on to write a tragedy, *Otho the Great.* Their hope was that it might reprise the West End success of *Narensky.* Certainly, a play in the Shakespearean mode had commercial potential at a time when Shakespearean actors such as Edmund Kean and Sarah Siddons were popular celebrities, and the Bard was so ubiquitous that his image graced the wall of an obscure Isle of Wight boardinghouse.

Keats, whose funds had by then run dry, was unable to pay his rent and had been borrowing from Brown, who said his own income was not sufficient to support them both, although he was happy to act as guarantor when Keats asked Taylor for a new loan. They hoped to share the profits from the play. "I feel every confidence that if I choose I may be a popular writer; that I never will be; but for all that I will get a livelihood," Keats told Taylor, conflictedly, on August 23, 1819. Brown eventually submitted *Otho the Great* to Drury Lane, but it was rejected.

Other poetry Keats wrote in 1819 also reveals the influence of Brown's rough-hewn sense of humor. "The Cap and the Bells," composed in November and December 1819, though never finished, is a burlesque modern fairy tale lampooning the Prince Regent, a provocative gesture from a protégé of Leigh Hunt, who had been jailed for libeling the royal. Only a few lines of the poem were published in Keats's lifetime. Highlights include a reference to the newfangled gas lamps which enabled Regency shoppers to satisfy their consumerist urges after dark:

> It was the time when wholesale houses close
> Their shutters with a moody sense of wealth,
> But retail dealers, diligent let loose
> The gas (objected to on score of health),
> Conveyed in little soldered pipes by stealth . . .

The versification is rougher than that of Byron's polished satire *Don Juan,* but in some ways it's tougher too.

Only specialist scholars read *Otho the Great* or "The Cap and the Bells" today. Yet it is worth remembering that 1819 was Keats's most productive year, which saw him experimenting with everything from light verse to epic, from sonnets, to satires, to romances, to plays, to the 700-plus-line *Lamia,* in addition to more than 500 lines of the unfinished "The Fall of Hyperion" and the eight-line fragment "This living hand . . ." On June 9, 1819, Keats told a correspondent in Devon, Sarah Jeffrey, "I have been very idle lately, very averse to writing." And yet he was halfway through his most productive year and had recently completed four of his five great odes.

In 1819, Keats wrote:

"The Eve of St. Agnes"
"The Eve of St. Mark"
"Gif ye wol stonden hardie wight"
"Why did I laugh tonight?"
"Faery Bird's Song"
"Faery Song"
"When they were come unto the Faery's Court"
"The House of Mourning written by Mr. Scott"
"Character of Charles Brown"
"A Dream, after reading Dante's episode of Paolo and
    Francesca"
"La Belle Dame sans Merci. A Ballad"
"Song of Four Faeries"
"To Sleep"
"If by dull rhymes our English must be chained"
"Ode to Psyche"
"On Fame (I)"
"On Fame (II)"
"Two or three Posies"
"Ode to a Nightingale"
"Ode on a Grecian Urn"
"Ode on Melancholy"
"Ode on Indolence"

Otho the Great: A Tragedy in Five Acts
Lamia
"Pensive they sit, and roll their languid eyes"
"To Autumn"
"The Fall of Hyperion. A Dream"
"The day is gone, and all its sweets are gone!"
"What can I do to drive away"
"I cry your mercy, pity, love—ay, love!"
"Bright star! would I were steadfast as thou art"
"King Stephen. A Fragment of a Tragedy"
"This living hand, now warm and capable"
"The Cap and the Bells; or, The Jealousies"

The dating of a small number of the poems on this list (taken from John Barnard's edition) is conjectural, including that of the famous sonnet "Bright star!" But the range among those which Keats is undisputedly documented to have composed in 1819 is immense. However, by the end of the nineteenth century, he was identified almost solely with the great odes. "The Odes are absolute perfection," declared William Graham in 1898, contrasting them with the rest of Keats's oeuvre, which he dismissed as "trash."

———

WAS THE "PERFECT" "Ode to a Nightingale" really written in "two or three hours," as Charles Brown recalled? His account foregrounds his own role as its savior, rescuing, as he put it, "four or five scraps" of paper on which, he said, it was illegibly scribbled, and which Keats had apparently thrust hurriedly behind some books on coming in from the garden. Dilke, however, later contested this story, calling it "pure delusion" on Brown's part and sarcastically noting in the margin of Milnes's 1848 biography, "We do not usually thrust waste paper behind books." By the time Milnes published his edition of Keats's works, he had completely removed Brown from the story, having no doubt heard of Dilke's skepticism.

The autograph manuscript of "Ode to a Nightingale" in Keats's hand is preserved today in the Fitzwilliam Museum in Cambridge. It is written on just two sheets of paper, which immediately casts doubt on Brown's tale of "four or five." The reason it survives is because Keats enclosed it in a letter to Reynolds, who subsequently passed it to his sister Marianne, who then passed it to their other sibling Charlotte, whose son went on to inherit it. Following the latter's death in 1899 it was sold at Sotheby's in 1901 before being acquired by the Fitzwilliam in 1932.

Brown's retrospective attempt to claim some sort of ownership over "Ode to a Nightingale" may suggest a hint of jealousy on his part of the fact that Keats had entrusted the original manuscript to Reynolds. If so, it would not have been the first time Keats's friends vied over him. Leigh Hunt and Benjamin Robert Haydon had done so in 1817. Keats inspired love but also conflict. Squabbles over his legacy among his circle continued long after his death.

Perhaps, as Robert Gittings once speculated, Brown was conflating his memories and confusing his odes. His account of the composition of "Ode to a Nightingale" might have more bearing on that of "Ode on Indolence," whose original manuscript does not survive. It was transcribed in different versions by Brown himself and by Woodhouse, with the stanzas in a different order, suggesting it was indeed felt to have required editorial shaping.

That is not, however, the case when you examine the manuscript of "Ode to a Nightingale." There are a few crossings-out, always changes for the better, but only minor, and the handwriting is, pace Brown, quite legible, if not as perfect as you would expect in a fair copy. That this is indeed a first draft is shown by the fact that upside down at the bottom on sheet two is what looks like a three-word-long false start that Keats had rejected in the moment. The manuscript, written on a couple of sheets torn from a cheap notebook, is material evidence that the ode was indeed written in one fell swoop.

Had Keats continued on from his false start, the ode, like so many others on the theme, would have opened with a direct address to the nightingale: "Small wingèd Dryad . . ." He went on to reuse that idea of the bird as a nature spirit out of classical mythology in line seven, when he refers to the bird as a "light-wingèd Dryad of the trees." But his new beginning went:

> Heart aches and a painful numbness falls

He soon changed "painful numbness falls" to "drowsy numbness pains" and he added a "My" to the start of the line, turning the compound noun of "heart aches" into the verbal, and personal, "My heart aches." But then he crossed out the "My," before reinstating it again in the published version which we still read today. His indecision over "My" seems, uncannily, to sum up the ode's shifting visions of self-erasure ending in the return to "my sole self" as the nightingale finally flies away.

The oxymoronic drowsy numbness that pains recalls a startling line in a much earlier poem, "In Drear-Nighted December," written in 1817: "the feel of not to feel it." Keats's medical training had made him alert to the physiology of sensation and its gradations. Here, the anesthetized ache is explicitly compared with the effect of narcotics:

> . . . as though of hemlock I had drunk,
> Or emptied some dull opiate to the drains.

It has been suggested that Keats was under the influence of such a drug when he wrote this, with a laudanum bottle at his elbow.

Laudanum—opium dissolved in alcohol—was the standard over-the-counter painkiller at the time. Given Keats's recurrent sore throats, it is inconceivable that he would not have used it at least on occasion for medicinal reasons. He must have spooned it out in quantities to his mother and his brother Tom as they were dying. The idea that Keats also used it recreationally, or to get himself in the mood to create poetry, is much more speculative, but not beyond possibility. The connection between creative writers and drug use was widespread in the period. Although De Quincey's *Confessions of an English Opium-Eater* was first published anonymously six months after Keats died, Byron and Shelley are known to have dabbled. Sufferers from depression—the "horrid Morbidity of Temperament" which afflicted Keats on and off—were also known to self-medicate with laudanum.

Certainly, attitudes toward its use were relaxed in Keats's circle and addiction was regarded as a low-risk danger. "I think in one of your letters you said you should like to take opium, but for the terrible penalty attending it, but I do not see why that should be a hindrance for it was only caused by the abuse of it. So—take it—if you can," wrote Fanny Brawne to Keats's eighteen-year-old sister Fanny in 1821, although she personally found the taste of laudanum so disagreeable that she thought it an odd idea to take it, unless in pain, simply in order to produce a "pleasant feeling."

Shortly before he wrote the ode, Keats had listened to

Coleridge's monologue which included, among other topics, "Nightingales." Coleridge's opiate addiction was well publicized; he had broadcast it himself when he published "Kubla Khan" in 1816 with a prefatory note explaining that it had come to him in a dream brought on by taking two grains of opium. The list of poets who admitted to using the drug is long, from Mary Robinson in the 1790s to Elizabeth Barrett Browning in the early Victorian period. According to the writer Harriet Martineau (who was born in 1802), "there was probably no author or authoress free from the habit . . . The amount of opium taken to relieve the wear and tear of authorship was . . . greater than most people had any conception of, and *all* literary workers took some."

It is not inconceivable, then, that "Ode to a Nightingale" was indeed written under the influence of laudanum. Rather than expecting it to spark hallucinatory visions, the writers Martineau refers to used it to dampen anxiety. An act of spontaneous composition—such as this ode—might depend on tuning out distraction and overly conscious self-critique. Certainly, the use of opiates by jazz performers in the twentieth century has been interpreted as a response to the stress of improvisation, and the idea that too much conscious cognition could interfere with the spontaneous flow—although that does not negate the fact that virtuoso improvisation is dependent on years of prior conscious practice.

We cannot know the extent of Keats's laudanum use. If he had had a serious habit, it would surely be indicated in the sources, which it isn't. Even if he was an occasional user, for recreational, or creative, rather than purely medicinal purposes, the idea of him downing a dose just after breakfast, if indeed that was the time of day at which he wrote the ode, seems a little de trop. Whether drug-induced or not, the text certainly shows him writing in a state of self-aware creative autopilot, devoid of the overthinking which is so apparent in *Endymion.* The words just come to him, unimpeded.

We do, however, know more about Keats's use of the next mood enhancer he alludes to in the poem:

> O, for a draught of vintage! that hath been
>   Cooled a long age in the deep-delvèd earth,
> Tasting of Flora and the country green . . .
>   . . .
> O for a beaker full of the warm South . . .

These lines have, inter alia, allowed scholars to narrow down the date of when "Ode to a Nightingale" was composed to around the first few days in May, owing to an echo in a letter he wrote to his sister Fanny on (almost certainly) May 1 in which he exclaimed, "please heaven, a little claret-wine cool out of a cellar a mile deep . . . a strawberry bed to say your prayers to Flora in."

On February 19, 1819, in his long letter to George and Georgiana, he had expatiated at length on his "palate-passion" for red wine:

> . . . now I like Claret whenever I can have Claret I must drink it.—'t is the only palate affair that I am at all sensual in . . . it fills the mouth one's mouth with a gushing freshness—then goes down cool and feverless—then you do not feel it quarrelling with your liver—no it is rather a Peace maker and lies as quiet as it did in the grape—then it is as fragrant as the Queen Bee; and the more ethereal Part of it mounts into the brain, not assaulting the cerebral apartments like a bully in a bad house looking for

his trul and hurrying from door to door bouncing against
the waist-coat; but rather walks like Aladin about his own
enchanted palace so gently that you do not feel his step—
Other wines of a heavy and spirituous nature transform a
Man to a Silenus; this makes him a Hermes—and gives a
Woman the soul and imortality of Ariadne for whom Bacchus always kept a cellar of good claret . . .

Yet Keats prefaced this by reassuring George and Georgiana
that his alcohol intake was under control, which suggests that
it previously hadn't been. "I now never drink above three
glasses of wine—and never any spirits and water," he assured
them. In his diaries, Haydon recalled of Keats a period in
which "for six weeks he was scarcely sober, & once he covered
his tongue & throat as far as he could reach with Cayenne
pepper, in order as he said to have the 'delicious coolness of
claret in all its glory'! This was his expression as he told me the
fact." Keats was probably teasing Haydon when it came to the
cayenne pepper, but not about his alcohol intake.

It makes some sense to imagine that the stresses of Keats's
life, with its frequent bereavements and instability, might
have prompted occasional recourse to the bottle. There was
certainly a susceptibility to alcoholism in the family, as his
mother Frances, according to Abbey, drowned her sorrows
in addiction to brandy. Yet it makes less sense to ascribe the
extraordinary literary craft on display in "Ode to a Nightingale" to chemical enhancement. It is much too alert, although
it depicts a "drowsy" state. The manuscript itself, so assured
though written on scrappy paper, pays testimony to Keats's
assertion, reported by Woodhouse, that "My judgment . . . is
as active when I am actually writing as my imagination."

Keats on his deathbed in Rome in early 1821, his hair plastered down with sweat, in an image by his artist friend Joseph Severn, who was looking after him.

Life mask of Keats made by Benjamin Robert Haydon in 1816, the year that Keats wrote "On First Looking into Chapman's Homer."

Keats's brother Tom. He died of tuberculosis in 1818 at the age of nineteen. Witnessing his decline was agonizing for the poet, who later began spitting blood himself and died of the same disease three years later.

Their other brother, George (1797–1841), emigrated to America with his wife in 1818. The long letters Keats wrote them contain some of his most vivid prose.

Compare the middle-class Keats with the upper-class firebrand Shelley. The latter's open-necked shirt was a brazen symbol of rebellion, but Keats has only unbuttoned his cuffs.

Keats in a miniature made by Joseph Severn in 1819.

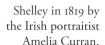

Shelley in 1819 by the Irish portraitist Amelia Curran.

Ode to the Nightingale

My Heart aches and a drowsy numbness pains
My sense, as though of hemlock I had drunk
Or emptied some dull opiate to the drains
One minute past and Lethe-wards had sunk:
Tis not through envy of thy happy lot
But being too happy in thine happiness
That thou light-winged dryad of the trees
In some melodious plot
Of beechen green, and shadows numberless
Singest of summer in full-throated ease.
O for a draught of vintage that has been
Cooling an age in the deep-delved earth
Tasting of Flora, and the country green
Dance, and Provencal song and sunburnt mirth
O for a Beaker full of the warm south,
Full of the true and blushful Hippocrene
With cluster'd bubbles winking at the brim
And purple stained mouth
that I might drink and leave the world unseen
And with thee fade away into the forest dim —
Fade far away, dissolve and quite forget
What thou among the leaves hast never known
The weariness, the fever and the fret
Here, where Men sit and hear each other groan
Where palsy shakes a few sad last grey hairs
Where youth pale and spectre thin and dies

Manuscript of "Ode to a Nightingale," 1819, almost certainly the first draft.

Keats, reimagined after his death, listening to a nightingale on Hampstead Heath in a staged-looking posthumous painting by Joseph Severn.

Fanny Brawne, with whom Keats fell, eventually, in love. When he first met her, he described her face unromantically: "a fine style of countenance of the lengthen'd sort—she wants sentiment in every feature—she manages to make her hair look well—her nostrils are fine—though a little painful—her mouth is bad and good—" This portrait was made in the 1830s, over a decade after Keats had died.

The street in which Keats bumped into the alluring Mrs. Jones in October 1818 still looks the same.

Wesleyan Place, where Keats, by then suffering from tuberculosis, lived briefly in 1820. There's not so much as a blue plaque to indicate that he was ever there.

Wentworth Place, now the Keats House museum. When Keats lived there, it was divided internally into two semidetached dwellings. The extension on the left was added later in the nineteenth century.

This Grave
contains all that was Mortal,
of a
YOUNG ENGLISH POET,
Who,
on his Death Bed,
in the Bitterness of his Heart
at the Malicious Power of his Enemies,
Desired
these Words to be engraven on his Tomb Stone
"Here lies One
Whose Name was writ in Water."
Feb 24ᵗʰ 1821

Keats's gravestone in Rome. His friend Charles Armitage Brown later called the epitaph "a sort of profanation."

BYRON LATER COMPLAINED to Leigh Hunt that he did not know what Keats meant by "a beaker full of the warm South." Hunt found this ludicrous, given that Byron was then living in Italy, "drinking its wine and basking in its sunshine." In a moment of superb clarity, Hunt brilliantly summed up why the over-rational Byron found fault: he was "not accustomed to these poetical concentrations."

That phrase sums up the extraordinary, repeated compressions of disparate ideas that make up the ode, with its plangent dissonances, mixed metaphors and contrarian impulses. Certainly, contemporary readers often found Keats a struggle as a result. "We frankly confess our dislike of his rhythm . . . and mistaken stringing together of compound epithets," opined the *London Magazine and Monthly Critical and Dramatic Review* in August 1820.

There is hardly an image in "Ode to a Nightingale" that doesn't melt into another to create an electric sense of instability and boundary-breaking, whether in "a beaker full of the warm South," or a "melodious plot / Of beechen green, and shadows numberless." In the latter phrase, musical sounds are relocated in the grass itself. "[S]hadows numberless" also contains a crunching ambiguity, meaning more than just "countless": "numbers" was a synonym for verses—writing to a rhythm with a certain number of beats in each line. Alexander Pope famously used the term in lines describing how his own natural talent for poetry appeared—as Keats's later did—in infancy. "Why did I write?" Alexander Pope had once asked in his *Epistle to Dr. Arbuthnot*: "As yet a child . . . / I lisp'd in numbers for the numbers came."

Keats is wittily opposing such optimistic Popian fluency by suggesting silence at this point in the ode. The poem will later open out into a Romantic vista of anti-Augustan, supra-rational, conflicted inspiration in which what can't be known for sure and pinned in clear-cut words becomes both the source and the end of the poet's creative task. At every stage, Keats mixes positive with negative, pleasure with pain and loss, through unexpected yokings and minglings that create a penumbra of fecund uncertainty.

In a moment of typically Keatsian synesthesia, the draught of vintage tastes of "Provençal song," an image which melds the senses of taste and hearing, and also the mouth-sensations of drinking and singing. In the phrase, Keats also self-alludes to the song played by Porphyro on Madeline's lute in "The Eve of St. Agnes," which is described as a "ditty . . . / In Provence called, 'La Belle Dame sans Merci.'" Porphyro's performance is both a seduction song and an enactment of seduction, since playing on Madeline's lute is a coy metaphor for what he does to her in bed. In his own "La Belle Dame sans Merci," however, Keats had reiterated the theme to evoke emptiness, not sexual satiation.

In "Ode to a Nightingale," however, he brings the ideas of pleasure and loss together in a bittersweet, almost Schubertian harmony. The wine, though cooled, has an undertaste of "sunburnt mirth," suggesting that laughter comes only with painfully scorched skin. The vintage then turns into the "blushful Hippocrene." According to Lemprière's *Classical Dictionary,* which Keats had known since school, the Hippocrene was "a fountain of Boeotia, near mount Helicon, sacred to the Muses." Unlike Jesus, who turned water into wine, Keats is turning wine into water, in his efforts to embrace the poetic muse. But this fountain is running with "blushful" water, as if turned pink by human blood running through it. He's indicating that his own notion of poetic inspiration is far from bloodless, rooted in the conflicts of the physical body.

There's a hint of eroticism in the very idea of the blush, but also one of embarrassment. In a classic couplet from his *Essay on Criticism,* Alexander Pope warned aspiring writers that:

> A little learning is a dangerous thing;
> Drink deep, or taste not the Pierian spring.

Pierides, according to Lemprière, was a name given by the ancient Greeks to the muses, so Pope too was alluding to the fount of inspiration, just as Keats later did with his reference to the Hippocrene. Keats himself—who knew a lot of Latin but had never studied the Greek language—had been humiliated for his insufficient "learning" in *Blackwood's,* which had dismissed him for knowing Homer only from Chapman—just as the grammar-school-educated Shakespeare had once been attacked by his contemporary Ben Jonson for knowing "small Latin and less Greek." Keats's reference to the "blushful Hippocrene" thus suggests a hint of his own blushfulness at making such a Greek allusion, while at the same time confidently asserting his ability and right to do so.

At every turn, the ode crushes images together in Keats's "teeming brain." Next, the wine becomes a "purple-stainèd mouth," transferring itself onto the lips of the drinker, crusted with red wine—but this is also the bloodied Philomela, whose tongue was cut out by her rapist before the gods turned her into a nightingale, forever singing her lament that no one could ever understand. The "flowers" and "fruit-tree wild" and "eglantine" that then appear are typical ideal nature images from the pastoral playbook. But the soundtrack is

ominous, the "murmurous haunt of flies on summer eves"
evoking decay and death. Negatives and positives coexist in
a flickering dialectic throughout this poem, in which every
idea spawns another and Keats's verbal creativity reaches what
many have considered to be its apex.

———

DID KEATS REALLY WRITE this ode on a chair he had taken
out onto the "grass plot" in the garden one morning after
breakfast? The poem itself begins in a "melodious plot," but
by stanza four it is clear that Keats is not literally depicting a
sunny morning, since it is now dark, whether in reality or in
his imagination: he explicitly tells us, "tender is the night, /
And haply the Queen-Moon is on her throne."

In fact, the poem will not allow us to distinguish between
what is out there in the world and what is in the mind, and
it is worth remembering that the nightingale was as much a
literary construct in the culture of Keats's day as an ornithological reality. Is he entering a real or an imagined nighttime
scene? The ode—almost aggressively, if implicitly—requires
its readers to access their own capacity for negative capability and to acknowledge the poetic imagination as a creative
rather than purely mimetic force. But then, in a volte-face,
Keats hits out at "fancy" as a "deceiving elf" rather than as a
bringer of truth. We are left as bereft in the end as the poet's
"Forlorn . . . sole self," unable to know what to trust, in a
poem whose writer is "half in love with easeful Death" and
yet which vibrates with so much verbal life.

"[T]he dull brain perplexes and retards," writes Keats. It
is as if he wants the reader to share his sensation of muzzy
perplexity and paradox, even as he describes his own efforts
to escape it in pitch-perfect language. No poem aspires more

than "Ode to a Nightingale" to the condition of music, gesturing to what cannot be said or logically defined. Through its silent harmonic slippage, composed of imagery rather than notes, it approaches in language the bittersweet sound world that Keats's contemporary (and fellow syphilis sufferer) Schubert was developing at exactly the same period.

Some recent critics have completely bypassed Brown's story, instead creating their own myths. "As the Ode begins, Keats stands, listening to the nightingale in the depths of the night, somewhere in the fields of Hampstead," goes one confident account written in 2011. Two hundred years ago, nightingales did indeed frequent the Heath, though they are not among the 180 species of birds now seen there, which include kingfishers, woodpeckers and, surreally, green parakeets of uncertain provenance. However, I can find no specific contemporary documentation to prove for sure that Keats listened to nightingales on the Heath after dark—although his artist friend Joseph Severn later painted a posthumous portrait of *John Keats Listening to the Nightingale on Hampstead Heath* in the 1840s. It is, however, a daytime scene. A somewhat stiff-looking Keats, who had by then been dead for more than twenty years, sits on a bank under some trees, resting one elbow awkwardly on a tuft of grass as he rolls his eyes theatrically skyward.

We cannot in the end know for sure exactly where or at what time of day Keats composed "Ode to a Nightingale." But as Brown was actually living with him when it was written, his account has more claim to being somewhere near the truth, despite its obvious holes, than subsequent speculations. More important is what Keats did, through his original artistry, to the Romantic genre of the nightingale poem. This is the only one that is still widely appreciated by nonspecialist readers today.

7

"Ode on a Grecian Urn"

I.

Thou still unravished bride of quietness,
    Thou foster-child of silence and slow time,
Sylvan historian, who canst thus express
    A flowery tale more sweetly than our rhyme:
What leaf-fringed legend haunts about thy shape
    Of deities or mortals, or of both,
        In Tempe or the dales of Arcady?
    What men or gods are these? What maidens loth?
What mad pursuit? What struggle to escape?
        What pipes and timbrels? What wild ecstasy?

II.

Heard melodies are sweet, but those unheard
    Are sweeter; therefore, ye soft pipes, play on;
Not to the sensual ear, but, more endeared,
    Pipe to the spirit ditties of no tone:
Fair youth, beneath the trees, thou canst not leave
    Thy song, nor ever can those trees be bare;
        Bold Lover, never, never canst thou kiss,

Though winning near the goal—yet, do not grieve:
   She cannot fade, though thou hast not thy bliss,
     For ever wilt thou love, and she be fair!

III.

Ah, happy, happy boughs! that cannot shed
   Your leaves, nor ever bid the Spring adieu;
And, happy melodist, unwearièd,
   For ever piping songs for ever new;
More happy love! more happy, happy love!
   For ever warm and still to be enjoyed,
     For ever panting, and for ever young—
All breathing human passion far above,
   That leaves a heart high-sorrowful and cloyed,
     A burning forehead, and a parching tongue.

IV.

Who are these coming to the sacrifice?
   To what green altar, O mysterious priest,
Lead'st thou that heifer lowing at the skies,
   And all her silken flanks with garlands dressed?
What little town by river or sea shore,
   Or mountain-built with peaceful citadel,
     Is emptied of this folk, this pious morn?
And, little town, thy streets for evermore
   Will silent be; and not a soul to tell
     Why thou art desolate, can e'er return.

V.

O Attic shape! Fair attitude! with brede
   Of marble men and maidens overwrought,
With forest branches and the trodden weed;

Thou, silent form, dost tease us out of thought
As doth eternity: Cold Pastoral!
When old age shall this generation waste,
Thou shalt remain, in midst of other woe
Than ours, a friend to man, to whom thou say'st,
"Beauty is truth, truth beauty,—that is all
Ye know on earth, and all ye need to know."

WHEN I WAS at school in the 1980s, I had two English teachers, who both taught Keats. One was a nature lover, somewhat authoritarian, a father of four, who enjoyed taking
pupils on energetic hiking expeditions to the Lake District.
No one could have impressed upon us more vigorously, as he
shepherded us outside into the garden to study the ode "To
Autumn" sitting on the grass under the trees, that what mat-
tered about Keats was the way in which his poetry connected
with the transcendent beauty and truth of the natural world.

The other teacher was younger, reluctantly single and far
less able to maintain class discipline. His chosen method for
retaining our interest—adopted with limited success—was
to regale us with lubricious anecdotes about his own sexual
humiliations. His take on Keats was less idealistic. He read
out the following in a mocking deadpan:

Beauty is truth, truth beauty.

We had previously supposed the words to be deep and metaphysical; now they were reconfigured as a sneering empty tau-
tology, even a sarcastic joke at the reader's expense.

That cryptic maxim about beauty and truth has become
one of Keats's most frequently quoted lines. It comes at the

end of "Ode on a Grecian Urn," in which he brings to life the images depicted on an artifact from classical antiquity.

Despite many attempts, no actual urn answering this description—featuring an orgiastic pursuit of maidens to the sound of pipes and timbrels (a sort of tambourine), a more intimate image of a lover leaning over to kiss his girl, and the image of a priest leading a heifer to its sacrificial death—has ever been identified. However, we do know that Keats saw the antiquities in the British Museum and that he was also familiar with other examples from illustrated books.

Keats made a surviving tracing of the Greek "Sosibios Vase," now in the Louvre, from just such a book of engravings, Henry Moses's *A Collection of Antique Vases, Altars, Paterae, Tripods, Candelabra, Sarcophagi,* first published in 1814. The side of the Sosibios vase drawn by Keats features a maenad, a frenzied female follower of the god Dionysus, wielding her thyrsus, a giant fennel staff plucked from the ground. However, none of the scenes Keats imagines on his own urn are depicted on the Sosibios vase, so named after the Athenian artisan who signed it. Most likely, the urn of Keats's ode was an imaginary composite. What he wrote refracts his complex response to the pagan past, which he uses as a springboard from which to interrogate—quite literally, given the number of question marks that punctuate the poem—the relationship between art and reality, immutability and transience, past and present, death and life.

Keats's interest in the relics of ancient Greece had first been inspired more than two years before, when the painter Benjamin Robert Haydon took him to see the Elgin Marbles, which had been put on display in the British Museum in 1816. Originally decorating the Parthenon in Athens, they had been removed and shipped to England by Lord Elgin with the agreement of the Turks, who had invaded Greece but whose lack of interest in the ancient temple was such that they were using it to store armaments.

After the Marbles arrived in London, they spent several desultory years in a damp shed in Park Lane while Parliament debated whether they were worth having for the nation and how much to pay for them. As an artist, Haydon had campaigned for them to be acquired, and he had testified to their incomparable value as artworks. He regarded their installation in the British Museum, where they rubbed shoulders with a miscellany of other exhibits, including three stuffed giraffes, as a personal triumph.

Keats had met Haydon for the first time at Leigh Hunt's birthday party, to which Charles Cowden Clarke had taken him on October 19, 1816. That "red letter day" had secured Keats not only the patronage of "Libertas," and his subsequent feature in Hunt's piece on young poets to watch, but also the support of the painter. Haydon was one of those men around a decade older—like Clarke and Hunt and Charles Brown—who were attracted by Keats's energy, and possibly by the orphan's unconscious need for approval. Although Keats had published only a single sonnet at the time Haydon met him, Haydon was instantly convinced of his "prematurity of intellectual and poetical power," and immediately "formed a very high idea of his genius." He set out to become his mentor, fueled by a combination of quasi-parental tenderness and egotistical desire to exert control.

Genius was a quality Haydon believed that he himself possessed in gigantic quantities—at least at those manic moments when he was feeling "like a man with air balloons under his armpits and ether in his soul." But he was volatile, bipolar even. The airborne episodes were interspersed with periods of self-loathing and disarray. He saw in Keats's determination to be a poet a similar commitment to his own vocation for painting, which he had adopted despite (perhaps, perversely, because of?) a childhood illness having left him with poor eyesight.

Haydon's surviving oeuvre—he specialized in vast history paintings—is weirdly patchy. Often there are brilliant corners in some otherwise leaden canvas. His market value was so low in the 1960s that my father and a student friend could afford to club together to buy a small oil study Haydon made for his massive *Alexander the Great Taming Bucephalus,* a canvas two meters wide that was made in the 1820s and is now in Petworth House, a National Trust stately home. My father's friend, who encouraged him to contribute, clearly had an eye. He subsequently became a distinguished art history professor.

Based on a subject from classical antiquity, the painting shows Alexander riding the wild horse he has tamed, though in Haydon's rendition there's a near-comical contrast between the stilted figure of the hero—hand on hip, one naked leg nonchalantly hanging—and that of the supposedly raging black steed he is sitting astride. But in the foreground there's the figure of a crouching woman, seen from behind, with a baby in her arms. She's rendered with startling tenderness, a human individual in the midst of a hyperbolic, theatrical scene. You can't see her face, but the baby's waxily fluffy head looks so real you want to stroke it—at least in the study for the picture that's now in my mother's sitting room.

Haydon's vivid literary voice has in the long term proved more valuable than his painting to cultural historians. His diaries tell his own tale of the agonies of failure amid the ecstasies of ambition. Inter alia, they also reveal much gossip about the art world and the books world of his era. Haydon might not have anticipated it, but today his most significant contribution to culture is what he recorded, in occasional bursts, of Keats.

When the twenty-year-old Keats met the thirty-year-old Haydon, the latter's career was already checkered. He had fallen out with the Royal Academy, at whose school he had studied, over a perceived slight concerning the exhibition of one of his works. To the young Keats at the time, however, Haydon seemed the embodiment of artistic high-mindedness, fighting for the "cause / Of steadfast genius." Haydon's grand claims for the creative arts as the pinnacle of human achievement, and for the nobility of fame, helped spur Keats on toward the "great thing" of poetry.

The mood swings Keats experienced while writing *Endymion*—one moment he felt dwarfed by the cliff of poetry, the next he felt himself towering over the mousy Pope—suggest that his chameleon nature had caught a whiff of Haydon's bipolar behavior at the time they were in frequent contact. However, the painter's feet of clay soon became more evident. Constitutionally unreliable, he went on to borrow money from Keats which he did not repay. Haydon's financial woes—his debts eventually mounted into the thousands—went on to contribute to his suicide in 1846 at the age of sixty. After misquoting from *King Lear* in his diary, he tried to shoot himself, missed, and then slit his throat.

Haydon's tendency to grandiosity pervades the rhetoric in which he expressed his enthusiasm for the Elgin Marbles: "Such a blast will Fame blow of their grandeur," he announced. Yet Keats's reaction when he was shown them by the painter in early 1817 was less triumphalist. In response, he sent Haydon two sonnets. One was called "On Seeing the Elgin Marbles"; the other, which was effectively a cover letter,

was titled "To B. R. Haydon, with a Sonnet Written on Seeing the Elgin Marbles." These poems reveal that, rather than
engendering a sensation of air balloons under the armpits,
the sight of the ancient Marbles, ripped from their original
context, had made Keats feel ambivalent and vulnerable. The
carved stones made him sense the weight of his own mortality. They made him realize, "I must die."

Couched in the form of a tribute to a mentor, Keats's sonnet to Haydon begins with what looks like an apology for the
inadequacy of his own response:

> Haydon! Forgive me that I cannot speak
> Definitively on these mighty things.

In fact, he was already inching away from Haydon's mega-
lomaniacal certainties toward the concept of "negative capability" that he went on to formulate later in the year, which
made uncertainties, mysteries and doubts the prerequisite
for creativity. "On Seeing the Elgin Marbles" makes art out
of what Keats calls the "undescribable feud" that seeing the
ancient sculptures had inspired in his own "heart." He min-
gles their "Grecian grandeur" with his own awareness of

> the rude
> Wasting of old Time—with a billowy main—
> A sun—a shadow of a magnitude.

The reference to the "billowy main" was an allusion to the
fact that some of the Marbles had been lost at sea during their
voyage to Britain, when the ship carrying them and other
antiquities, HMS *Mentor,* sank. Although the lost sculptures
were later salvaged, the shipwreck has continued to yield fur-

ther ancient treasures, including gold jewelry only brought to the surface by archaeologists as late as 2019.

In his sonnet, Keats was not responding to the sculptures, as Haydon had, as uncontested embodiments of eternal art. He's also aware of them as objects with their own history: as things within history, moving through time, and susceptible to its quirks and depredations. The play of movement against stasis would later be rewritten into "Ode on a Grecian Urn," in which the urn is there to "tease us out of thought," just as the Marbles made Keats feel "dizzy."

Dizziness suggests a bodily reaction, typical for Keats. It's as if he's suffering from vertigo, feeling wobbly and almost queasy with the intensity of his own mental effort to respond to sculptures made by human hands that had been dead for so many centuries. His hypersensitized and nuanced reaction—especially the way in which it arouses feelings of self-doubt which Keats then crystallizes into poetry—contrasts vividly with Haydon's bombast. It's worth wondering whether Keats, who loved puns, was privately making a silent play on words in his buried allusion to the wreck of the *Mentor.* Haydon, his self-styled mentor, was not a man to inspire full confidence from his chosen acolytes.

———

"Ode on a Grecian Urn" reflects at a tangent Keats's encounter with the Elgin Marbles, but it was inspired by literary as well as sculptural sources. His reading of Greek literature in translation was not confined to Chapman's Homer, although no other classical translator could match Chapman in his eyes. Recent scholarship has shown that, in describing the figures depicted on the Grecian urn, Keats was probably alluding to one of Theocritus's *Idylls,* which he could have read in the popular English translation by Richard Polwhele, first published in 1792.

We all know what "idyllic" means, but as a literary form in ancient Greek an idyll was a picturesque pastoral poem. In his third *Idyll,* Theocritus describes the images carved on a wooden drinking cup given by a goatherd to a shepherd. They include, in the 1792 translation, a "Female Figure," whose clothing ripples in the breeze, and two youths who compete for her romantic attention "by turns" as she redirects her "smiles" from one to the other, recalling the "Bold lover" on Keats's Grecian urn.

Obviously, a carved image is stationary. By making the girl on the drinking cup move, Theocritus was engaging in a traditional aesthetic contest: the rivalry between the visual and the verbal arts. Was a poem better because it could imagine time and movement, which a motionless picture could not? That sense of competition was invested in the topos of the ekphrasis, a depiction of a visual artwork in words, whose locus classicus was Homer's riff in the *Iliad* on the images depicted on the shield of Achilles. Virgil's *Aeneid,* which Keats had himself translated, also includes several set-piece ekphrases.

To write an imitation of Theocritus would have been standard fare for an Oxbridge-educated classicist. George Dyer, author of the pedestrian nightingale poem, footnotes Theocritus and announces himself on the title page of his wordily named book, *Poetics; or a Series of Poems, and Disquisitions on Poetry,* as "Formerly of Emanuel [*sic*] College, Cambridge." A scholar in late middle age at the time, he ascribed all his subsequent achievements—he spent his life as a classical scholar and editor—to the "academical predilections" fostered "when at Cambridge."

In contrast, Keats had been humiliatingly reminded by

Blackwood's that he had neither attended university nor learned Greek. "His knowledge of Greek and mythology seems to mystify him on every occasion," commented a condescending critic in 1820. It was one thing for a dusty old academic like Dyer to refer to ancient literature. But Keats's appropriation of Greek themes in *Endymion* had aroused scorn as vulgar pretension. He had, it was thought, no "nicety." His classical allusions were thought to rise no better than those of an overexcited schoolboy in the classroom.

During the Regency period, there was an uncomfortable feeling that the age in which so-called high art could dare to repurpose the Classics was over, not least since Greek and Roman themes and images had become so ubiquitously fashionable and mass-marketed that repurposing them had come to seem almost vulgar. Every middle-class terraced house being thrown up in London during the early-nineteenth-century building boom seemed to feature design motifs from ancient Rome or Greece on the balcony ironwork or ceiling moldings. In Jane Austen's *Emma* (1815), the parvenue Augusta Hawkins, who eventually weds the clergyman Mr. Elton, is pilloried for her vulgarity, and especially for describing marriage, in a classical circumlocution, as donning Hymen's saffron robe. That's an image Keats never used, but one can imagine him doing so. (Actually, he referred, in a canceled passage in *Lamia,* to "white robes hymeneal.")

Another aspect of Keats's attraction to pagan mythology that had the potential to discombobulate conservatives was its association with sexual license. Keats explicitly makes that connection in the first scene depicted on the urn, which features a band of "men or gods" in pursuit of fleeing maidens whom they are intent on ravishing. In popular culture, the debased use of classical language for erotic purposes had long since been a commonplace, used, say, in the late-eighteenth-century courtesan directory *Harris's List of Covent Garden Ladies,* in which sex is called "the Cytherean rites" and a prostitute is compared to the Venus de Medici. In the 1780s, the young Emma Hamilton had been employed as a scantily clad Hebe at the "Temple of Health." Later, having crossed class boundaries to marry Sir William Hamilton, a collector of antiquities, she became famous, or notorious, for her much satirized "attitudes" or *poses plastiques,* in which, draped in diaphanous fabrics, she became a living sculpture, personifying mythological characters. "She is a Whapper!" opined Lady Elgin, whose husband later gave his name to the eponymous Marbles after bringing them to England. "And I think her manner very vulgar."

Keats's attraction to classical themes and images not only seemed upstart and potentially libertine to some. It also attracted hostility from a religious and political viewpoint. His evident love of ancient pagan culture was read as antagonistic because it appeared to offer a rejection of the establishment Church and therefore the state. Oxbridge students in the early nineteenth century—many of whom, like Keats's friend Benjamin Bailey, were aspirant vicars—compartmentalized their scholarly study of Latin and Greek texts, erecting a mental barrier between their reverence for ancient authors and their adherence to Christian dogma. Keats, in contrast, broke down the fence between modern and ancient by creating a landscape in *Endymion* in which the English countryside and his own personal voice existed in the same space as Greek divinities, and in whose "Hymn to Pan" in Book One he extolled the mysteries of nature's life cycle.

How to process the legacy of the ancients was a question which often aroused anxiety, in the poet William Wordsworth among others. In 1814, he had addressed it in his modern epic *The Excursion,* set not on mythical Latmos, like *Endymion,* but in the Lake District and in the contemporary world. Wordsworth had settled in the Lakes to pursue his own sense of identification with nature. But by 1814, he felt ambivalent about old pagan nature worship.

Contemplating the "lively Grecian," who found in the hilly landscape of his birth "commodious place for every God," Wordsworth's reactions in *The Excursion* were painfully conflicted. He acknowledged the "unrivalled skill" with which Greek artists had bestowed a "fixed shape" in "[m]etal or stone" on the "fluent operations" of the natural world. But he also admitted that by embodying nature in the figures of gods, they were, worryingly, "idolatrously" motivated.

Wordsworth scathingly depicted Greek poets as "wandering Rhapsodists," their songs "gross fictions chanted in the streets." On the other hand, he also idealized the creative achievements of ancient Greece, seen for example in its "statues and temples," as "emanations . . . acts of immortality . . . mysteries." But later on in *The Excursion,* through the character of the "venerable Pastor," Wordsworth contrasted the pagans' worship of "Gods which themselves had fashioned, to promote / Ill purposes, and flatter foul desires," with "the true and only God" and "the faith derived through Him who bled / Upon the cross." As a young radical in the 1790s, Wordsworth had been attracted to revolutionary ideas which were then associated not just with political revolt but with pantheism and atheism. By 1814, he had become increasingly reattached to the establishment Church of England.

The many-angled ambivalence expressed in *The Excursion* is perhaps the context in which we should read the now famous anecdote, related by Haydon, about the time he introduced Keats to Wordsworth, which probably happened in late 1817, after Keats had written *Endymion* but before it had been published. Haydon relished his role as social broker and impresario, as he brought the new young poet together with the middle-aged literary grandee.

But as he recalled it in 1845, the encounter was embarrassing, the older poet treating the younger's "Paganism," as seen in *Endymion,* to a sarcastic put-down:

> Wordsworth received him kindly, & after a few minutes, Wordsworth asked him what he had been doing lately, I said he had just finished an exquisite Ode to Pan—and as he had not sent a copy I asked Keats to repeat it—which he did in the usual half-chant, (most touching) walking up & down the room, when he had done I felt really, as if I had heard a young Apollo—Wordsworth drily said
>
> "a Very pretty piece of Paganism—"
>
> This was unfeeling, & unworthy his high Genius to a young Worshipper like Keats—& Keats felt it deeply.

Modern biographers have questioned the credibility of Haydon's story, which he wrote down nearly thirty years after the event in a letter to the publisher Edward Moxon. Both Andrew Motion and Nicholas Roe follow Robert Gittings closely in rejecting its accuracy, suggesting that Keats might in fact have taken "pretty" as a compliment. Certainly, there is nothing in Keats's correspondence to indicate that he felt slighted by Wordsworth at the time. But it is equally possible that he did not refer to the incident in his letters because the experience was so embarrassing that he wanted to edit it out.

There's no doubt that Wordsworth is on record as expressing his disapproval of Keats, whom he regarded as a young man who, though talented, was prey to corrupting influences. "How is Keates," he asked Haydon on January 15, 1820, "he is a youth of promise too great for the sorry company he keeps." It is also on record that Keats himself later became disillusioned with Wordsworth, during his northern walking tour with Brown in the summer of 1818. On calling at Wordsworth's house in the Lake District, Rydal Mount, Keats was disappointed to find him out but flagrantly dismayed to discover the reason. Wordsworth, who had been a radical in his youth but had become increasingly conservative, was away electioneering on behalf of the local Tories. "Sad—sad—sad . . . What can we say?" wrote Keats to Tom on June 26, 1818.

Haydon's recall at a distance of three decades is unlikely to have been fully accurate, and it's moreover hard to imagine Wordsworth being quite so ill-mannered and ungenerous. However, the anecdote as Haydon told it in 1845 is not nugatory in terms of its cultural meaning. It registers the discomfort felt by many, in the ideologically repressive era following the Napoleonic Wars, toward the appropriation of ancient pagan culture. It's even possible that, in describing Keats reciting the "Hymn to Pan" in a "half-chant" as he walked up and down the room, Haydon was half-remembering those lines from Wordsworth's *Excursion* about the "wandering" rhapsodists "chanting" their "gross fictions."

Whatever Wordsworth really thought of Keats's use of pagan images and ideas in his poetry, it is certainly the case that Keats overtly expressed a preference for ancient religion over Christianity in his private correspondence. In his long letter to George and Georgiana of February 14 to May 3, 1819, he bemoaned the fact that the Christian faith had not introduced "Mediators and Personages in the same manner as in the hethen [*sic*] mythology abstractions are personified." Unlike Wordsworth, he was uninhibitedly attracted to the seemingly idolatrous way in which the Greek artists used the images of gods to give a metaphorical "fixed shape" to aspects of nature.

Rather than naïvely assuming that Greek and Roman poets had believed literally in their gods, Keats saw the ancient mythologies as allegories or metaphors for the human condition, a view which fitted his own instinctive tendency to think in images and "poetical concentrations." In the same letter, he also denied the divinity of Christ, a heretical position at the time, although he also viewed Jesus, along with Socrates, as a uniquely inspired human being.

Keats's attraction to radically heterodox opinions and his opposition to establishment religion, thus, fed his interest in ancient mythology. This was picked up on by the *Eclectic Review* in its notice of his 1820 collection, which stated that "Mr. Keats, seemingly, can think or write of scarcely anything else than the 'happy pieties' of Paganism," concluding disapprovingly that the poet lacked "the regulating principle of religion."

The *Eclectic Review* sarcastically singled out the gnomic and now famous ending of "Ode on a Grecian Urn" to demonstrate that what it dismissed as Keats's schoolboy attraction to paganism had led him into a void of ignorance:

A Grecian Urn throws him into an ecstasy: its "silent form," he says, "doth tease us out of thought as doth Eternity,"—a very happy description of the bewildering effect such subjects have had at least upon his own mind; and his fancy having just got the better of his reason, we are the less surprised at the oracle when the urn is made to utter:

"Beauty is truth, truth beauty,—that is all

Ye know on earth, and all ye need to know."

That is all Mr. Keats knows or cares to know.—But till he knows much more than this, he will never write verses fit to live.

Yet Keats's morphing reputation was such that by 1857, following Richard Monckton Milnes's rehabilitating biography of 1848, "Ode on a Grecian Urn" was championed in the *Encyclopædia Britannica* as "perhaps the most exquisite specimen of Keats's poetry." It was, according to that Victorian repository of establishment wisdom, the high point of Keats's art because "it breathes the very spirit of antiquity;—eternal beauty and eternal repose." Keats's own reputation had, within a few decades, been subject to the "billowy main" of public opinion and was by then riding the crest of a wave.

————

FEW POEMS HAVE inspired such disparate responses as "Ode on a Grecian Urn." Yet the fact that it has aroused so much conflicting commentary is perhaps unsurprising, since it is implicitly a poem about reading or interpreting a work of art. Keats's numerous questions emphasize the viewer's ignorance. Neither he, nor we, know who the characters depicted on the urn are, or what their story is. Only the viewer's imagination can supply the answer.

"What leaf-fringed legend haunts about thy shape . . . ?" Keats asks. "What men or gods are these?" As readers, we are left on our own to make sense of the Delphic statement at the end, supposed to be the imagined speech of the urn itself, a "friend to man." Is the urn—which has often been taken to be a funerary urn—really so friendly? Does it "speak / Definitively," unlike Keats himself, who could not do that in responding to the Elgin Marbles? And what do its strange words mean?

Keats's most intimate knowledge of the classical ekphrasis came not from reading Theocritus's third *Idyll* in translation, but from Virgil's *Aeneid*, which he had personally translated word for word. The *Aeneid* includes several set-piece ekphrases. What marks them is Virgil's sophisticated and sometimes ironized literary consciousness of viewpoint. When, for example, Aeneas looks at the frieze on the temple of Juno depicting the fall of Troy, he interprets it as sympathetic to the plight of his own people, the Trojans. Virgil, however, makes it clear that this is a misreading prompted by his hero's wishful thinking. Thus, the meanings Virgil invests in the ekphrasis require the reader to hold two perspectives in mind at once.

Multiple or uncertain meanings abound in Keats's ode. The idea that it channels the spirit of "eternal repose" can only be a Victorian taming of Keats's text, which is much less complacent and much more anxious and equivocal than that suggests. Its questions never let the reader rest in the way in which the movement of the characters depicted on the urn is literally arrested. Even the word "still" in the opening line is semantically unstable, meaning both "motionless" and "as yet."

Theocritus had given movement to the stationary carved figures, by making the girl's clothing ripple as she turns her smiles from one youth to another. Keats, in contrast, keeps his figures frozen in a state of suspended animation and relocates the sense of mobility in poetic language itself. Keats's silent piper plays "ditties of no tone," but his ode has no fixed tone either, in the sense that its moods are changeable, its pathos freighted with moments of near-comedy.

The anonymous critic in the *Monthly Review* bewailed Keats's failure to live up to the "high being" of poetry and found deplorable "triteness" in the lines:

> Heard melodies are sweet, but those unheard
>   Are sweeter; therefore, ye soft pipes, play on;
> Not to the sensual ear, but, more endeared,
>   Pipe to the spirit ditties of no tone.

He was probably recoiling from the pun in "endeared" ("end eared" to riff on "unheard"). To use a pun, the lowest form of wit, in a high-flown classical context would have seemed indecorous—and antiestablishment. Indeed the ode's tone, hovering between the comic and the tragic, is provocatively ambiguous. Another contemporary reviewer, in *The Guardian,* described it, unsympathetically, as having the "stimulating properties of a Christmas riddle."

This tendency to find puzzles and comical wordplay in the ode was subsequently lost after it was canonized by the Victorians as an ideal representation of "eternal beauty." In more recent times, however, criticism has doubled back. The punning echo in "O Attic shape! Fair attitude!" was emphasized by Jeffrey N. Cox in 1998, who also felt he could spot in the phrase an echo of the shapely Emma Hamilton's titillating "attitudes." He concluded that Keats was playing with mixing ancient and modern registers, high and low art, in a period of history which saw endless Greek-style vases pour out of the Wedgwood factory into middle-class homes, and in which classical themes were becoming, potentially subversively, democratized.

Irony is certainly an undersong in Keats's so-called representation of "eternal beauty." The whole poem is mired in, yet strangely celebrates, frustration. The human urge to connect or grasp, even when stymied, is valued for itself. The "Bold lover" who can "never, never" kiss is no more able to satisfy his desire than Keats was when he lunged at Mrs. Jones in her Bloomsbury rooms. Sexual frustration would also underlie Keats's increasingly desperate attachment to Fanny Brawne, to whom he wrote his first love letter a few weeks after writing this ode. His own frustration may have been exacerbated by his belief that he had contracted syphilis, which would have meant that consummating his passion with a woman he loved might have put her at risk if the "little Mercury" he had "taken" had not fully "corrected the Poison."

The aesthetic fetishization of frustration comes because, throughout the ode, Keats is engaged in a conceptual duel, one that can never be resolved, between the claims of the earthly yet transient and the capacity of artworks to defy death by remaining the same as human generations come and go. Can the mortal poet escape the "burning forehead" and the "parching tongue" of his mortality by imaginatively identifying with the urn's longevity? Or does the urn mock him and inspire his envy by reminding him that he "must die," as Keats put it in his Elgin Marbles sonnet?

When my romantically frustrated young English teacher read out the ode, giving voice to the "silent form" of Keats's words printed in our textbook, his face contorted with satire as he enunciated:

More happy love! more happy, happy love!

That line comes immediately after the "happy, happy boughs" and the "happy melodist," with the result that Keats repeats the word "happy" six times in the space of five lines.

Keats's "happy melodist" is "For ever piping songs for ever new," but "happy" indeed seems somewhat rictus by the sixth repetition, like a cracked record, stuck rather than moving forward. The more the word is repeated, the less it means, or perhaps the more we question what it means. Keats was never a cynic but he could be an ironist, always more inspired by the shape-shifting potential of language than by its capacity to be "definitive." For him, words themselves were not inert, like the urn, but had the quality of living things whose semantics he, as a poet, could mutate or arrest at will.

———

SO WHAT DOES the urn's final message tell us? It has become so widely disseminated that even Google recognizes it, and will give you an answer of sorts, if grammatically garbled, when you ask it:

> **Beauty** is **truth. Truth** is **beauty.** This philosophical statement means that the real **beauty** of a thing lies on its permanence and that there is only one ultimate **beauty** in this world is **truth** which never perishes. The remaining, though they seem to be **beautiful**, is not really **beautiful** as they are perishable.

In Keats's time, the ideas of beauty and truth were frequently yoked in contemporary aesthetics, by Leigh Hunt and Hazlitt among others. Indeed, the pairing had become such a commonplace by 1817 that Byron mentioned the terms together in a comical aside in *Beppo,* in which he compared the fleshly charms of "pretty-faced" Venetian lovelies with Italian Old Master paintings by Titian or Giorgione, whose tints are "truth and beauty at their best." In the same passage he alluded to the ancient Greeks' reputation for sexual license in noting that the Italians had "copied from the Grecians."

The moments in his letters where Keats links the terms "beauty and truth" have subsequently become some of his most quoted pronouncements. Many critics have tried to find in them some schematic philosophy. "What the imagination seizes as Beauty must be truth . . . The Imagination may be compared to Adam's dream—he awoke and found it truth," Keats wrote to Benjamin Bailey, for example, on November 22, 1817, alluding to Milton's portrayal of Adam, who dreams of having a partner and wakes to find that God has indeed created Eve for him.

The extended passage in which these sentences by Keats occur reads like a conversational monologue that captures the reeling energy with which he and Bailey enjoyed sharing their thoughts at speed as they arose. We should be mindful of the fact that Keats goes on to question the value of philosophical rationalism as a route to truth—"I have never yet been able to perceive how any thing can be known for truth by consequitive reasoning"—before bursting out, "O for a life of Sensations rather than of Thoughts!"

He goes on to reference what sounds like a quasi-Platonic idea when he suggests that it is sensations not thoughts that form "a Shadow of reality to come." He then treats Bailey to an extended riff on a "favourite Speculation of mine": that an ideal afterlife might exist—but only for those who "delight in sensation rather than hunger, as you do, after Truth"—in which our moments of "what we called happiness on Earth" might be endlessly repeated in a "finer tone."

In a beautiful proto-Proustian image, Keats compares this to hearing an old melody and remembering the time you first heard it, and how much more beautiful the original singer's face might seem in imaginary recall than it could have really been when you first experienced it in real time and physical proximity. The silent pipes and timbrels on the urn uncannily echo this image of music that's better in memory than in real time.

When Keats talks about having heard a melody and subsequently remembering it when hearing a second, less enchanting, performance, he makes me feel he is at his most engaging not when he is philosophizing about abstractions but when he is talking about something previously experienced, as he elsewhere put it, "on the pulses." This is the individual, very human, twenty-two-year-old Keats thinking aloud, rather than a calculated theorist setting out a philosophical program. "What a time! I am continually running away from the subject," he concludes.

Another well-known passage on beauty and truth comes in a letter Keats wrote to George and Tom on December 21, 1817: "the excellence of every Art is its intensity, capable of making all disagreeables evaporate, from their being in close relationship with Beauty & Truth." This comment, like some of his other seemingly philosophical statements, has often been quoted out of context. When he wrote it, he was in fact very specifically referring to Shakespeare: he went on to cite *King Lear* as the paradigm of what he meant. In doing so, he was expressing admiration for the way in which Shakespeare represents ugly emotions and human situations in poetic language that is both aesthetically beautiful and true to life. Shakespeare, for Keats, was a genius because he embraced the negatives of human experience—what Keats later called the "fever, and the fret"—and cathartically transformed them into art without denial.

That Keats himself rejected the abstruse abstractions of philosophy, and preferred those poets who rendered the muddle of human experience, should make us question whether he intended the final chiasmus of "Ode on a Grecian Urn" to be taken as a meaningful leap into metaphysics. The lines are hoveringly ambiguous:

> "Beauty is truth, truth beauty,—that is all
> Ye know on earth, and all ye need to know."

All ye know? Are we being invited to reflect on the summation of human knowledge, or on how little humans really understand?

The aesthetic symmetry of the phrase enacts the idea of closure in its very circularity. And yet the whole dynamic of the poem has been to imagine the "disagreeables" that are *not* enclosed in the idealized images on the urn: the (offstage and never to be actuated) rape of the "maidens loth," the "burning forehead" and the "parching tongue," the heifer's bloody death. Keats looks beyond, in true ekphrastic fashion, to what the urn cannot tell us and gives voice to what has been emptied out, just as the "little town" depicted in the background will remain "desolate" forever: its absent inhabitants, who have left it to attend the sacrificial rite, can never return, as they are stuck in the world of the urn, implied but not represented. This is a poem about the failure of art as well as its potential to image an ideal. But it also links to how art can imply more than it states, how it gives suggestive life to things beyond the frame in the mind of the viewer or reader.

"Ode on a Grecian Urn" ultimately offers no definitive

answer. It is indeed there to "tease us out of thought." It shows Keats using his by now astonishing verbal dexterity to hold art and grubby human reality in suspension. As Helen Vendler carefully puts it, with some understatement, "The attribution of truth to representational art, and the coupling, common in aesthetics, of the terms Truth and Beauty, as the desiderata of art, did not, for Keats, render the terms unproblematic." This ode tells us less about the abstract ideas of "beauty and truth" than about Keats's game-changing concept of "negative capability," as he challenges us, his readers, to take in his words without irritably reaching after fact or reason, while at the same time provoking us to do just that.

In assessing Keats's work in 1820, the *Monthly Review* concluded that "though he is frequently involved in ambiguity . . . we are yet sure of finding in all that he writes the proof of deep thought and energetic reflections." That assessment still stands. However, today the ambiguities are regarded no longer as a problem but as the core of the ode's achievement. The urn Keats depicts is conceived to have survived far longer than a human life span. So, by now, has Keats's poem, which continues to tease us not just out of, but into, thought.

We will never know the full truth about the meeting in which Wordsworth allegedly slighted Keats's "Hymn to Pan" as a "pretty piece of Paganism." But we do know that, long after Keats had died, at a time when his reputation was on the rise, the by then elderly Wordsworth had no qualms about keeping poetic company with him. Indeed, he even laid claim to having got there first when it came to the themes treated in "Ode on a Grecian Urn," which was by then coming to be regarded as a masterpiece. According to a local clergyman friend, Wordsworth evinced "a peculiar satisfaction" in asserting the "priority" of his own poem, "Upon the Sight of a Beautiful Picture," thus implying, without actually saying so, that Keats had borrowed the idea for the ode from him. In that minor effusion, first published in 1815, Wordsworth had eulogized a landscape painting in his own collection by Sir G. H. Beaumont, Bart, as "soul-soothing art" which captured "one brief moment" to give it the "appropriate calm of blest eternity." "Ode on a Grecian Urn" indeed deals with the dialectic between the trapped moment and eternity. But it is far from calm and often inappropriate.

———◦◦◦◦———

8

"To Autumn"

I.

Season of mists and mellow fruitfulness,
   Close bosom-friend of the maturing sun,
Conspiring with him how to load and bless
   With fruit the vines that round the thatch-eves run;
To bend with apples the mossed cottage-trees,
   And fill all fruit with ripeness to the core;
     To swell the gourd, and plump the hazel shells
   With a sweet kernel; to set budding more,
And still more, later flowers for the bees,
Until they think warm days will never cease,
     For Summer has o'er-brimmed their clammy cells.

II.

Who hath not seen thee oft amid thy store?
   Sometimes whoever seeks abroad may find
Thee sitting careless on a granary floor,
   Thy hair soft-lifted by the winnowing wind;
Or on a half-reaped furrow sound asleep,
   Drowsed with the fume of poppies, while thy hook

Spares the next swath and all its twinèd flowers;
And sometimes like a gleaner thou dost keep
  Steady thy laden head across a brook;
  Or by a cider-press, with patient look,
    Thou watchest the last oozings hours by hours.

III.

Where are the songs of Spring? Ay, where are they?
  Think not of them, thou hast thy music too—
While barrèd clouds bloom the soft-dying day,
  And touch the stubble-plains with rosy hue:
Then in a wailful choir the small gnats mourn
  Among the river sallows, borne aloft
    Or sinking as the light wind lives or dies;
And full-grown lambs loud bleat from hilly bourn;
  Hedge-crickets sing; and now with treble soft
  The red-breast whistles from a garden-croft;
    And gathering swallows twitter in the skies.

APART FROM WORDSWORTH'S "Daffodils" ("I wandered lonely as a cloud"), Keats's ode "To Autumn" is probably today's most widely read Romantic-era nature poem. Its cultural ubiquity is such that in the film *Bridget Jones's Diary*, the heroine, trying to be arty, recites its opening lines in an attempt to impress her potential paramour while in a rowing boat, with typically comedic consequences.

Readers respond to the way in which this ode humanizes nature. Autumn is personified, but not as a classical deity. It's not even clear what gender Autumn is. There's something of a nurturing female mother figure there. Autumn provides a "store" of food. Yet behind Keats's address to the season hover

Edmund Spenser's Elizabethan lines on the same subject, in which Autumn is gendered male, a "he" who "joyed in his plentious store / Laden with fruits that made him laugh." Keats's "abstraction personified" is in fact too close to the earth to be a person with a gender.

The language too is earthy, far less high-flown than in the other odes. We are not charioted by Bacchus and his pards, and we are invited to drink English cider rather than water from the Hippocrene spring. We are not in Tempe or the dales of Arcady, but in fact in a field just outside Winchester, where Keats wrote "To Autumn" on Sunday, September 19, 1819.

"To Autumn" has been called the "greatest" of his odes: "So compact, masterful, and yet gentle." The biographical backdrop to its composition was, however, freighted with stress, and Keats had little mastery over his personal circumstances when he wrote it. Not only was he increasingly plagued by his "irritable state of health"—those recurrent sore throats. His deteriorating financial situation was also a cause for anxiety. Moreover, the national mood in which he composed his paean to the English countryside was far from placid. Only a month before, the body politic had been rocked by the Peterloo Massacre.

Despite his incipient health problems, Keats had been working frenetically on various projects since completing the other great odes in the late spring, hoping to publish a new collection by the end of the year. "Within these two months I have written 1500 Lines, most of which, besides many more of prior composition, you will probably see by next Winter," he told Benjamin Bailey on August 14, getting in touch after a lapse to bring him up to date with his latest news.

It is notable that Keats does not even mention the odes

when he goes into detail about what he has been doing over the last year or so: "I have written two Tales, one from Boccaccio call'd the Pot of Basil; and another call'd St. Agnes Eve on a popular superstition; and a 3rd called Lamia—(half-finished—I [hav]e a[l]so been writing parts of my Hyperion and [c]ompleted 4 Acts of a Tragedy."

Looking at it from posterity's perspective, it seems poignant that Keats failed to foresee that the great odes would come to be regarded as his most significant works. Yet his letter to Bailey also indicates the sensual delight he took in poetic language, which the odes so profoundly embody. "I look upon fine Phrases like a Lover," he confessed. The manuscript of "To Autumn"—either written al fresco or after he returned to his lodgings from his walk in the fields—reveals the physical pleasure he took in words.

As Helen Vendler once pointed out, the very handwriting shows this, in the stretched-out way in which Keats writes down the word "winnowing" in the line "Thy hair soft-lifted by the winnowing wind," making the flowing W's and N's almost resemble corn in a field being flattened by the breeze. Even misspellings, Vendler adds, indicate the way that words were protean living things for Keats, concentrations of ideas. There's a delightful dyslexic moment when he miswrites "aloft" as "afots" in the line that was published as:

Among the river sallows, borne aloft.

"Afots" is an anagram of "a-soft." We can see his linguistic creativity running ahead of itself as he anticipates the word "soft" with which he is intending to rhyme "aloft," three lines later, in the "treble soft" of the robin's song.

On June 27, Keats had left Hampstead for an extended,

and indeed enforced, writer's retreat on the Isle of Wight, since Brown was planning as usual to rent out his half of Wentworth Place for the summer. Keats's companion on this trip was his lawyer friend James Rice, who was unwell and needed to convalesce, and whose company Keats found both genial and steadying. Then on July 20 Brown arrived to work with Keats on their play *Otho the Great.* On August 12 the two set off for Winchester, where they remained in lodgings together until Brown left on September 6. By the time he wrote "To Autumn" on September 19, Keats was on his own in Winchester, living with daily "fatigue and trouble," as he put it to Fanny Brawne five days earlier on September 14.

During 1819, Keats's financial troubles snowballed. On June 17, he had begged Haydon to repay a loan: "I know you will not be quite prepared for this, because your Pocket must needs be very low . . . but what can I do? mine is lower." Having gone to Abbey "for some Cash," out of the dead Tom's portion, he had discovered that his uncle's widow was suing the Jennings estate and that Abbey could pay out no more as a trustee since he might end up liable if the widow won her case.

While in Winchester, Keats had then received a desperate letter from George, informing him that he had lost everything, having been fleeced by Audubon. As a result, Keats hurried up to London on September 10, in the hope of getting Abbey to release some funds for George and also of persuading Taylor & Hessey to publish his new poems immediately, keen as he was to make some instant money from his pen. The meetings did not yield any concrete results. Abbey felt his hands were tied and Taylor's adviser Woodhouse was still worrying about the sexual content of "The Eve of St. Agnes." Keats as a result returned to Winchester empty-handed on September 15. Then, on Sunday the 19th, after a morning working on *Hyperion,* he walked out into the fields, which had recently been harvested. The following Tuesday he wrote to Reynolds:

> How beautiful the season is now—How fine the air. A temperate sharpness about it. Really, without joking, chaste weather—Dian skies—I never lik'd stubble fields so much as now—Aye better than the chilly green of the spring. Somehow a stubble plain looks warm—in the same way that some pictures look warm—this struck me so much in my sunday's walk that I composed upon it.

That earth-warmth feels embodied in "To Autumn," with its simple, loamy Anglo-Saxon vocabulary: thatch, moss, ripe, apple, winnow, reap, gnat, sallow, hedge, bleat and so forth. Lovers of the poem have long since regarded it as quintessentially English, rooted in the English countryside. The atmosphere Keats depicts in his letter to Reynolds seems calm; the skies are "chaste," as if released from the "mad pursuit" of the erotic drive. And yet the oxymoronic "temperate sharpness" hints that the season offers a beauty that incorporates, rather than denies, the "disagreeables."

The critic Christopher Ricks, writing in 1974, regarded "To Autumn" as the greatest of the odes because it was the one which "most naturally, subtly, and unmisgivingly accommodates the ambivalence of feeling which I consider characteristic of Keats's truest imagination." Far from being a simple idealization, the poem indeed contains uneasy images: "oozings" has a fetid feel, as do the "clammy cells" of the bees; the soundtrack is provided by a "wailful choir" of gnats. The mood of the ode is not perhaps as "mellow" as it at first appears.

Over the last few decades, the question of how we should read Keats's poetry, especially when it comes to the ambivalences in "To Autumn," has become a site of debate. Should we analyze the odes as self-contained artworks, as the formalist critic Helen Vendler contended in the 1980s? Or should we, as has since become more fashionable, attempt to re-embed them in their historical moment and, if so, how?

"To Autumn" was certainly written against the backdrop of the personal troubles Keats was experiencing in September 1819. Yet it is the ode's immediate political context that has intrigued scholars in recent times. On August 16, 1819, a month before it was written, about 60,000 demonstrators had attended a rally on St. Peter's Fields in Manchester to demand democratic reform. The cavalry, armed with sabers, was sent in to disperse the crowd. In the resulting Peterloo Massacre, up to fifteen people were killed and at least four hundred injured. The radical orator Henry Hunt, one of the scheduled speakers and a man from a farming background, was arrested for high treason. Having being released on bail, he arrived in London on September 13, where he was met by huge crowds of supporters, numbering "not less than 200,000" in the estimate of the *Gentleman's Magazine*. He was later acquitted of high treason but convicted of seditious conspiracy and sentenced to prison.

In 1998, the poet and critic Tom Paulin detected, in the final, "subtly queasy" stanza of "To Autumn," an "oblique" reference to the "deserted field" of Peterloo "with its hewn flagstaffs and torn banners":

> While barrèd clouds bloom the soft-dying day,
>   And touch the stubble-plains with rosy hue:
> Then in a wailful choir the small gnats mourn . . .

Paulin did not extrapolate further, but if you are tempted to think his reading far-fetched (which, in the detail, it indeed is), it is worth remembering that Keats's poetic imagination had always been linked with his politics, nurtured as it had originally been in the soil of a dissenting academy.

It certainly looks overly specific to find hewn flagstaffs and torn banners haunting Keats's "stubble-plains." It could also be objected that St. Peter's Fields in Manchester was a tract of waste ground, marked for building development, rather than a harvested field of wheat. Yet there is a definite bloody hint in "rosy hue" and one might add that the "clammy cells" and "barrèd clouds" transpose ideas of imprisonment—Henry Hunt's fate following his arrest—on to a natural scene.

Does this political interpretation of one of the best-loved nature poems in the English language have traction? The context of Peterloo is incorporated as a given by Keats's most recent major biographers, Andrew Motion in 1997 and Nicholas Roe in 2012, in their readings of the ode. Let's assess the idea by delving deeper into the biographical micro-context, to see where Keats's mind was moving at the moment he composed it.

The very day before he wrote "To Autumn," Keats had, in fact, explicitly alluded, in a letter to George, to the fallout from Peterloo. "You will hear by the papers of the proceedings at Manchester and Hunt's triumphal entry into London," he wrote, referring to Henry Hunt's arrest, and his subsequent public appearance in the capital. Hunt's progress through the metropolitan streets had been witnessed by Keats himself on Monday, September 13, during the few days he spent in London before returning to Winchester. "The whole distance from the Angel Islington to the Crown and anchor [in the Strand] was lined with Multitudes," he reported to George.

This account of Londoners coming out to support Henry Hunt comes just after a longer passage in which Keats contemplates the cycles of history. He sets up, in liberal, Enlightenment fashion, the notion of historical progress: "All civiled [*sic*] countries become gradually more enlighten'd and there should be a continual change for the better." At the same time, he notes the setbacks to which the democratic instincts of "the common people" have been repeatedly subjected since the Middle Ages. Looking at more recent history, he notes that "liberal writers . . . sowed the seed" for the "rapid progress of free sentiments in England" against "Tyranny."

This movement, Keats avers, was "swelling in the ground" until the French Revolution. But the excesses of the latter put a stop to the organic progress of democracy in England, prompting the British state "to make a handle" of it, and to use it as an excuse for repression at home: to "undermine our freedom" and spread "a horrid superstition against all innovation and improvement." The nature images of sowing the seed and swelling in the ground have their obvious analogues in "To Autumn" with its swelling gourd.

Keats saw the "present struggle," embodied in the tragedy of Peterloo and the people's subsequent support of Henry Hunt in the streets of London, as being to "destroy this superstition" in favor of democracy. He also acknowledged that "What has rous'd them to do it is their distresses." Following the end of the Napoleonic Wars in 1815, Britain had experienced an economic collapse leading to bankruptcies among the middle classes and abject poverty and unemployment lower down the scale. In "To Autumn," Keats images a "gleaner," an emblem of the impoverished outsider, scavenging on the fringes of the field by collecting the crops that the harvesters have missed. Andrew Motion pointed out that gleaning—a vegetable form of poaching—had been made illegal in 1818, a seeming attempt to buttress landowners' rights against the people.

The people's distresses, Keats speculates in his letter to George, may turn out to be a "fortunate thing," though "horrid in the[i]r experience," because they have led to the popular politicization, seen in Henry Hunt's triumphal procession through London, which might lead to "progress." The mixed moods of "To Autumn," with its sense that things are "maturing," yet still haunted by wailing gnats, seem to reflect the paradox Keats perceived in the political situation in England at the time. Although he admitted to George that "I know very little of these things," Keats was "convinced that apparently small causes make great alterations" and that democratic evolution would, in the end, prevail.

The letter is also interesting because it shows how Keats was particularly exercised about the current government clampdown on free speech. In an extended passage, he returned again to the case he had previously referred to, in his earlier letter to George and Georgiana written in the spring, of Carlisle the bookseller, imprisoned for publishing Deist pamphlets along with the politically radical works of Thomas Paine "and many other works held in superstitious horror." He notes that Carlisle has been given bail but surmises that the authorities are "affraid to prosecute" because his defense would spark a "flame they could not extinguish."

The clampdown on free speech in post-Napoleonic Britain made the atmosphere there feel as repressive as that under the Metternich regime in the Austrian Empire at the same period, which impacted artists from the poet Heinrich Heine, who was born, just two years after Keats, in 1797 and later became a political exile in Paris, to the composer Franz Schubert, also born in 1797, who set many of Heine's poems to music. Heine's lyrics mingle irony and idealism to the extent that their tone can never be pinned down. Schubert mixed moods in a similar vein, making the major key sound sadder than the minor by some sleight of hand. Both were responding—Heine more directly, Schubert more obliquely—to contemporary political pressures on artists' voices, resulting in works of consummate creativity.

Back in the English literary world, in 1819, the confidently upper-class firebrand Shelley responded poetically to the Peterloo Massacre by writing *The Mask of Anarchy*, an angry, explicitly political indictment of the authorities. It was much too incendiary to publish in his lifetime. Keats, for his part, displaced his political sentiments into a nature poem because of his outsider status as a lower-middle-class democrat in authoritarian times. By the time he wrote "To Autumn," he had been publicly humiliated as an aspirational emerging writer by the reactionary ruffianism of *Blackwood's Magazine* and the conservative de haut en bas of the *Quarterly Review*—not just for his upstart classical allusions, but for his ideological allegiances.

Modern Shakespeare scholars, most notably Stephen Greenblatt and James Shapiro, have wondered whether the playwright's unique linguistic fertility was powered by his historical circumstances. Shakespeare's equivocations, the way his words always mean so much more than their literal sense, have been linked to the repressive political climate in which they were written: the Elizabethan police state in which Catholics, among whom Shakespeare's relatives were numbered, were at risk of legal sanction and even execution. So too has the way in which Shakespeare enters the subjectivity of every character as an individual—he is, as Keats put it in his letter on the "camelion poet," equally at home in embodying an Iago as an Imogen—with the result that it is impossible to infer a clear ideological position even from those plays that were explicitly written for the Court.

Keats's creativity also coincided with a historical period of repression and unease. It is certainly worth wondering whether his Shakespearean-inflected preference for ambiguities, paradoxes and "poetical concentrations" was connected to his own context as a young man whose social status and ideological views set him outside the establishment. His protean poetic language seems linked, at some inchoate level, with the fact that he knew he was living at a time when free speech was under threat, demonstrated by Leigh Hunt's imprisonment for libel long before Peterloo. Keats certainly regarded the creative liberties he took with words as politically charged acts even when their content was not explicitly political. The son of a working-class father and a middle-class mother, and educated in an alternative, dissenting academy, Keats remained an amorphous outsider.

To represent the English countryside in old English words, as Keats does in his ode "To Autumn," was, at the time, no exercise in cozy nostalgia. His preference for the language of the older English writers—Chaucer, Spenser, Chapman, Shakespeare, Milton—had always had a radical edge. They were associated in the "Cockney" mind not just with poetic, but with political freedom. At the time he wrote "To Autumn" Keats was specifically thinking about Chatterton, the "marvellous Boy, the sleepless Soul that perished in his pride," as Wordsworth had put it in his poem "Resolution and Independence," written in 1802 before the latter's conservatism had begun to solidify. Chatterton's medieval imitations made him, as Keats put it to Reynolds on September 21,

1819, at the time he wrote "To Autumn," "the purest writer in the English Language," who wrote "genuine English Idiom in English words."

It may be too much to find a specific allusion to the bloodstained, discarded banners of the Peterloo demonstrators in Keats's stubble-plains. But it is certainly the case that in embodying the English countryside in unapologetically English vocabulary, Keats was making his own political statement about old English liberties. Winchester, where it was written, was where the Anglo-Saxon king Alfred the Great, who fought off the Vikings and united England, had been buried in AD 899. In the early nineteenth century, Alfred was regarded as a heroic freedom fighter by liberals, including Leigh Hunt, who kept a portrait of him on the wall of his Hampstead home, which Keats had seen when visiting.

Keats's celebration of the English countryside was thus not ideologically neutral. It was an expression of English nationalism with a political edge. At the time, nationalist movements all over Europe were arising, with associated radical demands for freedom and democracy. In 1816, Keats had penned a sonnet celebrating the Polish patriot Andrzej Tadeusz Kościuszko, who had fought against the imperial Russian yoke—after also fighting on the American side in the U.S. War of Independence—and had died a hero to English liberals. His portrait, along with Alfred's, was displayed in Leigh Hunt's sitting room, which prompted Keats to write the sonnet shortly after first visiting Hunt.

"To Autumn" is indeed quintessentially English, but Keats was not unaware of the international context. In describing the streets of London filled with supporters of Henry Hunt on September 13, 1819, he went on to make another reference to the fight for radical political reform abroad, then associated with nationalism. He noted in passing that when he walked by the print dealer Colnaghi's shop it had a portrait of "Sands the destroyer of Kotzebue" in the window, which "must interest every one in his favour."

The German dramatist August von Kotzebue was responsible for the racy play about a love child, *Lovers' Vows,* that features in Jane Austen's *Mansfield Park,* to the author's evident disapproval. In Austen's novel, published in 1814, testy rehearsals for an amateur production of *Lovers' Vows* expose the moral inadequacy of her novel's characters, and their unfitness to support the traditional family structures that Austen regarded as essential to the smooth running of society.

Yet though Austen saw Kotzebue's play as worryingly libertine, he was, by the time Keats noted seeing a print of his destroyer in a shop window, regarded in his home country as a virulent conservative, due to his subsequent opposition to political reform. Karl Ludwig Sand, who stabbed Kotzebue to death in 1819, was a militant student who saw the older writer as a traitor to the German people and was consequently regarded as a heroic martyr by radicals. Sand's much-disseminated portrait, which Keats saw, shows him in profile with long hair, his clothing inspired by the styles of the sixteenth or seventeenth century. Such historicism was symbolic of subversion in the European context, just as, for Keats, the use of old poetic forms and themes seemed more radical than backward-looking.

Sand's assassination of Kotzebue led to the former's execution in 1820 and gave Metternich the pretext to crack down on the liberal press, restrict academic freedom and consolidate state control—which would not have pleased Keats. It's noteworthy that in September 1819, Keats saw in the assassin's portrait a possible hero. "He seems to me a young

Abelard—A fine Mouth, cheek bones (and this is no joke) full of sentiment," he told George, referencing the medieval philosopher famous not just for his brains but for his star-crossed, rebellious love affair with his pupil Eloise. It's unclear from his comments whether Keats is expressing his own surprised admiration for Sand, now revealed by the portrait to be a romantic and sensitive young man, or whether he is criticizing the artist for having idealized a terrorist.

It is one thing to laud Keats's sympathy for democratic reform, but another to paint him uncomplicatedly as a hero of modern liberal values. To be true to the Keats of history we have to burrow into the contradictions of his often not fully formulated political positions. "To Autumn," his paean to the English earth, needs to be read in the wider European context of Romantic nationalism: the Greek War of Independence against the Turks, for which Byron volunteered, although he died of fever at Missolonghi soon after his arrival in Greece in 1824; the project of the Brothers Grimm to collect and preserve the folktales of the people as a means of embodying the spirit of Germanness; the work of exiled Italian poets such as Ugo Foscolo, in the run-up to Garibaldi's successful campaign for Italian unification; the Irish nationalism of the poet Tom Moore; Chopin's use, a little later, of musical forms such as the polonaise and mazurka to express the voice of the oppressed Polish people then under Russian control.

Nationalism in Europe went on to develop an ugly name. German Romantic nationalism subsequently inspired Wagner and thence Hitler. But in 1819, nationalism was a liberal ideal, which Keats leveraged at a tangent by using Winchester, where King Alfred was buried, as the inspiration for his celebration of the English countryside. Earlier in 1819, Keats had expressed his interest in idealistic nation-building by briefly toying with throwing up everything to join Simón Bolívar's insurgents in South America. It's something of a relief to posterity that he decided on a month on the Isle of Wight, followed by Winchester, instead, since he might not otherwise have written "To Autumn."

In its contradictory yet unhurried moods, "To Autumn" registers the conflicted response of a young liberal of 1819. Its shifting emotional tones indeed hint at the political tensions dramatized at Peterloo: the sense that democratic fruition is in the cards sometime soon, but that the body politic is decaying in the meanwhile. At the same time, it is also, as it is taken by most people who come across it out of context in anthologies, an ineffably moving and subtle depiction of nature.

In fact, recent trends in criticism might be seen to be moving away from readings which root the poem within the political complexities of 1819 toward a more future-looking approach. "To Autumn" is ripe to become a key text in what's now called "ecocriticism," that seeks to read the nature poems of the past to address current anxieties about the planet while charting how literary culture has represented the relationship between humans and the natural world. The truth is that Keats achieves such multifaceted poetic mastery that his ode, though he did not know it at the time, has proved fertile enough to be ever meaningful in new contexts.

"To Autumn" was the last great poem that Keats ever wrote, although he did not die for another seventeen months. It has, as a result, been hard for literary biographers to resist the temptation to regard it, with its reference to the "maturing sun," as the ultimate summation of Keats's own achievement: as a testimony, in the words of Jack Stillinger in 1990, to Keats's "unparalleled touch in the face of death, and his moral resilience"; and as the apogee of what Robert Gittings, writing in 1970, called his "spiritual triumph."

There's a desire here to canonize Keats not simply as a poet of astonishing talent and extraordinary verbal invention, which he was, but as a moral hero, a sort of secular saint who miraculously managed to penetrate the meaning of life before he was twenty-five. Such a view would have provoked guffaws in Keats's hostile contemporaries, such as John Lockhart. But by the twentieth century, it had become the norm.

During the Victorian period, the idea of "English Litera-ture" was elevated from the rebel realm that it had occupied during the Romantic era, into the moral center, most notably by Matthew Arnold in his influential *Culture and Anarchy.* Arnold offered literature almost as a moral alternative to reli-gion, at a time when what he called the "sea of faith," tradi-tional religious belief, was showing incipient signs of ebbing out.

Keats had once enjoyed ad hoc, informal lessons on verse form with Charles Cowden Clarke. A century on, his own poetry was being studied in schools and universities, and regarded as iconic within the establishment structure which had rejected Keats himself in his lifetime. By the twentieth century, Arnold's vision of literary studies as an alternative theology with a moral purpose had become normalized, as in the attitude of my older English teacher in the 1980s, the one who made us sit on the grass and read "To Autumn" as a hymn to the beauty and truth of nature.

I don't see Keats as a spiritual guru who can tell me how to live. What I value in his surviving poetry and letters is that they show us how *he* lived. In doing so, they dramatize, rather than dogmatize, a humanistic moral position. Unlike

Shakespeare, Keats is alive to us as an individual because he recorded so much of his inner as well as his external life. Even the fact that there are historical losses—things that were not recorded—adds to the visceral sense that we are dealing with a real human being with his feet firmly planted in the lived experience of what was his present but is now our past.

The "wasting" process of "old Time," as he put it in his sonnet on the Elgin Marbles, makes Keats himself, from the perspective of two centuries on, paradoxically more real. He does not belong to the abstract realm of spirituality and eternity but to his own here and now: to the "knowledge of contrast, feeling for light and shade, all that information (primitive sense) necessary for a poem" which he regarded, unpretentiously and without any sense that he was offering a philosophical insight, as the building blocks of his creativity.

———

BY SEPTEMBER 22, 1819, Keats's finances were so rocky that he was on the verge of abandoning poetry, instead hoping to become a pen for hire by writing magazine pieces for money, which he regarded as tantamount to prostitution or "to venture on the common" (the phrase, like "going on the game," referred to women selling sex). He had given up all thoughts of returning to the apothecary profession as a fallback, noting that Reynolds was not yet making money in his newfound legal career. "I am fit for nothing but literature," he concluded, simultaneously proudly and self-dismissively.

He had once been inspired by the "great thing" of poetry. By "literature" he now meant "shining up" articles for a fee, manufacturing opinions on subjects he knew nothing about. Two years ago, he said, he would have spoken his mind "with the utmost simplicity," but he no longer had faith in the value of the integrity of his own voice. He was instead planning to "cheat as well as any literary Jew of the Market," as he put it in terms repulsive to the modern eye.

As it turned out, Keats did not adopt a new career in journalism. That is hardly a surprise, given his attitude. Even the most cynical hacks have to believe at some level in their own spin, and Keats admitted to feeling timid about selling himself as a pen for hire. Yet the slowing of Keats's poetic productivity by the end of 1819 shows he had indeed lost faith in the "great thing" to which he had once aspired. "I have no trust whatever on Poetry . . . the ma[r]vel i[s] to me how people read so much of it," he wrote bitterly.

KEATS'S ANDROGYNOUS FIGURE of Autumn seems openended and sexless. In his letter to Reynolds, in which he depicted the walk in the fields that inspired him to write the ode, he exclaimed at the clear "Dian skies," alluding to Diana, the classical goddess both of the hunt and of chastity. So it comes as a jolt to register that at the time he wrote it Keats himself was "deep in love," as he had put it on July 25, with Fanny Brawne.

By September 19, 1819, he had written her no fewer than seven love letters: from the Isle of Wight on July 1, July 8, July 15, July 25 and August 5–6; from Winchester on August 16; and from London on Monday, September 13, while on his flying visit, during which he refused to go and see her. "I love you too much to venture to Hampstead," he told her in a note written from his publishers' office on Fleet Street, where he had gone to press them to publish his poetry forthwith. "I feel it is not paying a visit but venturing into a fire."

Fanny Brawne had in fact been in the background all the

while Keats was writing his great odes. From now on, until his death in February 1821, his life would be dominated less by poetry than by his tormented passion for her and by his own increasingly failing health. It would have surprised Matthew Arnold to find Keats being valued in the twentieth century as an icon of "moral resilience." On reading the latter's love letters to Fanny Brawne, following their publication in 1878, he recoiled in disgust. In his view, the letters proved that Keats lacked the "character and self-control" required to achieve true "greatness."

9

"Bright star!"

Bright star! would I were steadfast as thou art—
    Not in lone splendour hung aloft the night
And watching, with eternal lids apart,
    Like nature's patient, sleepless Eremite,
The moving waters at their priestlike task
    Of pure ablution round earth's human shores,
Or gazing on the new soft-fallen mask
    Of snow upon the mountains and the moors—
No—yet still steadfast, still unchangeable,
    Pillowed upon my fair love's ripening breast,
To feel for ever its soft swell and fall,
    Awake for ever in a sweet unrest,
Still, still to hear her tender-taken breath,
And so live ever—or else swoon to death.

KEATS'S SONNET BEGINNING "Bright star!" was once thought to be the last poem he ever composed. He wrote it out for Joseph Severn, who accompanied him on his final, fateful voyage to Italy in September 1820, while they were on board the ship. Severn believed that Keats was extemporizing and saw himself as the privileged beneficiary. However, a manuscript version in Brown's hand, dated 1819, was subsequently discovered and scholars have since concluded that Keats must have written it out from memory, on the flyleaf of Severn's copy of Shakespeare, during the voyage.

It is now generally accepted that this sonnet was in fact written sometime in July 1819 and inspired by Keats's love for Fanny Brawne. The poem's star image reflects the language of the letters he wrote to her that month from the Isle of Wight. "I have seen your Comet," he told her on July 8, identifying her with a comet that had been seen in the skies over England that week. "I will imagine you Venus tonight and pray, pray, pray to your star like a Hethen," he went on to add on July 25, signing off, "Your's ever, fair Star."

In "On First Looking into Chapman's Homer," written nearly three years previously, Keats had compared his own dynamic discovery of literary potential to the excitement of an astronomer looking at a newly discovered planet. In "Bright star!," he is, in contrast, looking for the stasis of comfort: "still unchangeable, / Pillowed upon my fair love's ripening breast, / To feel for ever its soft swell and fall." Yet the lines are infused with what had by now become typically Keatsian uncertainties and ambiguities—quite literally with the ups and downs of his lover's bosom as she breathes in and out—that are contrasted with the unchanging star. There's an oxymoron in "sweet unrest," and the ending of the sonnet hovers without resolution between a fantasized eternity of breathing and the finality of death.

KEATS'S PASSION FOR Fanny Brawne has become an essential part of his image as the most romantic of the Romantic poets, not least in recent times as a result of the film *Bright Star*. We know how Keats felt about her because he expressed his feelings in a series of thirty-nine surviving letters that he sent her between July 1, 1819, and the summer of 1820, including the two, reflected in his "Bright star!" sonnet, in which he compared her to an astral body.

In 2009, the movie *Bright Star*'s director Jane Campion described their relationship, as depicted in Keats's letters to Fanny, as the embodiment of a near-unattainable ideal: "the first love most of us dream of enjoying." Yet Keats's feelings for Fanny were more complex and less conventional than that suggests. Matthew Arnold recoiled from them in the Victorian age not just, perhaps, because they didn't fit the gentlemanly, stiff-upper-lip culture of his own period, but because they are actually quite painful to read, infused as they are for us with the sense that they are written by a conflicted young man in his early twenties who is—though he and his doctors try to deny it as long as possible—terminally ill.

Keats was so aware of his confused feelings about women that he had previously held himself aloof from emotional attachment. He had been interested in "warming" with Mrs. Jones, and presumably in seeking a sexual outlet with prostitutes or barmaids. He had written about romantic love as a Neoplatonic union of mortal and immortal in *Endymion*; as a form of mental illness in *Isabella; or, The Pot of Basil*; as a predatory seduction scenario in "The Eve of St. Agnes"; and as a risky business that might lead to eternal alienation in "La Belle Dame sans Merci." But he had previously scoffed at the idea of being in love himself. As he put it to Fanny Brawne on July 8, 1819, "I never knew before, what such a love as you have made me feel, was; I did not believe in it; my Fancy was affraid of it, lest it should burn me up."

It is an index of Keats's ambivalence that only a couple of months later, on September 18, 1819, we find him mocking the very idea of romantic love, telling George and Georgiana that "Nothing strikes me so forcibly with a sense of the rediculous as love—A Man in love I do think cuts the sorryest figure in the world. Even when I know a poor fool to be really in pain about it, I could burst out laughing in his face." Unbeknownst to George and Georgiana, with whom he had not been open about his feelings for Fanny, Keats was laughing in his own face.

There are many gaps in the record when it comes to trying to chart the progress of Keats's intimacy with Fanny Brawne. Neither of them kept a diary in which their every meeting and conversation was documented, and Fanny's replies to Keats's letters are not extant. Nor did any of Keats's friends leave a detailed account of what was in fact his most important relationship with a woman outside his family. Their reticence was due to the fact that they disapproved of the relationship, which they regarded as somehow off-limits. The few comments they made in private suggest they thought Fanny herself was unworthy of Keats's love, and that his obsession with her was deleterious to his mental stability and physical health.

According to the painter Joseph Severn, who went on to accompany Keats on his final journey to Rome, Fanny "always seemed a cold, conventional mistress." In 1875, Dilke's son Charley, by then Sir Charles Wentworth Dilke, was told by his uncle William, who appears to have met Fanny Brawne at the time she knew Keats, that she was unattractively sallow and most definitely not "a lady with whom a Poet so sensitive as John Keats would be likely to have fallen in love with." He also claimed that Fanny was a bit of what Lady Elgin might have called a whapper: that she had made "all the advances to him without really caring much for him."

However, when Fanny Brawne's letters to Keats's sister, also called Fanny, were finally published in 1936, her own voice was revealed. The two women had never met in Keats's lifetime, but just before he left for Rome, where he was to die, he asked Fanny Brawne to get in touch with his sister, which resulted in a lengthy correspondence. The letters show her to have been intelligent and articulate, though "by no means a great poetry reader," as she put it, though she loved Shakespeare and was encouraged by Keats to read Spenser. They also demonstrate that she was far from cold in revealing how agonizingly affected she was by Keats's final illness and death.

———

THE BRAWNES HAD MADE friends with the Dilkes when they rented Charles Brown's half of Wentworth Place during the summer of 1818, while the latter was away in Scotland with Keats. After that summer rental came to an end, the family had moved to another house only a couple of minutes away, Elm Cottage in Downshire Hill. Keats first met Fanny Brawne, according to her own testimony, in September 1818, not long after he had returned to Well Walk from the Scottish hiking tour. He had come home prematurely with a serious chill only to find Tom's condition worse. Once his own health had improved, Keats had called on the Dilkes at Wentworth Place, half a mile down the hill. It was there that he first encountered Fanny. At the time, she was eighteen to Keats's twenty-three, the eldest of three children. Her siblings Margaret, known as Tootts, and Sam were fourteen and nine, respectively.

No account of Keats's first meeting with Fanny survives, and it is not clear how often they saw one another in the autumn and winter of 1818. Keats's first reference to her comes on December 16, 1818, in a letter to George and Georgiana— the next letter he wrote to them after the one in which he described his encounter with Mrs. Jones in her "tasty" rooms. He tells them about the Brawnes as recent acquaintances:

> Mrs. Brawne, who took Brown's house for the Summer, still resides in Hampstead—she is a very nice woman— and her daughter senior is [I t]hink beautiful and elegant, graceful, silly, fashionable and strange we [h]ave a li[ttle] tiff now and then—and she behaves a little better . . .

It sounds from this as though Fanny Brawne is already flirting with Keats in a frisky, Beatrice and Benedick fashion, although it is also clear that Keats finds her arch repartee "strange," hard to make sense of. In his correspondence with male friends, Keats was playfully relaxed when it came to making obscene jokes. But he regarded females of his own class with confusion, unable, as he had been in Mrs. Jones's rooms, to read the signs.

We can perhaps detect in Fanny's "fashionable" conversation a submerged echo of that of the witty, metropolitan, although rather more socially elevated, Mary Crawford in Jane Austen's *Mansfield Park*. Certainly, in the next sentence Keats evokes a somewhat Austen-like scenario, although it took place in a middle-class London circle a slight step down from the gentry caste in which Austen set her novels. "I find . . . I am to be invited to Miss Millar's birthday dance—Shall I dance with Miss Waldegrave? Eh, I shall be obliged to shirk a good many there," Keats wrote. Concerned that he would be one of only a few men at the party, he jokingly announced he would dress like a dandy "with the list [of] the beauties I have conquered embroidered around my Calv[es]." He was clearly inclined to "shirk" those young ladies who, like Austen's Bennet sisters, would have regarded a dance as a courtship ritual, a step on the road to marriage.

Fanny Brawne, like Keats, came from the insecure, emerging London middle class. Like his, her family background was mixed. Her grandfather Samuel Brawne had, like Keats's father, kept a prosperous livery stable in central London, and had gone on to invest in property. According to Joanna Richardson's 1952 biography of Fanny, he was related to the Regency dandy Beau Brummell (1778–1840), the grandson of a valet who re-created himself as an arbiter of taste and powered himself into the circle of the Prince Regent, until debts forced him to leave the country in 1816. Fanny's own interest in fashion is apparent in the sketches of dress designs she included in her letters to Keats's sister Fanny.

It is not clear what Fanny's father Samuel did for a living, if anything much. But he had married money in the shape of Frances, née Ricketts, before he died of tuberculosis in 1810. The widowed Mrs. Frances Brawne's income derived from a legacy from her father, John Ricketts, who had interests in the City and family in positions of administrative power in Jamaica and Barbados, where fortunes were made from slave plantations. Keats vigorously attacked the slave economy in *Isabella; or, The Pot of Basil,* but the reality of the slavery background to much British wealth in the early nineteenth century was rarely acknowledged in polite company, as in Austen's *Mansfield Park,* where nothing about the actual day-to-day meaning of Sir Thomas Bertram's interests in the West Indies, the source of his wealth, is mentioned.

Mrs. Brawne and her children thus relied—like Keats and his siblings—on modest unearned income. Like the Keats siblings, they were not securely rooted. Mrs. Brawne's frequent moves between rented properties reflect the restlessness of the metropolitan "middle classes" of the period, whose identity was not vested in bricks and mortar, let alone in the landed property on which the gentry and aristocracy relied for their sense of identity. You only have to read the novels of Jane Austen to see how important property security, in the form of an inheritable home, was felt to be at the time: the anxieties, for example, in *Pride and Prejudice* surrounding the fact that the Bennet property is entailed, meaning that after Mr. Bennet dies his wife and daughters will have nowhere to live. Neither Keats nor Fanny had property security, and they shared a similarly amorphous social position.

Keats clearly found the strange and fashionable Fanny an attractive distraction, as he returns to the subject of her two days later in the next installment of his letter to George and Georgiana. "Shall I give you Miss Brawn?" he asks them on December 18, less than three weeks after Tom died on the first of that month:

> She is about my height—with a fine style of countenance of the lengthen'd sort—she wants sentiment in every feature—she manages to make her hair look well—her nostrills are fine—though a little painful—her mouth is bad and good—he[r] Profil is better than her full-face indeed is not full [b]ut pale and thin without showing any bone— Her shape is very graceful and so are her movements—her Arms are good her hands badish—her feet tolerable—she is not seventeen—but she is ignorant—monstrous in her behaviour flying out in all directions, calling people such

names—that I was forced lately to make use of the term
Minx—this is I think no[t] from any innate vice but from
a penchant she has for acting stylishly. I am however tired
of such style and shall decline any more of it.

This description of Fanny's bodily attributes sounds a little
like a medieval *blazon,* the verse form in which troubadours
expressed their stylized chivalric love for unattainable ladies,
while at the same time subtly dehumanizing the female
objects of their devotion by clinically itemizing their features.

That Christmas, following Tom's death, Keats was invited
to spend the day with the Brawnes. Mrs. Brawne, whose own
husband had also died of tuberculosis, was clearly concerned
that the recently bereaved young man had no family to go
to. Writing to Keats's sister in 1821, ten months after he died,
Fanny Brawne later described that Christmas Day as "the
happiest day I had ever then spent." Some have taken that
to mean that December 25, 1818, was the day on which Keats
and Fanny plighted their troth to one another and became
engaged.

However, it may simply have been the first day on which
Fanny had spent several relaxed hours at a stretch in Keats's
company, without the presence of his other friends from
Wentworth Place, the Dilkes and Brown. Her words "ever
then spent" suggest that, in retrospect, she regarded the day's
happiness as a harbinger of subsequent moments of intenser
joy, not as the date on which a definite understanding was
reached. In Keats's next letter to George and Georgiana, on
February 14, comes his somewhat unengaged report that
"Miss Brawne and I have every now and then a chat and a
tiff."

After April, however, came the chance for Keats to see much more of her. When the Dilkes vacated their half of Wentworth Place to move closer to Charley's school, the Brawnes moved in, although it's not quite certain when. Keats and Fanny thus became next-door neighbors until Brown rented out his house for the summer and Keats departed for the Isle of Wight. We cannot trace the day-to-day progress of their relationship, but by the time Keats writes his first letter to Fanny from the Isle of Wight, she has become his "beautiful Girl whom I love so much." He asks her to write back immediately, and to kiss the page, so that he can "at least touch my lips where yours have been."

————

KEATS'S LOVE LETTERS to Fanny almost form an oeuvre in themselves. They are extraordinary survivals from the past in which he strips himself emotionally naked, exposing his vulnerabilities, his overwhelming needs, his jealousy and possessiveness, his insecurities. They are conflicted, as he seeks infinite intimacy while simultaneously trying to hold his beloved at bay. In his focus on Fanny, he seems to have found a real-life counterpart to the paradoxes that pervaded his poetry, a way of combining agony and ecstasy "upon the pulses," and of keeping the relationship at a perpetual level of high intensity without any prospect of easy closure or definition. They show his self-confessed morbidity of temperament given free rein.

What is most striking about the letters, in the context of social history, is that they are very much love letters, not courtship letters. They read more like a case study out of Stendhal's *De l'Amour*—his classic 1822 treatise on the psychopathology of love—than like the letters of a typical English Regency suitor who was hoping to gain a lady's hand in marriage. Jane Austen would not have approved. It is often said that Keats and Fanny's tragedy was that they were unable to marry because his health was failing and he did not have the means to support a wife. That was indeed true, and became increasingly so as his financial situation, and his physical condition, deteriorated. Yet at the time he began writing to her in early July 1819, his chronic sore throats were not yet incapacitating. On July 6, five days after writing his first love letter to Fanny Brawne, he reassured his sister that he was confident that he could always fall back on his medical training if he ever needed to make a stable living, to "ensure me an employment & maintainance."

Had marriage been his overwhelming goal in July 1819, Keats might have at least held out that same promise to Fanny Brawne. Marriage, the goal of every Jane Austen heroine, was the only respectable life choice for a girl from her background. But at no point in his letters does Keats even mention it as a possible option to Fanny—except when, on July 25, he effectively tells her it is *not* something that appeals to him. "I look not forward with any pleasure to what is call'd being settled in the world," he confesses, adding, "I tremble at domestic cares—yet for you I would meet them." The truth is that Keats did not really want to give up his life as a bohemian poet and become a bourgeois husband like Dilke. So what was he expecting from his relationship with Fanny?

Keats's first letter to Fanny is self-consciously literary. In the opening sentence, he alludes to Jean-Jacques Rousseau's epistolary novel, *Julie; ou, la nouvelle Héloïse,* and his words sound rather like the opening of an epistolary novel themselves:

My dearest Lady,

I am glad I had not an opportunity of sending off a Letter which I wrote for you on Tuesday—'twas too much like one out of Ro[u]sseau's Heloise. I am more reasonable this morning. The morning is the only time for me to write to a beautiful Girl whom I love so much: for at night, when the lonely day has closed, and the lonely, silent, unmusical Chamber is waiting to receive me as into a Sepulchre, then believe me my passion gets entirely the sway.

The allusion to Rousseau's eighteenth-century bestseller would have made quite a statement at the time. In contrast to the polite world of Jane Austen's fiction, in which the heroes and heroines sustain the social order by marrying and living happily ever after, *Julie* told a tragic, and socially disruptive, tale of star-crossed and illicit love. Julie falls for her tutor, but after they consummate their passion for one night only, she has to marry another man to please her family. In the end she dies of a broken heart. It is as if Keats is both identifying his love for Fanny as illicit and willing it into high tragedy from the start, even though she was an eligible girl of his own class.

The teacher-pupil relationship depicted by Rousseau may also have had personal resonances for Keats, who romanticized the figure of Abelard, famous for his tragic love affair with his student Eloise. He took it upon himself to direct Fanny's reading and to inform her taste, marking up choice passages in Spenser for her. He had once offered to be of service to Mrs. Jones in matters of knowledge and taste, but the latter was perhaps too sophisticated to accept his tutelage. Fanny—whom Keats perceived as even younger than she was, describing her as "not seventeen" at a time when she was actually eighteen—proved more responsive.

The allusion to Rousseau also had political undertones. The latter's promotion of the "cult of sensibility" was by 1819 regarded with suspicion by conservatives, including Jane Austen. Keats's ideal of authentic emotional unbuttoning, as opposed to artificial social control, was associated in the public mind with revolution. Following Peterloo, radicals in England were in retreat. The private world of the anarchic emotions remained one arena in which sedition could still flourish, as is shown by William Hazlitt's *Liber Amoris* of 1823, in which he, though still formally married, flew in the face of social propriety by exposing in print the excruciating details of his tormented sexual obsession with his landlord's daughter. Consisting of reported conversations, diaristic passages and letters, one entry was supposedly written on the flyleaf of *Endymion,* suggesting that shortly after Keats's death he was regarded by Hazlitt as a byword for subversive sensuality. Keats himself, in his lifetime, had looked up to Hazlitt as a radical guru and Shakespeare critic, copying out reams of his writings in a letter to George and Georgiana. Now his memory was being used by Hazlitt as a way of signaling his own resistance to social and political conservatism.

In his letters to Fanny, Keats is not playing the role of a middle-class suitor but identifying with the sexually anarchic figures of Shelley and Byron. Writing to Fanny on August 6, he fantasizes about going away to Switzerland with her: "We might spend a pleasant year at Berne or Zurich—if it should please Venus to hear my 'Beseech thee to hear us O Goddess.'" In 1819, Switzerland was not associated with the bourgeois image of society that it might represent today. Instead, it symbolized an exotic escape into unrestrained sexual license.

It was where Byron and Shelley had ended up in 1816 with their young lovers Mary Godwin and Claire Clairmont.

Those two bohemian teenage stepsisters had thrown themselves, rebelliously, into out-of-wedlock sexual relationships with poets, as Keats must have known on the gossip vine through Leigh Hunt. Keats is fantasizing that Fanny Brawne, too, might be open to seeking unwedded bliss. "Better be imprudent moveables than prudent fixtures," he tells her; "god forbid we should what people call, *settle*—turn into a pond, a stagnant Lethe—a vile crescent, row or buildings." It is free love, not bourgeois marriage, that is Keats's heart's desire. It sounds like a frank erotic invitation when he tells Fanny, "But if you will fully love me, though there may be some fire, 'twill not be more than we can bear when moistened and bedewed with Pleasures." One recalls the "slippery blisses" of *Endymion.* This time those ecstasies were imagined in the context of a real individual woman.

"I am indeed astonish'd to find myself so careless of all cha[r]ms but yours—remembring as I do the time when even a bit of ribband was a matter of interest to me," Keats told Fanny on July 25, all his desires centered on her. Erotic frustration became the motor of his imagination, intensified by Fanny's physical absence. Nevertheless, sexual escapades with lower-class women appear to have continued on the Isle of Wight after Brown arrived, as is suggested by a passage in a letter from Keats to Dilke of July 31. "When I come to town I shall have a little talk with you about Brown and one Jenny Jacobs. Open Daylight! he don't care," Keats wrote. "I am affraid the[r]e will be some more feet for little stockings," he went on, at which point Brown, who was looking over his shoulder, added in his own hand, "—of Keats' making (I mean the feet)." Brown was insinuating that Keats himself had been up to something that might result in his having "made" an untoward baby—just as Severn had earlier done.

Fanny had originally feared that Keats only loved her for her "Beauty"—her body—but she had in no way been put off by his rhapsodies, as he called them. In fact, she had been hooked by them. "So you intend to hold me to my promise of seeing you in a short time," Keats wrote to her on August 5 as he was setting out for Winchester, promising to pop down from there to Hampstead.

In the event, he did make that brief visit to London, but decided not to see her. Reality, in the shape of his money troubles, had begun to bite as he cantered to the end of the last act of *Otho the Great,* contemplated trying his hand at making a journalistic living by his pen, and finally put all thoughts of ever going back to medicine behind him, as he told Brown. "Remember I have no idle leisure to brood over you," he told Fanny coldly on August 16. He lacked the means either to marry her respectably or to take her off to unwedded bliss in Switzerland.

When he returned from Winchester to London for good, he decided not to go back to Wentworth Place, because Fanny's presence would be too great a temptation. As he explained to Brown, "I like [Miss Brawne] and I cannot help it." Instead, simultaneously commitment-phobic and terrified of the intensity Fanny had inspired in him, he rented a room in Westminster close to the Dilkes. However, his determination to stay away did not last long. By mid-October he was back in Wentworth Place, next door to Fanny. It would remain his base for the next seven months, until Brown once again rented out his house for the summer and Keats had to find an alternative lodging.

The young couple's intimacy became a matter of concern to others. Their "engagement," if such it was, was not a conventional one in which Keats made a formal proposal and sought the permission of Fanny's family before being accepted. He was a nonstarter as a potential husband. Her mother was driven to distraction by the young couple's mutual attraction. According to Dilke, "It is quite a settled thing between Keats and Miss [Brawne]. God help them. It's a bad thing for them. The mother says she cannot prevent it, and that her only hope is that it will go off." Mrs. Brawne was clearly afraid that her daughter would marry an ailing pauper. She may also have feared that Fanny's reputation was in danger, or even that she might get pregnant.

The fact that Keats and Fanny exchanged rings has often been interpreted as evidence that they were engaged. The one he gave to her, an inexpensive garnet in a gold openwork setting, is now in a glass case in the Keats House museum. It is usually referred to as her engagement ring, but it is worth remembering that the romantic exchange of rings did not necessarily denote any expectation of marriage in the period. In none of Jane Austen's novels does the hero present the heroine with a ring on proposing. Indeed, at that time ritual ring exchanges often denoted a pact between lovers who were forbidden from legalizing their union. Nelson and Emma Hamilton, for example, exchanged rings in an informal ceremony in 1805 because they could not wed as, although she was by then a widow, he was still married to Lady Nelson. The assumption that what Keats "longed for" above all was an "early marriage" dates from William Michael Rossetti's Victorian biography of 1887, the first to incorporate Fanny into his story. Keats's own letters to her suggest otherwise.

In December 1829, when he was working on his biography of Keats, Charles Brown wrote to Fanny Brawne for help with the project, though it was never published in his lifetime. He directly alluded to her relationship with Keats in terms that suggest how close they had actually been. "As his love for you formed so great a part of him, we may be doing him an injustice to be silent on it," he told her, but he was worried that it would be inappropriate to make their relationship public:

> We live among strange customs; for had you been husband and wife, though but for an hour, every one would have thought himself at liberty to speak of, and all about you; but as you were only so in your hearts, it seems, as it were, improper.

It is hard to see how a formal engagement, which failed to end in marriage only as a result of the tragic premature death of one party, could have seemed improper even to the strictest moralist. By saying that Keats and Fanny had been "husband and wife . . . only so in [their] hearts," Brown, who had had a live-in lover himself, was implicitly suggesting that the couple's intimacy had approached what only husbands and wives should have. In 1820, Keats expressed anger in a letter to Fanny that his friends had become "tattlers, and inquisitors into my conduct," spying upon his "secret" and laughing at Fanny herself. Was his male friends' gossip a little bawdy?

Their reticence on the subject of his love affair after his death, and the dismissive attitude to Fanny displayed by some, make better sense if they regarded the relationship as more torrid than chaste, fueled by physical rather than intellectual attraction, and inappropriate as a result. Certainly, some genteel Regency girls were as sexually reckless as Lydia

Bennet in *Pride and Prejudice*. In 1820, on the other side of London, another middle-class teenager, Letitia Landon, who was hoping to make her career as a poet, began sleeping with the married editor of the *Literary Gazette*. But by the mid-1820s, the "free love" philosophy of the radical Romantic era had been decisively relegated to the realm of the unsayable as proto-Victorian hypocrisy began to kick in.

After Brown wrote to Fanny in 1829, eight years after Keats died, stating that they had been like husband and wife, although they had not married, her own reply was pointedly noncommittal: "I was more generous ten years ago, I should not now endure the odium of being connected with one who was working up his way against poverty and every sort of abuse . . . I should be glad if you could disprove I was a very poor judge of character ten years ago and probably overrated every good quality he had but surely they go too far on the other side." There was clearly something about their youthful indiscretions that made Fanny feel ambivalent and excruciated in retrospect, at a time before Keats had been widely established by Milnes's *Life and Letters* as a significant cultural figure. Perhaps Fanny recoiled from Brown's implication that the relationship would be considered improper.

———

WE CAN NEVER KNOW the extent of the couple's "warming," but Keats's frequent references to their kisses make it clear that this was not a relationship that denied the body. Keats's own body was meanwhile increasingly betraying him. On Thursday, February 3, he went into London and came back ill, having taken a cheaper seat on the outside of the stagecoach, leaving him vulnerable to the cold. As Brown recalled:

I asked hurriedly, "What is the matter—are you fevered?"
"Yes, yes," he answered. I was on the outside of the stage
this bitter day till I was severely chilled,—but now I don't
feel it. Fevered! of course, a little. He . . . yielded to my
request that he should go to bed . . . I entered his chamber as he leapt into bed. On entering the cold sheets, he
slightly coughed, and I heard him say,—"That is blood
from my mouth," I went towards him; he was examin-
ing a single drop of blood upon the sheet. "Bring me the
candle, Brown; and let me see this blood." After regarding
it steadfastly, he looked up into my face, with a calmness of
countenance that I can never forget, and said,—"I know
the colour of that blood; it is arterial blood; I cannot be
deceived in that colour;—that drop of blood is my death-
warrant;—I must die."

With his history of medical training, and of nursing both
his mother and Tom through terminal tuberculosis, Keats
was only too aware of the prognosis when it came to actual
blood-spitting.

Doctors were called in, but to little ultimate avail. Keats
was forbidden to go out, told to avoid any possible excitement. Immediately after the hemorrhage, Keats scribbled a
note to Fanny. "They say I must remain confined to this room
for some time. The consciousness that you love me will make
a pleasant prison of the house next to yours." Brown went on
to become his effective jailer, barring Fanny from seeing him,
though she lived next door, except by showing herself at the
window.

Keats's friends increasingly feared that his obsession with
her was inimical to the calm state of mind which his health
required. In his poem "To Fanny" Keats called love his physi-

cian. But, among his friends, even Brown, who had no time for propriety when it came to love relationships, suspected that the poet's fevered feelings for her were far from therapeutic. Keats went on to offer to release Fanny from their informal engagement, so informal that it was never explicitly discussed in his letters to her. He was briefly relieved from anxiety when she demurred.

"How illness stands as a barrier betwixt me and you!" he wrote to Fanny. "Even if I was well—I must make myself as good a Philosopher as possible," he added, aspiring to Stoicism and at the same time half-admitting that the barriers, even had he been in full health, were part of the attraction. He confessed to her the thoughts that now intruded on his insomniac mind at night. The perceived failure of his poetic career was uppermost:

> "If I should die," said I to myself, "I have left no immortal work behind me—nothing to make my friends proud of my memory—but I have lov'd the principle of beauty in all things, and if I had had time I would have made myself remember'd." Thoughts like these came very feebly when I was in health and every pulse beat for you—now you divide with this (may *I* say it?) "last infirmity of noble minds" all my reflection.

The "last infirmity of noble minds" is what the young Milton called the desire for fame in his poem "Lycidas." It was a pastoral lament written in memory of a fellow student who had died at twenty-five before achieving the earthly fame he had deserved. Keats, who was now in his twenty-fifth year, could not have missed the irony, although his third book, *Lamia, Isabella, The Eve of St. Agnes, and Other Poems,* which

included the major odes, was due to be published in the summer. In the event, its critical reception would be better than
Keats might have hoped for, in the light of the earlier attacks
on *Endymion*. "My book has had good success among literary people, and, I believe, has a moderate sale," he informed
Brown in August. But by then, Keats himself was in such a
depleted state of health that he would soon be leaving the
country for the warmer climate of Rome, never to return.

Yet he had seemed to rally initially in the wake of his first
hemorrhage, in February. "I am nervous, I own, and may
think myself worse than I really am," he told Fanny Brawne,
hoping his health fears were more paranoid than rationally
grounded. Given Keats's experience with Tom, it is hard,
however, to see how he could have genuinely believed he had
any realistic chance of cheating his death warrant, despite
periods in which the symptoms appeared to recede.

———

AT THE BEGINNING of May 1820, when Keats had to move
out of Wentworth Place, since Brown had sublet it for the
summer, he chose new lodgings at 2 Wesleyan Place in Kent-
ish Town, about a mile away on the other side of the Heath.
Leigh Hunt—whom Keats no longer hero-worshipped, but
who remained a friend—was living around the corner with
his chaotic family at 13 Mortimer Terrace.

Wentworth Place is now, of course, the Keats House museum, but there is nothing in Wesleyan Place today to indicate that Keats ever lived there, not so much as a blue plaque.
It's a short, quiet, cobbled cul-de-sac, directly off the traffic-
heavy thoroughfare of Highgate Road, with a terrace of two-
story Georgian cottages. Though stucco-fronted, they look a

little down-at-heel compared to the upmarket houses in Keats Grove.

In my childhood, the shop on the corner of Wesleyan Place and Highgate Road was a takeaway, called the Sun Wah Fish Bar, where we used to buy delicious salty chips wrapped in newspaper, soft inside but so hot they burnt your mouth. Then it was boarded up and abandoned for about twenty years. Recently, however, it has reopened as an organic store called Goods Grocery. As it is less than a minute from my front door, I often find myself in the shop on the corner of Wesleyan Place, tempted by the fresh fruit and vegetables at Goods Grocery, including nectarines as juicy as the pulpy one Keats described enjoying in a letter to Dilke, written from Winchester on September 22, 1819.

One evening, after buying a bunch of basil in the corner shop, I decided to knock on the door of the house in Wesleyan Place where I thought Keats had once rented a room. It was answered by a girl of about ten, who called her father. He knew about the Keats connection but thought the houses had since been renumbered and he was not sure which was the right one. He also thought the stucco had been added to the facade of the terrace later in the nineteenth century. If so, when Keats stayed here, these modest cottages would have been plain brick, and a lot less bijou than Wentworth Place.

So I walked around the corner to see if 13 Mortimer Terrace, where Leigh Hunt lived, could offer anything more. There are only four tall, thin, flat, brick-faced, six-story terraced Georgian houses in Mortimer Terrace now, truncated by a Victorian railway bridge, under whose arches a car mechanics' workshop now sits. From my own home over the road I can hear the rumble of the trains at night. Number 13, where the Hunts lived, must have been demolished to make way for the bridge.

Still, I rang one of the bells on the only house that showed signs of life, now divided into single-dwelling units. It was answered by a young man who kindly invited me in. I followed him up the stairs to his top-floor studio. There was not a hint of a Regency banister in sight, only utilitarian white walls, fluorescent lighting and vinyl stair treads.

But when we got to the top, the door opened into an arty room with kilims on the floor, guttered candles in wine bottles by the bed and a cello in the corner. The man who lived here turned out to be a musician—just the sort of young, freelance bohemian who was living here two hundred years ago in the era of Leigh Hunt and Keats. When I walked back along Wesleyan Place, I wondered whether Keats had walked on the same cobblestones, or whether the street had still been a dirt track back in 1820.

———

FROM WESLEYAN PLACE, Keats wrote repeatedly to Fanny, the ring she gave him on his finger, his focus on her increasingly demanding. "I am greedy of you—Do not think of any thing but me," he wrote. "Do not think as if I was not existing—Do not forget me—." He had always suffered from mood swings, but now they were increasingly concentrated in single moments of heightened, conflicted anxiety, focused on Fanny, reprising the mood of the five-year-old who had threatened his mother with a sword, a sign of his desperate yet aggressive need.

He acknowledged that he had no right to assume Fanny had forgotten him. "Perhaps you think of me all day," he admitted. But his jealousy and possessiveness were by now such that the news that she had been to a party without him felt scorching: "If you could really what is call'd enjoy yourself at a Party—if you can smile in peoples [*sic*] faces, and wish them to admire you *now,* you never have nor ever will love me." Behind his sexual jealousy—his fear that she had displayed her charms to others at the party—was a more basic fear: his envy that she had independent life and health when his own were so compromised.

Keats's constitutionally empathetic nature had previously made it a struggle to deal with suffering medical patients, although his driven self-control had won out, allowing him to extract the bullet from Jane Hull's neck with professional sangfroid in March 1816. But the boundaries around his self were never secure, and, as a poet, he had cultivated that skinlessness, whether he was identifying with a sparrow or with a billiard ball, or making inventive "poetical concentrations" in which one word or idea bled into another.

"I cannot exist without you . . . I have a sensation at the present moment as though I was dissolving," he had told Fanny from 25 College Street, while he was briefly lodging near the Dilkes in Westminster, on October 18, 1819, recalling the desire to fade away and dissolve which he had aestheticized in "Ode to a Nightingale." "I should be affraid to separate myself far from you," he went on, even at a time when he had deliberately chosen to put five miles' distance between himself and her.

By the summer of 1820, with his tubercular condition by then a certainty, he came to believe that his very life depended on the absent Fanny, as every hour he became "more and more concentrated in you." But nothing she said could ever be enough. He became desperate and controlling, even asking her to rewrite a passage in one of her letters to him because her expressions of love were too cold in his eyes. He enclosed the passage for her convenience, and went on to compare his twisted state of mind to that of Hamlet "when he said to Ophelia 'Go to a Nunnery, go, go!' " Keats in love could be cruel.

In late June he had had another serious blood-spitting incident. He left Wesleyan Place to stay around the corner with the Hunts at Mortimer Terrace. Irritations there included a caller who bored on about the miraculous lung capacity of a legendary opera singer, not a particularly tactful choice of conversation in front of a consumptive. Haydon had written to Keats at Wesleyan Place saying that he had been trying to reach him, had called and heard from his landlady that he was "very poorly." Haydon wrote again on July 14, admitting that his main purpose in getting in touch was to get back a copy he had lent Keats of Chapman's Homer. The book—which had inspired Keats with so much sense of future possibility less than four years before—had gone missing. Keats had to buy Haydon another, although it's uncertain as to whether the painter had paid back any of the money Keats had lent him.

Things came to a head in mid-August when Keats stormed off from Mortimer Terrace after a misunderstanding. A note—probably from Fanny—had been delivered to him, but the Hunts' maid had failed to pass it to him directly and, when he finally got it, via one of the Hunts' children, the seal had been broken. Apparently, there was nothing sensitive or personal in the content of the note itself. But it made Keats feel "nervous," as he put it in a letter to his sister on August 13: violated, paranoid, as if his very being was being threatened— which it in fact was, though by tuberculosis rather than by an unreliable, distracted maid or young child.

Weak as he was, Keats took off and walked the mile to Hampstead. He was taken in by Mrs. Brawne at Wentworth Place. As a biographer, it is hard to know how to find the balance between scholarly detachment and compassion. Amy Lowell's excessive imaginings about the child Keats's supposed weeping into his pillow at boarding school stand as a rebuke. Yet I now have a son of twenty and am thus of Mrs. Brawne's parental generation.

In my less scholarly moments, I think about her. Her teenage daughter had fallen in love with an unsuitable young man, "quite the little poet," who had no family and few prospects. Mrs. Bennet would have been up in arms. But by now Keats was clearly so ill that he represented no threat. Even today, a single mother might balk at inviting her daughter's unsuitable, and now evidently terminally ill, boyfriend to live in her house. But as Fanny later attested in a letter to Keats's sister, her mother "nursed" him for the last five weeks he was in England. It's notable, but perhaps not unsurprising, that Fanny, still a teenager when she first fell in love with Keats, didn't do the nursing herself. In contrast to Keats, who nursed his own dying mother at fourteen, she had a mother to rely on.

By July 5, Keats had written to Fanny, "They talk of my going to Italy." He would indeed leave for Rome, where the climate was believed to be of help to consumptives, in September, by then little caring about the reception of his last poetry collection that had been published in the summer. There is no on-the-spot evidence as to how Fanny Brawne experienced those last five weeks in England when he was staying in her family home under the care of her mother. It is likely that the intensity of living cheek-by-jowl with him, when he was evidently on the road to death, was the most intimate and traumatic period in her relationship with Keats.

Fanny later told Keats's sister that, had he returned alive from Rome, the plan was for them to marry and that he should live "with us." If Mrs. Brawne was anything like Mrs. Bennet, this was not what she might have imagined for her daughter, which would, conventionally, have been the hope to settle Fanny in her own independent home, supported by a solvent husband. Had Keats returned, the only prospect was a marriage which would make him, instead, a surrogate child in Mrs. Brawne's home. The idea sounds like something said to soothe, rather than a meaningful plan. Having seen her own husband die of tuberculosis, Mrs. Brawne was perhaps unconvinced that Keats would survive, although Fanny continued to hope.

What may have started for Fanny as a flippant flirtation eventually became an intense experience. She was devastated by Keats's death in 1821 and kept his ring for the rest of her life. However, the claim that she cut off her hair and wore black for three years is a late-nineteenth-century myth. It is disproved by her letter to Fanny Keats of November 1821 in which she refers to having put her hair in curling papers for the night, and by another, written in summer 1822, in which she refers to her own "red and black" dress. However, she did not marry until 1833, when she was thirty-three. Her chosen husband was twelve years her junior, closer in age to Keats when he died than to Fanny herself at the time she married. His name was Louis Lindo, who anglicized his name to Lindon. He was a Sephardic Jew from Portugal whose grandfather had once been a wealthy merchant in the morally dubious West India trade. No future man in Fanny's life would have been acceptable to Keats, who was possessive of her in the extreme. His own prejudices against "close Hebrews," possibly enhanced by the fact that his profligate mother had a Jewish lover, would have made Louis doubly offensive in his eyes.

Yet in marrying someone so much younger, it was as if Fanny was still identifying with the period of her life in which she had experienced her most intense emotions. With Louis, whom she met in France, she later lived abroad, in Heidelberg among other places. Like Keats's sister Fanny— and Byron's former lover Claire Clairmont, who went on to live in Russia—she became a wanderer away from England, though she returned in 1859. Many of Keats's contemporaries sought refuge abroad after the Romantic heyday, though a more typical country of choice was Italy, where Byron and Shelley sought exile and where Leigh Hunt, Charles Brown and Joseph Severn lived for a time.

———

KEATS'S RELATIONSHIP WITH Fanny Brawne was kept under wraps until long after he died. His first biographer, Richard Monckton Milnes, omitted all reference to her name in his 1848 biography. Fanny's letters to Keats were still in her possession, but it is unlikely that Milnes would have used them even had they been given to him on a plate. As a Victorian gentleman, he was keen to be as reticent as possible about the private life of his subject. He wanted to establish Keats as a name to conjure with among the English poets, as Keats himself had once, in a throwaway letter to his brother of 1817, expressed the hope he might be after his death. But Victorian culture had, meanwhile, erected a cordon sanitaire around the private life. Milnes only made a single, obscure, embarrassed reference to "one intense affection" in Keats's life, which he did not explain and which no reader who was not in the know would have picked up on.

Yet the fact that Keats had died before being able to marry Fanny was not necessarily a bar to her being mentioned. The 1858 painting *Too Late* by William Lindsay Windus was acceptable to the Victorians. It shows an inconstant fiancé returning to the woman to whom he has promised marriage, only to find her emaciated by consumption, on the road to death. The relationship between Keats and Fanny was also brought to a tragic premature end by consumption, but it was never a formal engagement, though they exchanged rings. The new Victorian attitude toward privacy was one reason why Milnes did not investigate Keats's romance with Fanny. Just as significant was the fact that it had been regarded as suspect in their own circle at the time.

When Keats's letters to Fanny were finally published in 1878, the literary establishment was horrified by their emotional abandon. The Dilkes' son Charley, by then Sir Charles Wentworth Dilke, wrote an article in the *Athenaeum* in which he decried the exposure as beyond belief. "In life's battle," he wrote, "an English gentleman would as soon think of picking the pocket of a dead comrade as of making public his love letters." Somewhat ironically, his own son's scandalous sexual affairs were soon to be exposed in the press.

Keats's letters to Fanny failed to conform to the Victorian ideal of the stiff upper lip, which had taken over from Rousseauesque permissiveness. The poet Algernon Charles Swinburne had previously regarded Keats as a "man so perfect." He was disgusted to read the letters to Fanny, although his own private inclinations included sexually sadomasochistic tendencies, as indeed did those of Keats's first biographer,

Richard Monckton Milnes. "If they ought never to have been published, it is no less certain that they ought never to have been written," Swinburne spluttered. "A manful kind of man, or even a manly sort of boy, in his love-making or in his suffering, will not howl and snivel after such a lamentable fashion."

The only reason why Milnes had felt he had to make even the slightest, most obscure allusion to Keats's love for Fanny in his biography was because Leigh Hunt had already made reference to it in print, though without naming the woman concerned. In his 1828 memoir, *Lord Byron and Some of His Contemporaries,* Hunt—who was by then reduced to trading on the reflected glory of literary gossip to establish his own onetime position at the heart of English Romantic culture— had alluded coyly to "a very tender circumstance" in Keats's life.

He had vividly glossed it by recalling a moment when he and Keats had sat together on a bench in Hampstead's Well Walk, probably sometime after Keats moved to Wesleyan Place. Tom had died in the Bentleys' house in Well Walk less than two years before, in 1818. Hunt specified that the bench was the one against the wall nearest to the Heath. He remembered that Keats had burst into tears, confessing that his heart was breaking. His feelings over the "hopelessness" of his love affair and the perceived failure of his poetic career were, Hunt attested, "more than he could bear . . . he feared for his senses."

———

I'VE JUST COME back from taking a mind-clearing walk over to Hampstead, across the fields and through the wooded parts of the Heath, which remain as wild as they must have been in 1820. I ended up at Well Walk. The house in which Keats and

Tom lived with the Bentleys was subsequently demolished to make way for a Victorian pub, though other houses in that stretch of the terrace would have been there in the period.

And there's still a bench against the wall at the end of the street nearest to the Heath. The wooden planks which form the seat are obviously new, but the wrought-iron ends, with leaf motifs, look, from a style perspective at least, as though they could date from the Regency period, though, if so, they must have been vigorously sandblasted and repainted since then. The whole bench is, more likely, a replacement. But it's in the same spot as the one on which Keats told Hunt his heart was breaking. I think about this as I sit on it, with the cars going by along the street which briefly separates it from the wooded half-wilderness of Hampstead Heath.

Epitaph

Here lies One Whose Name was writ in Water

KEATS'S FINAL TRIP to Rome was organized for him by his friends, but it was only at the last moment that Joseph Severn agreed to accompany him. In two passages of later reminiscences, Severn offered conflicting accounts. In one, he described how he had boarded the ship with Keats on the very day after the idea was initially mooted. He had hurriedly called on the painter Sir Thomas Lawrence to get a couple of letters of introduction to influential artists in Rome, before rushing home to his parents after midnight, and leaving the following morning. In Severn's second version, he said he had three or four days' grace before their departure.

In both accounts, however, Severn says that he was asked to accompany Keats by William Haslam. Haslam was, according to Brown, an old school friend of Keats's and the man who had first introduced the embryonic poet to the embryonic painter. Haslam himself had gone on from Clarke's Academy to train as a solicitor, before taking over his father's position in business at a wholesale grocer's in Leadenhall Street in the

City. In 1819, he married. He had followed the route of bourgeois security rather than the bohemian path of his painter and poet friends, though he was also compassionate and open-minded enough to help Severn find somewhere to place his illegitimate son.

As little correspondence survives to chart Keats's friendship with Haslam, we can know almost nothing about its texture. It is one of those lost relationships on the fringes of history that might have been more significant than the record suggests. While Keats was away on his hiking holiday up north in 1818, Haslam showed such kindness to the lonely Tom, as Keats put it, that it "endeared him to me for ever." Haslam's concern in 1820, now that Keats himself was also suffering from life-threatening tuberculosis, seems characteristic.

On July 27, 1820, Shelley, in response to a hint from a friend of Leigh Hunt, sent a letter to Keats inviting him to join him in Italy, where he was by then living with his unconventional household. He had heard that Keats continued "to wear a consumptive appearance" and suggested a winter in a warmer clime might help. Shelley and Mary Godwin had by then finally married, following his abandoned wife Harriet's suicide, but Mary's stepsister Claire, who had given birth to an illegitimate daughter by Byron in 1817, lived with them. Claire was rumored—perhaps with justification—to be Shelley's lover too. Their ménage was later mocked, by *Blackwood's* in December 1821, as a free-love commune in which they were playing "the Bacchanal beside the Tuscan sea."

The year before, Keats had fantasized about going with Fanny Brawne to Switzerland, where Shelley and Mary had shared the summer of 1816 with Byron and Claire. But six days after Shelley's letter reached him at Wesleyan Place on August 10, 1820, he wrote back, politely declining the invitation. He had met Shelley in London, through Leigh Hunt, but had not felt quite comfortable in his company, and no real friendship between them developed.

The differences between the two poets are visually evident if you compare two portraits of them made in 1819. Amelia Curran's image of Shelley shows him with an upright quill in his hand and wearing a defiantly open-necked shirt. In the miniature made by Severn that same year, Keats has unbuttoned his jacket cuffs, but he is swathed up to the chin in the conventional white cravat of the period and looks a little tense. Unlike the entitled Shelley, he is not quite able to dispense with the proprieties of dress. Rather than holding a quill, his right hand cups his chin and his left fist is clenched on an open folio. Ironically, shortly after Keats's death, the *Literary Gazette,* in a tirade against anarchistic poets, flippantly surmised that Keats had only died because his bohemian habits were so ingrained that he refused to wear a neckcloth and had caught cold as a result.

Severn's motivation for going with Keats was enhanced by the fact that he also wanted to pursue his painting career in Rome. He had recently been awarded the annual gold medal by the Royal Academy and assumed he would be able to get a travel grant. Rome was then an international center for art students, who created a vibrant culture there. The Académie de France, for example, had a scheme to put emerging artists up in the Villa de Medici. In 1817, the young painter Jean Alaux produced canvases of his contemporaries, François-Édouard Picot and Louis-Vincent-Léon Pallière, in their rooms there, studios that doubled as bedrooms. The images conjure up carefree young artists enjoying their freedom.

Pallière is sitting on the edge of his single bed strumming a guitar. Two typically Italian cypress trees are seen at a distance in the vista through the window, and the room itself features unframed prints and a tambourine nonchalantly hung on the wall. The painting is now in the Metropolitan Museum in New York. But when it was made by Alaux in 1817, its image of a guitar-strumming student—with a tambourine on the wall—had a Bob Dylanish feeling of youth rebellion.

Severn may have had the ulterior motive of wanting to pursue art in Rome. But, at twenty-six, he cannot have believed that agreeing to take care of a seriously ill contemporary would be an altogether carefree experience. His *Life and Letters,* published by William Sharp in 1892, contains an intriguing anecdote about his childhood. When Severn was eight, he went with a schoolmate to swim in a water-filled quarry pit. The friend got into difficulties and drowned. Severn, alone, had to take the dead boy's clothes back to his parents and tell them the terrible news. One has to wonder whether, at some possibly unconscious level, his willingness to take on the burden of Keats was related to his earlier guilt at having failed to save a friend.

Contemporary evidence unavailable to Sharp shows that Haslam in fact approached Severn on September 12, five days before the painter and the invalid poet boarded the ship, the *Maria Crowther,* on the 17th. They were seen off by Haslam and also by Keats's publisher Taylor and the latter's loyal adviser Woodhouse. Keats had left Wentworth Place for Fleet Street a few days earlier, where he was to stay before he embarked. On quitting her, he gave Fanny Brawne his miniature by Severn. She gave him a penknife, a pocket diary and a new silk lining for his traveling cap that she had sewn herself, along with an oval carnelian stone that she used to hold to cool her hand when it was hot with needlework. Keats could hold it in his own "living hand," still warm and "capable of earnest grasping," a sensuous reminder. He also had a locket containing some of her hair, cut from her actual body.

Keats left the country broke. On Sunday, August 20, he had applied to Abbey for more funds but had been refused. "Dear Sir," Abbey wrote back, "I have yours of Sunday and am exceedingly grieved at its contents." He complained that George had drawn an extra £50 more than he had agreed to, and that the profits from his own business had been reduced by bad debts to the extent that his own private expenses were under pressure. "It is therefore not in my power to lend you any thing," he concluded.

Abbey may not have been fully cognizant of Keats's desperate state of health. Fanny Keats, who was living with him as his ward, had received only carefully optimistic accounts from her brother. In a postscript, Abbey added, "When you shall be able to call I shall be glad to see you, as I should not like to see you want 'maintenance for the day.'" But Keats gave up on Abbey, his pride wounded by the idea that he was a charity case in desperate need of daily bread, and unwilling to expose his true medical condition.

Reading all the contemporary material relating to the last months of Keats's life, it is hard not to be distracted by the frequent expressions of hope, or at least the refusal to express despair of his case, even by his doctors. But it had been far from paranoid of him to regard his first blood-spitting as a "death warrant," given his family history. That he was almost certain he was going to die in Italy is clear from the fact that he made an informal will before he left, in a note to his publisher John Taylor:

> In case of my death this scrap of Paper may be serviceable in your possession.

> All my estate real and personal consists in the hopes
> of the sale of books publish'd or unpublish'd. Now I wish
> Brown and you to be the first paid Creditors—the rest is
> in nubibus [in the clouds], but in case it should shower
> pay my Taylor the few pounds I owe him.
> My chest of books I divide among my friends—

This is Keats in his own voice. His "scrap" of a will is notable for its casualness and brevity, its nature metaphor of clouds and rain, its conversational use of a Latinism, and its wide-open embrace of "friends," with no thought to name them. Even the way in which he misspells "tailor" as "Taylor" reflects his habit of verbal plasticity. The word becomes almost a pun, as the tradesman whose petty bill he hasn't settled merges in a moment of near-irony with the publishing patron, John Taylor, on whom he so relied.

We can almost hear Keats speak. This highly personal "will," which he did not even sign or date, has none of the features conventionally associated with a legally binding document. It reflects his almost phobic resistance to thinking practically about matters of finance, a reaction to his family history. And it contrasts markedly with the formal "assignment of copyright" to Taylor & Hessey, drawn up by the lawyer Richard Woodhouse and written in careful legalese, that Keats signed on September 16, 1820. According to its terms, there were two assignments of copyright, each worth £100, one (belatedly) for *Endymion,* the other for the 1817 *Poems* and the 1820 volume, *Lamia, Isabella, The Eve of St. Agnes, and Other Poems.* However, Keats received only £30 of that £200, since Taylor & Hessey had already advanced him the rest. Nevertheless, on September 19, they forwarded a further £150 to a bank in Naples to cover Keats's expenses in Italy. Given how uncertain it was that the poet would live to write any more books, this was an act of pure generosity on John Taylor's part, not the equivalent of a publisher's advance which he hoped to recoup.

Keats and Severn boarded the *Maria Crowther* at Tower Wharf on the Thames on September 17. As bad luck would have it, one of the other passengers was a consumptive young woman far gone in the disease, a reminder to Keats of his own mortality. It took until October 31 for them to land in Naples, after a protracted spell sailing along the English coast waiting for fair winds. Then, when they arrived at Naples, the ship was held in quarantine for ten days, a stifling, floating prison.

Severn kept his spirits up until, on November 1, after they had finally disembarked, he told Haslam that the experience had made him cry a "plentiful shower of tears," but without letting Keats see. "I am horror struck at his sufferings on this voyage," he confided in a letter that was subsequently circulated among Keats's circle. When Isabella Jones read it, having been shown it by John Taylor shortly after Keats's death, she reacted cynically, dismissing Severn's tears as "cant," a "disgusting" fake show of feeling. That, perhaps, tells us more about Mrs. Jones's distrustful attitude to emotion than it does about Severn. There is no reason to doubt the authenticity of his response to the stress of the situation.

That same day, Keats wrote to Brown of the "load of WRETCHEDNESS which presses upon me." His most agitating thoughts were about Fanny: "The persuasion that I shall see her no more will kill me . . . Oh, God! God! God! Every thing I have in my trunks that reminds me of her goes through me like a spear. The silk lining she put in my traveling cap scalds my head. My imagination is horribly vivid about her—I see her—I hear her . . ."

On October 24, while still on the quarantined ship, Keats,

too distressed to address Fanny directly, had written a letter to the by now sympathetic Mrs. Brawne: "I dare not fix my Mind on Fanny," he told her, "I have not dared to think of her . . . if ever there was any person born without the faculty of hoping I am he . . . O what a misery it is to have an intellect in splints!" he added, still bringing mind and body together in a medical metaphor. It's striking that Keats wanted connection with Mrs., not Miss, Brawne: with the older woman who, during his last weeks in England, had played the role of the nurturing mother he believed he had never had. He must have assumed that Fanny would read what he wrote to her mother, but he effectively rejected her attempts to soothe him. The ambivalence he had always expressed concerning women was being replayed at a level of heightened pain.

They reached Rome, traveling overland from Naples, on around November 14, soon finding lodgings at 26 Piazza di Spagna in what is now the Keats–Shelley museum. Their small, high-ceilinged apartment was on the second floor of the building, which was originally erected in the seventeenth century but remodeled in the 1720s. They also made contact with the local English doctor, James Clark, who lived nearby. His diagnosis was confusing and falsely optimistic. He seemed to think that the problem was with Keats's stomach and recommended horse rides for exercise, with which Keats was able to comply at the start. Clark also recommended a starvation diet consisting of a single anchovy with a morsel of bread a day. One thinks of the roots of relish sweet, the jellies soother than the creamy curd, the nectarines, the roasted game fowls and the claret that Keats's appetite, both poetical and culinary, had previously appreciated. Later, he could take nothing but bread and milk, which Severn prepared for him.

The latter's letters home, recording Keats's physical decline, make for painful reading.

A massive pulmonary hemorrhage on December 9, in which Keats "vomited near two Cup-fuls of blood" was followed by nine days of serious blood-spitting. Following the standard, if unhelpful, medical practice of the day, the doctor bled him, extracting a further eight ounces of blood from his arm. It was "black and thick in the extreme." Keats's distended stomach could digest nothing, leaving him "in perpetual hunger or craving." His eyes were staring and glassy, and his mental horrors so extreme that Severn feared for his sanity. Then there were the night sweats, the chattering teeth, the diarrhea. Keats's sufferings were so great that he said he wanted to kill himself, prompting Severn to hide the laudanum bottle in case he deliberately overdosed. In his delirium, Keats seemed convinced that "the continued stretch of his imagination [had] killed him," or that his illness had been caused by "the exciting and thwarting of his passions": that his two great loves, poetry and Fanny Brawne, were responsible. "I should have had her when I was in health, and I should have remained well," he had told Brown, as if the fact that he had not actually slept with Fanny, despite their kisses, had been his undoing.

Severn, meanwhile, sought much-needed refuge from the sickroom in the restaurants of Rome. Keen not to worry his family too much, he regaled his sister on February 19, 1820, about how much he was enjoying the local cuisine, in contrast to the slops he was preparing for his invalid friend:

I make bread and milk three times a day for Keats—
for myself—sometimes tea—sometimes Chocolate—or

Coffee—my dinner now I go out for—I have 1st dish macarona—it is like a dish of large white earth worms—made of Flour with butter &c—very good—my 2nd dish is fish—and then comes Roast Beef or Mutton—a cutlet of Pork or wild boar—their vegetables are very beautiful—cabbage—cauliflower—broccola spinach—every thing good—and very well cooked—and then I have pudding every day.

Three days later, on February 22, Severn revealed more to Haslam than he had to his sister about his sickroom duties, which prevented him from painting, though on January 28 at 3 a.m. he had made the now famous sketch of Keats on his deathbed:

here I am by our poor dying friend—my spirits—my intellects and my health are breaking down . . . no one will relieve me—they all run away . . . and even if they did not poor Keats could not do without me . . . Last night I thought he was going—I could hear the Phlegm in his throat—he bade me lift him up in the bed—or he would die with pain—I watchd him all night—at every cough I expected he would suffocate . . . he opens his eyes in great horror and doubt but when they fall on me they close gently and open and close until he falls into another sleep—The very thought of this keeps me by him until he dies.

By now Keats regarded the prospect of "easeful death," as he had called it in "Ode to a Nightingale," as his only comfort. It came the next night. When it did, he approached it with calm and courage. In Severn's words:

He is gone—he died with the most perfect ease—he seemed to go to sleep—on the 23rd (Friday) at half past 4 the approaches of death came on—"Severn—S—lift me up for I am dying—I shall die easy—dont [*sic*] be frightened—thank God it has come"—I lifted him up in my arms—and the phlegm seemed boiling in his throat—this increased until 11 at night when he gradually sunk into death—so quiet that I still thought he slept.

Severn organized for a death mask and casts of Keats's hands and feet to be taken. When an autopsy was performed on February 25 by three doctors, including Clark, Keats's lungs were revealed to have been so totally destroyed that they could not believe how he had continued alive for the previous two months. Keats was buried in Rome's Cimitero Acattolico—the burial ground reserved for non-Catholics—shortly after dawn on Monday, February 26, 1821, with Fanny's unopened letters tucked into his shroud.

On the evening of February 14, a week before he died, Keats composed his own epitaph. As with so many of his poems, we have direct testimony relating to the actual moment of its composition. The words were not written down by Keats himself, who was by then too ill to use a pen, but by Severn, who relayed them to Brown in a letter he wrote later that very night, which sets the scene in which the words were imparted:

To-night he has talked very much to me, but so easily, that he, at last, fell into a pleasant sleep. He seems to have comfortable dreams, without the night-mare . . . Among the many things he has requested of me to-night, this is the principal one,—that on his grave-stone shall be this,—

HERE LIES ONE WHOSE NAME WAS WRIT IN
WATER.

Keats's self-epigraphic words were indeed later carved on his
grave in the Cimitero Acattolico, in the distinctly solid and
unwatery medium of stone. They have subsequently been
quoted endless times in the black certitude of printers' ink.
They suggest he thought he would disappear into nothingness, unremembered. His grave has, on the contrary, since
become a literary pilgrimage site.

Oscar Wilde and Thomas Hardy later wrote their own,
very different, poems about paying their respects at Keats's
graveside, while countless visitors, myself included, continue
to make their way there, weaving through the other tombs
of those non-Catholics who happened to die in the city in
the nineteenth century, from British Anglicans, to Orthodox
Greeks or Russians, to Jews, to Muslims, to Scandinavian
Protestants. Keats himself, although he was baptized in the
Church of England, had no religious affiliation. Unconventional for his era, he died with no faith in a Christian afterlife.
"I wish to believe in immortality," he had told Fanny in June
1820, after saying that he rested his only idea of "heaven" in
"life and health" with her, by then an impossible prospect.

His chosen epitaph suggests the idea of dissolving into
invisibility, yet its mood and meaning remain ambiguous.
Was he railing against fate, acerbically angry that he had not,
as he believed, achieved the lasting poetic fame he had so
striven for as the only way for an atheist to cheat death? Or
was he expressing acceptance of death's dissolution: letting go,
as it were, of the "fever and the fret," including the feverish
excitement he had once felt when writing poetry?

Designed by Severn, and erected in 1823, Keats's gravestone

features an image of a Grecian lyre half-strung, to represent
a life half-lived, cut off in its prime. But it's a little botched.
The date of death recorded on it is out by a day. The words
Keats entrusted to Severn a week before his death are given as
a quotation, beginning with quotation marks. But there's no
room on the stone for the closing quotation marks, leaving
it feeling somehow unfinished, which seems symbolic of the
fact that there would be no closure for Severn himself, who
was haunted by Keats for the rest of his life.

Moreover, Keats's self-invented epitaph is presented at the
end of a much longer inscription, which was not of Keats's
own making but the result of a confabulation between Severn,
Brown and Keats's publisher John Taylor. It reads thus:

This Grave
contains all that was Mortal
of a
YOUNG ENGLISH POET
Who,
on his Death Bed,
in the Bitterness of his Heart,
at the Malicious Power of his Enemies
Desired
these Words to be engraven on his Tomb Stone
"Here lies One
Whose Name was writ in Water.

Feb. 24th 1821

This is a monument which, rather than speaking to eternity, is
mired in its own moment. It shows that Keats's own friends,
people who knew him intimately, were perhaps influenced by

Shelley's elegy *Adonais,* published in 1821, a couple of months after Keats died. Though Keats himself had hardly known Shelley, felt awkward around him, and had politely turned down his invitation to Italy, Shelley went on to appropriate him as the ultimate Romantic martyr. In the preface to the elegy, he had portrayed Keats as "delicate and fragile," claiming that he had suffered a rupturing of the lungs directly as a result of the "savage criticism . . . wantonly inflicted" on *Endymion* by the "poisoned shaft" of that "murderer," the conservative press.

The inscription on Keats's gravestone is less idealized than *Adonais* with its images of the dead poet as a "pale flower," a "broken lily" or "a portion of the loveliness / Which once he made more lovely." It presents Keats as the eternal underdog, as a puny pugilist destroyed by "the malicious power of his enemies," dying in the "bitterness of his heart." That sentiment sits uneasily with Severn's on-the-spot account of the night Keats came up with the phrase "HERE LIES ONE WHOSE NAME WAS WRIT IN WATER." At the time, he recorded that Keats, who had previously been in a state of suicidal distress, fell into a "pleasant sleep," undisturbed by nightmares, after imparting the words to him. Moreover, the inscription fails to do justice to those who had in fact fully appreciated Keats's genius in his lifetime.

I made my own pilgrimage to Keats's grave sometime before I started working on this book. I had gone to Rome for a half-term break with a friend and our respective daughters. After a grueling visit to the Forum, we had taken the children across the city to the Cimitero Acattolico. Stroking the tame stray cats wandering among the graves was a welcome distraction for them, but we insisted that they pay their homage to Keats, explaining what an important poet he was. "But why hasn't it got his name on?" one of them asked when we reached the grave.

Her question is worth pondering. A grave without a name? Keats asked for the words "Here lies one whose name was writ in water," but he never mentioned that he wanted his name to be omitted. It was Taylor who decided that. "Neither name nor date is requisite," he wrote to Severn in August 1821, believing that Keats's own epitaph was enough to "stand alone" because the details would later be supplied by his biographer. Taylor had his own plans to publish a biography, though they came to naught. "I foresee that it will be as clear an indication to posterity as the plainest, every-day inscription that one may find in Westminster Abbey," he added, perhaps hoping that anonymity on his gravestone might in the long term enhance Keats's romantic image as a tragic unacknowledged genius on an analogy with Chatterton, to whose memory *Endymion* had been dedicated.

Brown and Severn later regretted the rest of the inscription. On November 26, 1836, Severn described it as "an eyesore to me," while Brown referred to it as a "sort of profanation." They both came to the conclusion that the wording on the grave, setting grievances in stone, was too crude to be true to Keats.

But what was true to him? In the last letter he wrote to Brown, dated November 30, 1820, Keats expressed the idea that he felt he was already leading a "posthumous existence." His actual posthumous life would lead to his establishment at the heart of the English canon. The infighting between the liberal and reactionary press at the time he was alive, which led to the attacks on Keats by *Blackwood's* and the *Quarterly,* and to the inscription on his gravestone, would be forgotten once his poems, especially the odes, were enshrined out of context in anthologies.

Like his hero Shakespeare, Keats created literary artifacts which went on to speak beyond their time, able to say so much because their fertile language resolutely resists any final definition. In doing so, his poetry continues to unlock our own creativity as readers. Yet, at the same time, everything he wrote, especially his letters, embodies his individuality too. He may be a "camelion Poet," but he is defiantly not a poet with "no self."

Acknowledgments

My main debt is to fellow Keatsians. Thank you to the organizers of the international Keats Bicentenary Conferences, which have been held annually in the handsome lecture room of the library next door to Keats House since 2014: Professor Nicholas Roe, Professor Richard Marggraf Turley and Professor Sarah Wootton, along with the conference administrator Dr. Hrileena Ghosh. I have benefited so much from their research and insights, particularly those of Nicholas Roe and Richard Marggraf Turley. I was honored to be asked by them to deliver a keynote lecture at the 2019 event. It forms the basis of my chapter on "The Eve of St. Agnes." Sadly, the 2020 and 2021 conferences had to be canceled due to the COVID-19 pandemic.

Keats himself had a gift for friendship; the Keats experts I have encountered have been unfailingly warm, welcoming, supportive and keen to share. I would like to express my particular gratitude to Professor John Barnard, whose scholarly knowledge of Keats is unsurpassed. He generously read this book in manuscript (I need hardly add that any errors that remain are my own). Giuseppe Albano, curator of the Keats–Shelley museum in Rome, was kind enough to show me, and some friends, around. We hugely enjoyed the experience and learned so much from him. I am grateful to Rob Shakespeare, the principal curator of Keats House, for allowing me to photograph it, and to my brother Charlie for actually taking the photo that we eventually used in this book. Thanks too to Sofie Davis for her help and advice on the Keats deathbed image; also to Professor Seamus Perry for the information about Coleridge at Highgate and to Ned Campbell for his typographical insights.

Bea Hemming at Cape has been more than supportive as an editor: unfailingly calm, cheerful and reassuring, yet with an eagle eye. My thanks to her and her team, especially Daisy Watt. Mary Chamberlain's focus and precision as a copy-editor were likewise a boon, while my agent Georgina Capel has remained, as ever, a rock.

Most of the writing of this book was done at the height of the pandemic, when it was impossible to visit libraries. I could not have done it without the digital library archive.org, which offers scanned out-of-copyright books online for free. Nor could I have written it without breaks on Hampstead Heath, where I was able to walk every day, following in Keats's footsteps. Beautifully maintained by the City of London Corporation, it provided a lifesaver to many Londoners during lockdown.

My old friends Alexander Bird and John Mullan, professors both, provided helpful conversation on relevant intellectual or scholarly issues, sometimes while walking on the Heath. My son Oliver shared his insights on the classical ekphrasis in Virgil; my daughter Ottilie offered a healthily skeptical perspective on whether Keats really wrote "Ode to a Nightingale" under a plum tree one morning after breakfast; my husband Ian offered stimulating parallels between Keats and Schubert. But thanks most of all to my mother, Lisa, who first took me to Keats House many years ago.

References

All quotations from Keats's poetry are taken from *John Keats: The Complete Poems,* ed. John Barnard (London: Penguin, third edition, 1988).

The full details of each text cited can be found in the Bibliography.

ABBREVIATIONS

CH: *John Keats: The Critical Heritage,* ed. G. M. Matthews (London: Routledge, 1971).

KC: *The Keats Circle: Letters and Papers and More Letters and Poems of the Keats Circle 1814–1879,* ed. Hyder E. Rollins, 2 vols. (Cambridge, Mass: Harvard University Press, 1965).

LJK: *The Letters of John Keats 1814–1821,* ed. Hyder E. Rollins, 2 vols. (Cambridge, Mass: Harvard University Press, 1958).

Poems: *John Keats: The Complete Poems,* ed. John Barnard (London: Penguin, 1988).

PROLOGUE: BODY AND SOUL

4 "prescriptive language": *Monthly Review,* July 1820, CH, p. 160.
4 "own originality": Ibid.
4 "unintelligible": *Literary Chronicle and Weekly Review,* July 29, 1820, CH, p. 164.
4 "avoid coining new words": Ibid.
4 "a subject for laughter or for pity": *London Magazine and Monthly Critical and Dramatic Review,* August 1820, CH, p. 183.

5 "the candles are burnt down": LJK, II, p. 73.

5 "no self": Keats to Richard Woodhouse, October 27, 1818, LJK, I, p. 387.

5 "camelion Poet": Ibid.

7 "four or five in number": Brown, *Life of John Keats*, p. 54.

7 "writing was not well legible": Ibid.

7 "With his [Keats's] assistance": Ibid.

9 "I think I shall be among the English Poets": LJK, I, p. 394.

10 Over the course of the last hundred years: The titles are listed in the Bibliography.

10 "cumulative process of collaboration": Nicholas Roe, "Undefinitive Keats," in Chantler et al. (eds.), *Literature and Authenticity 1780–1900*, p. 50.

10 Essay topics plucked at random: see Bibliography for details of these titles from the *Keats–Shelley Journal* and for the book titles subsequently quoted.

12 "young[,] writing at random": LJK, II, p. 80.

13 "Jack Keats or Ketch or whatever his names are": *Byron's Letters and Journals*, vol. 7, p. 217.

13 "a sort of mental masturbation": *Byron's Letters and Journals*, vol. 7, p. 225.

13 "to give the very age and body of the time": *Hamlet*, III.ii.24–5.

14 "north Pole—with the icebergs": LJK, II, p. 95.

14 fewer and fewer British high-school students: "Students Don't See the Value: Why A Level English Is in Decline," *The Guardian*, August 16, 2019.

15 "cash-recourses": LJK, II, p. 141.

15 "thought very little of these matters": Ibid.

15 "on Primrose Hill": *London Magazine*, August 1820, CH, p. 201.

16 "my only life": LJK, I, p. 370.

16 "possessed of much less than I thought": LJK, II, p. 54.

17 "This living hand": *Poems*, p. 459.

17 "generally supposed to be a fragment": *Poems*, p. 711.

18 Edward Holmes, who was at school: KC, II, pp. 163–4.

18 "He was under the middle height": Leigh Hunt, *Lord Byron and Some of His Contemporaries*, p. 246.

20 "a Nectarine": LJK, II, p. 179.

22 "men who had been bosom friends": LJK, II, p. 208.

23 "cures for clap": Richard Marggraf Turley, *Bright Stars: John Keats, "Barry Cornwall" and Romantic Literary Culture*, p. 124.

23 "foolish young man": *Literary Gazette*, December 1, 1821, p. 772.

23 "orgasm of . . . intellect": William Howitt, *Homes and Haunts of the Most Eminent British Poets*, p. 293.

1. "ON FIRST LOOKING INTO CHAPMAN'S HOMER"

27 "when he could just speak": Benjamin Robert Haydon, *Neglected Genius: The Diaries of Benjamin Robert Haydon,* p. 48.

27 "If Poetry comes not as naturally": LJK, I, p. 238.

28 "jumbled heap / Of murky buildings": from Keats's sonnet beginning "O Solitude!," *Poems,* p. 50.

29 Leigh Hunt, a high-profile: For Leigh Hunt's incarceration, see Gregory Dart, *Metropolitan Art and Literature, 1810–1840, Cockney Adventures,* pp. 1–2.

30 "strike up a blithe defiance": *Poems of Leigh Hunt,* p. 42.

30 "red letter day": Charles Cowden Clarke, *Recollections of Writers,* p. 133.

31 "mere smoothness for harmony": *Poems of Leigh Hunt,* p. xiv.

32 "Then forth he came": Chapman passage, with interpolated italics, Clarke, *Recollections of Writers,* p. 130.

33 exact date of his birth: For the uncertainties surrounding Keats's birth date, see Roe, "Undefinitive Keats," in Chantler et al. (eds.), *Literature and Authenticity 1780–1900,* p. 41.

34 "the humblest description": Hunt, *Lord Byron and Some of His Contemporaries,* p. 247.

34 "personal soreness": Ibid.

35 "the upper rank of the middle class": Richard Monckton Milnes, "Memoir," *The Poetical Works of John Keats,* p. xii.

35 "the coarse-bred son": From the poem "Ego Dominus Tuus," in *The Collected Poems of W. B. Yeats* (1933; London: Macmillan, 1958), p. 182.

36 "What a thing to be in the Mouth of Fame": LJK, I, p. 139.

38 "without money": Nicholas Roe, *John Keats: A New Life,* p. 35.

38 "probably an alcoholic": Ibid.

38 "sat up whole nights": Haydon, *Neglected Genius: The Diaries of Benjamin Robert Haydon,* p. 49.

39 "I have never known any unalloy'd Happiness": LJK, II, p. 123.

39 "Whenever I find myself growing vapourish": LJK, II, p. 186.

42 "in one of his moods": Clarke, *Recollections of Writers,* p. 123.

43 medicine was the lowest of the professions: See Rory Muir, *Gentlemen of Uncertain Fortune* (London: Yale University Press, 2019), for a sociological analysis of the professions in early-nineteenth-century England.

44 "ramping": Clarke, *Recollections of Writers,* p. 126.

48 "potential sharing": Helen Vendler, *Coming of Age as a Poet: Milton, Keats, Eliot, Plath,* p. 52.

48 "unacknowledged legislators of the World": Percy Bysshe Shelley, *Selected Poems and Prose,* p. 678.

50 "When not a breath—disturbs the deep serene": For a discussion of Keats's appropriation of Pope, see John Kandl, "The Politics of Keats's

Early Poetry," in Wolfson (ed.), *The Cambridge Companion to Keats,* p. 3.

52 During the week, Keats was still working all hours at the hospital: Understanding of Keats's hands-on experience as a young medic has been vastly enhanced by new research presented in Roe (ed.), *John Keats and the Medical Imagination.*

53 "noble sonnet": Hunt, *Lord Byron and Some of His Contemporaries,* p. 248.

53 "fairly surprised us with the truth of their ambition": *Examiner,* December 1, 1816, CH, p. 42.

2. "A THING OF BEAUTY IS A JOY FOR EVER"

56 "passed into a proverb": Clarke, *Recollections of Writers,* p. 131.

56 "One evening, in the twilight": Benjamin Ward Richardson, *Disciples of Aesculapius,* vol. 1, p. 27.

57 "some dozens": Roe, *John Keats: A New Life,* p. 167.

58 "ensure me an employment & maintainance": LJK, II, p. 125.

58 notoriously hard apothecaries' exam: Roe (ed.), *John Keats and the Medical Imagination,* p. 32.

59 promoted to the role of "dresser": Roe (ed.), *John Keats and the Medical Imagination,* p. 60.

59 "a test, a trial of my Powers of Imagination": LJK, I, pp. 169–70.

60 "John Keats, who was killed off by one critique": Byron, *Don Juan,* canto 11, stanza 60, *Lord Byron: The Major Works,* p. 735.

61 "gross": *British Critic,* June 1818, CH, p. 94.

62 "foul language": *British Critic,* June 1818, CH, p. 93.

62 "farmy fields": *Poems of Leigh Hunt,* p. 87.

62 "pillowy fields": Ibid.

62 "piny": *Poems of Leigh Hunt,* p. 21.

62 "scattery light": *Poems of Leigh Hunt,* p. 2.

62 "pranksome": *Poems of Leigh Hunt,* p. 18.

62 "lightsome": *Poems of Leigh Hunt,* pp. 4, 7, 48, 82.

62 "passion-plighted spots": *Poems of Leigh Hunt,* p. 21.

62 "the utterance of a passion for truth": Leigh Hunt, quoted in Duncan Wu, "Keats and the 'Cockney School,'" in Wolfson (ed.), *Cambridge Companion to Keats,* pp. 40–41.

63 "The woe was earthly": *Poems of Leigh Hunt,* p. 42.

63 "Happy Poetry Preferred": CH, p. 62.

64 "transparent": Walter Jackson Bate, *John Keats,* p. 177.

65 pulmonary conditions: Roe (ed.), *John Keats and the Medical Imagination,* p. 59.

65 "axioms in philosophy are not axioms": May 3, 1818, LJK, I, p. 279; discussed in Roe (ed.), *John Keats and the Medical Imagination,* p. 35.

65 "fever, and the fret": "Ode to a Nightingale."
65 "I scarcely remember counting upon any Happiness": LJK, I, p. 186.
65 "I have never yet been able to perceive": LJK, I, p. 185.
67 "over capable": LJK, I, p. 138.
67 "upper Stories": Ibid.
67 "down in the Mouth": LJK, I, p. 139.
67 "I have asked myself so often": Ibid.
68 "the Cliff of Poesy": LJK, I, p. 141.
68 "seem[ed] like Mice to mine": Ibid.
68 "horrid Morbidity": LJK, I, p. 142.
68 "greatest Enemy": Ibid.
69 "pack of scattered cards": LJK, II, p. 323.
69 George and Tom Keats lost money playing rouge et noir: Nicholas
     Roe, *John Keats: A New Life*, p. 181.
71 "no inward feel of being able to finish": CH, p. 76.
71 "undersong of disrespect to the Public": LJK, I, p. 267.
71 "London drizzle or a scotch Mist": CH, p. 77. Both the canceled and
     the published prefaces to *Endymion* are reprinted in CH.
72 "conversation": Ibid.
72 "extravagant pretensions": "On the Cockney School of Poetry No. 1,"
     Blackwood's Edinburgh Magazine, ii, 1817, p. 38.
72 "exquisitely bad taste": Ibid.
73 "the Cockney school of versification": *Blackwood's*, iii, August 1818,
     CH, p. 101.
73 "the Reputation of Hunt's elevé [*sic*]": LJK, I, p. 170.
73 The review was published: *Blackwood's*, iii, 1818, CH, pp. 97–110.
76 "Twenty years ago": Charles Wentworth Dilke, unsigned review of
     Lady Morgan's *Dramatic Scenes*, *The Athenaeum*, No. 293, July 13,
     1833, p. 1.
77 "powers of language, rays of fancy": *Quarterly Review*, xix, September
     1818, CH, pp. 110–14.

3. ISABELLA; OR, THE POT OF BASIL

101 "mawkish": Keats refers to "mawkishness," in the Preface to *Endym-
     ion*, CH, p. 78.
101 "finest thing": Charles Lamb, unsigned review, *New Times*, July 19,
     1820, CH, p. 157.
102 "—but I saw / Too far into the sea:" *Poems*, p. 238.
103 "E'en tales like this, founded on real woe": *Poems of Leigh Hunt*, p. 42.
104 "the favour of the public": LJK, II, p. 144.
104 "a cloying treacle": Ibid.
106 "ghastly": Barry Cornwall, *A Sicilian Story, with Diego de Montilla,
     and Other Poems*, p. 177.

106   "And then she wept": Cornwall, *A Sicilian Story,* p. 20.

107   "smokeable": LJK, II, p. 174.

107   "There are very few would look to the reality": Ibid.

108   Astley Cooper: Druin Birch, "The Beauty of Body Snatching," in Roe (ed.), *John Keats and the Medical Imagination,* Chapter 3.

109   "great pleasure in alleviating suffering": R. H. Horne, "Keats at Edmonton," *Daily News,* April 8, 1871, p. 5.

110   "if a Sparrow come before my Window": LJK, I, p. 186.

110   "he has affirmed that he can conceive": LJK, I, p. 389.

110   "smother": LJK, II, p. 12.

110   "everlasting restraint": Ibid.

110   "unfit to perform": Brown, *Life of John Keats,* p. 43.

111   Jane Hull, who was brought: Nicholas Roe, "Dressing for Art: Notes from Keats in the Emergency Ward," *TLS,* May 27, 2015, pp. 14–15; also "Mr. Keats," in Roe (ed.), *John Keats and the Medical Imagination,* pp. 65 ff.

112   similarities of theme have been noted: Roe, *John Keats: A New Life,* pp. 226 ff.

112   "suspected every Body": LJK, I, pp. 292–3.

112   "loss of [his] parents": Ibid.

113   "irritable morbidity": LJK, I, p. 292, note 4.

113   "his suspicions to excess": Ibid.

113   "fine things": LJK, I, p. 279.

113   "feel them to the full": Ibid.

113   "relish Hamlet more than . . . ever": Ibid.

113   "jealous rivals": Roe, *John Keats: A New Life,* p. 227.

114   "a Jew at Enfield, named Abraham": Robert Gittings noted that a J. Abraham lived at Edmonton rather than Enfield, and surmised that Abbey had confused the two places. Gittings, *John Keats,* p. 47.

114   "that his great misfortune": William Sharp, *The Life and Letters of Joseph Severn* (1892; New York: Cambridge University Press, 2013), p. 5.

115   "not too flush of cash": Manuscript letter of Fanny Keats de Llanos to Harry Buxton Forman, March 3, 1886, and draft letter to Ralph Thomas, cited in Roe, *John Keats: A New Life,* p. 25, note 22.

115   "no property whatever": Ibid.

116   "Mr. Benjamin a Jew": LJK, II, p. 215.

118   According to University College, London's recent research project: For Smith, Payne & Smith and the legacies of slave ownership, see https://www.ucl.ac.uk/lbs/firm/view/1816453197.

118   "I have all my life thought very little of these matters": LJK, II, p. 141.

121   John James Audubon . . . exposed as a slaveholder: see https://www.audubon.org/news/the-myth-john-james-audubon.

122   "liberality in the Shape of a manufactu[r]ed rag value £20": LJK, I, p. 145.

123   "Maidenhead with respect to money": LJK, I, p. 147.

4. "THE EVE OF ST. AGNES"

139 "I am certain I have not a right feeling towards Women": LJK, I, p. 341.

139 "warmed with her . . . and kissed her": LJK, I, p. 403.

140 During the course of its reception history: see the summary in Susan J. Wolfson, *Reading John Keats,* p. 73.

141 "Decency & Discretion": John Taylor to Richard Woodhouse, September 25, 1819, LJK, II, p. 183.

141 "unfit for ladies": Richard Woodhouse to John Taylor, September 19, 1819, LJK, II, p. 163.

141 "the Suffrages of Women": John Taylor to Richard Woodhouse, September 25, 1819, LJK, II, p. 183.

141 "he should despise a man who would be such an eunuch": LJK, II, p. 163.

142 "opening for doubt what took place": Ibid.

142 In the idiom of the day: "Keats's use of Bawdy," Robert Gittings, *John Keats,* Appendix 4, pp. 650–52.

142 as described in William Houlston's medical textbook: Turley, *Bright Stars,* p. 124.

143 "The little Mercury I have taken": LJK, I, p. 171.

143 "Women being a little profligate": LJK, I, p. 132.

143 "a secret she gave you on the nail": LJK, I, p. 256.

144 "Severn has had a little Baby": LJK, II, p. 205.

145 "the effort of furious gratification": Haydon, *Neglected Genius: Diaries of Benjamin Robert Haydon,* p. 46.

145 "Fill for me a brimming bowl": *Poems,* p. 38.

146 "Her brest like to a bowle of creame uncrudded": Spenser allusion noted by Barnard, *Poems,* p. 569.

147 "The breasts are slung upon the chest": Astley Cooper, quoted in Roe (ed.), *John Keats and the Medical Imagination,* p. 54.

148 "inference": LJK, II, p. 163.

148 "had a fancy for trying his hand": Ibid.

148 "She has always been an enigma to me": LJK, I, p. 402.

148 "You once favoured me with the most amusing": Edmund Blunden, *Keats's Publisher,* p. 96.

149 Further research by Robert Gittings: *John Keats: the Living Year,* Appendix D, "Letters from Isabella Jones to John Taylor, with A Note on Mrs. Jones"; *The Mask of Keats,* Chapter 3, "More about Mrs. Jones," pp. 45–53.

149 a long and vivid letter: the passage on Mrs. Jones is in a letter to George and Georgiana, LJK, I, pp. 402–3.

151 "What is more gentle than a wind in summer?": "Sleep and Poetry," *Poems,* p. 82; Benjamin Britten, *Nocturne.*

152 "When I have fears that I may cease to be": *Poems,* p. 221.

155　"Oat-cakes": LJK, I, p. 362.

155　"despair": Ibid.

155　"long[ed] for some famous Beauty": LJK, I, p. 360.

155　"I must plead guilty to the breast of a Partridge": LJK, II, p. 65.

155　"favourite": Isabella Jones to John Taylor, quoted in Edmund Blunden, *Keats's Publisher*, p. 97.

155　"one of the Misses Porter": LJK, I, p. 410.

156　"My dear Woodhouse": LJK, I, p. 412.

156　"I equally dislike the favour of the public": LJK, II, p. 144.

157　"What think you of £25,000?": LJK, II, p. 62.

157　"try the public again": LJK, II, p. 65.

157　"fine mother Radcliff": LJK, II, p. 62.

158　"utter aversion": William Hazlitt, "On Great and Little Things," reprinted in *Table-talk; or, Original Essays*, vol. 2, p. 168.

158　*"bluestockings"*: Ibid.

158　"knowledge and taste": LJK, I, p. 403.

158　After he died: see Charles Brown's "List of Keats's Books," KC, I, p. 122.

158　In the search for her identity: see Roe, *John Keats: A New Life*, p. 171.

160　"some times through shabby, sometimes through decent Street[s]": LJK, I, p. 402.

160　The fact that her friend: for the loucheness of such establishments as her friend's boarding school, see Lucasta Miller, *L.E.L.: The Lost Life and Mysterious Death of the "Female Byron,"* (New York: Knopf, 2019) p. 41.

161　"Hush, hush, tread softly": *Poems*, p. 311.

161　She told Taylor: "The Magdalen," see Blunden, *Keats's Publisher*, p. 97.

161　"pettish": LJK, II, p. 163.

162　"In her home / (Which she did once desert)": Barry Cornwall, "The Magdalen," in *Dramatic Scenes and Other Poems*, p. 151.

5. "LA BELLE DAME SANS MERCI. A BALLAD"

169　It survives because Keats's brother: see Haydon, *Neglected Genius: The Diaries of Benjamin Robert Haydon*, p. 48.

169　"in one of his moods": Clarke, *Recollections of Writers*, p. 123.

170　"Poor little shaver": Quoted in William Henry Marquess, *Lives of the Poet: The First Century of Keats Biography*, p. 101.

170　"Indeed, we do not": Ibid.

170　"I am sitting opposite the Shakspeare": LJK, II, p. 62.

171　"When I am among women": LJK, I, p. 341.

171　"and put all this perversity": Ibid.

176　"beautiful Mrs. Jones": Reynolds to Taylor, October 31, 1837, LJK, II, p. 468 a.

177 "I see ~~death's~~ lilly on thy brow": LJK, II, p. 95.

178 "Why four kisses—you will say": LJK, II, p. 97.

178 "Chorus of Fairies": LJK, II, pp. 97–100.

179 "[S]ome kind of letters": LJK, I, p. 279.

180 "they kickit & jumpit with mettle extraordinary": LJK, I, p. 307.

180 "There was a naughty boy": LJK, I, pp. 312–3.

182 "for the most part dash'd of[f]": LJK, II, p. 106.

183 "smoak'd . . . a Segar": LJK, II, p. 78.

183 "I am still at Wentworth Place": LJK, II, p. 58.

184 "Brown and Dilke are walking round their Garden": LJK, II, p. 59.

184 "very little of Reynolds": LJK, II, p. 60.

184 "Miss Brawne and I have every now and then": LJK, II, p. 59.

184 "She made me take home a Pheasant the other day": LJK, II, p. 65.

185 "O, he is quite the little Poet": LJK, II, p. 61.

185 "abominable": Ibid.

185 "I do think better of Womankind than to suppose": LJK, I, p. 342.

185 "pluck up": LJK, II, p. 65.

186 "the boy has nothing in his ears all day": LJK, II, p. 84.

187 "I joined them, after enquiring by a look": LJK, II, pp. 88–89.

188 Their unfortunate son: see Lucy Watson, *Coleridge at Highgate*, p. 3.

189 "It looks so much like rain": LJK, II, pp. 88–89.

190 "vale of Soul-making": LJK, II, p. 102.

190 "Man who cannot feel he has a personal identity": LJK, II, p. 213.

190 "only means of strengthening one's intellect": LJK, II, p. 231.

190 "I am however young writing at random": LJK, II, p. 80.

191 A surviving early letter: see Edward B. Hinckley et al., "On First Looking into Swedenborg's Philosophy: A New Keats-Circle Letter," *Keats–Shelley Review*, vol. 9, no. 1, Winter 1960, pp. 15–25.

192 "Carlisle, a Bookseller": LJK, II, p. 62.

192 "I can scarcely express what I but dimly perceive": LJK, II, p. 102.

192 "I wonder how people exist with all their worries": LJK, II, p. 83.

193 "several things dovetailed in my mind": LJK, I, p. 193.

193 "*Negative Capability*": Ibid. The professional philosophers referred to are Professors Alexander Bird of Oxford and Alison Hills of Cambridge.

193 "As to the poetical Character itself": LJK, I, p. 387.

194 "this is the 3d May & every thing is in delightful forwardness": LJK, II, p. 109.

6. "ODE TO A NIGHTINGALE"

199 "modern ode": John Aitken, *Essays on Song-Writing*, quoted in Paul D. Sheats, "Keats and the Ode," in Wolfson (ed.), *Cambridge Companion to Keats*, p. 86.

199 "the assistance of every figure": Ibid.

200 "Child of melancholy song / O yet that tender strain prolong!": Ann Radcliffe, *The Romance of the Forest,* Chapter 19; quoted in Duncan Wu, *Immortal Bird: The Nightingale in Romantic Poetry,* p. 26.

200 "Sweet songster!": George Dyer, *Poetics,* p. 141.

201 "melting strains": Mary Robinson, *Poems,* p. 32.

203 "In these lines": Dyer, *Poetics,* p. 141.

203 Richard Woodhouse, who transcribed the poem: For transcriptions by Woodhouse and Dilke, see Suzanne Reynolds, " 'Some Scraps of Paper,' " pp. 141–2.

204 "He was the most scrupulously honest man": KC, p. lxix.

204 "to lead a life of literary leisure": Manuscript memoir of Charles Armitage Brown by his son, quoted in KC, pp. lv–lvi.

205 It is an outlandish concoction: LJK, II, p. 61.

206 "I feel every confidence that if I choose": LJK, II, p. 144.

206 "It was the time when wholesale houses close": *Poems,* p. 466.

207 "I have been very idle lately, very averse to writing": LJK, II, p. 116.

208 "The Odes are absolute perfection": William Graham, *Last Links with Byron, Shelley and Keats,* p. 54.

208 "trash": Ibid.

208 "pure delusion": Quoted in Gittings, *The Odes of Keats & Their Earliest Known Manuscripts in Facsimile,* p. 65.

209 "We do not usually thrust waste paper behind books": Ibid.

209 Keats enclosed it in a letter to Reynolds: For the history of the manuscript's provenance, see Reynolds, " 'Some Scraps of Paper.' "

210 "In Drear-Nighted December": *Poems,* p. 217.

211 "I think in one of your letters you said": Fred Edgcume (ed.), *Letters of Fanny Brawne to Fanny Keats,* p. 32.

212 "there was probably no author or authoress free": Harriet Martineau, quoted in Alethea Hayter, "The Laudanum Bottle Loomed Large," p. 37.

213 "please heaven, a little claret-wine": LJK, II, p. 56.

213 "now I like Claret": LJK, II, p. 64.

214 "I now never drink above three glasses": Ibid.

214 "My judgment . . . is as active": Keats's comment reported by Woodhouse, July (?) 1820, KC, I, pp. 128–9.

215 Byron later complained to Leigh Hunt: Hunt, *Lord Byron and Some of His Contemporaries,* p. 266.

215 "We frankly confess our dislike of his rhythm": CH, p. 183.

215 "Why did I write?": Pope, *Poetical Works,* p. 331.

216 "a fountain of Boeotia": *Lemprière's Classical Dictionary* (1788; London: Routledge and Kegan Paul, 1978), p. 283.

219 "As the Ode begins, Keats stands": Wu, *Immortal Bird: The Nightingale in Romantic Poetry,* p. xii.

7. "ODE ON A GRECIAN URN"

224 "red letter day": Clarke, *Recollections of Writers,* p. 133.
224 "prematurity of intellectual and poetical power": Elwin (ed.), *Autobiography and Journals of Benjamin Robert Haydon,* p. 295.
224 "formed a very high idea": Ibid.
224 "like a man with air balloons under his armpits": Elwin (ed.), *Autobiography and Journals of Benjamin Robert Haydon,* p. 240.
226 "cause / Of steadfast genius": Keats, *Addressed to Haydon, Poems,* p. 74.
226 "Such a blast will Fame blow of their grandeur": *Examiner,* March 17, 1816, p. 174.
226 "On Seeing the Elgin Marbles": "To B. R. Haydon, with a Sonnet Written on Seeing the Elgin Marbles," *Poems,* pp. 99–100.
227 "the shipwreck has continued to yield": see https://www.archaeology.org/news/8121–191021-greece-kythera-mentor-shipwreck.
228 Recent scholarship has shown: Theresa M. Kelley, "Keats and Ekphrasis," in Wolfson (ed.), *Cambridge Companion to Keats,* pp. 172–3.
229 "academical predilections": Dyer, *Poetics,* p. ix.
230 "His knowledge of Greek and mythology": CH, p. 183.
230 "nicety": CH, p. 162.
230 "white robes hymeneal": Becker et al., *A Concordance to the Poems of John Keats,* p. 263.
231 "the Cytherean rites": *Harris's List,* p. 40.
231 "She is a Whapper!": *The Letters of Mary Nisbet of Dirleton, Countess of Elgin,* ed. Nisbet Hamilton Grant (New York: Appelton, 1928), p. 22.
232 "lively Grecian": *The Excursion,* Book 4, *Complete Poetical Works of William Wordsworth,* pp. 461–2.
232 "Gods which themselves": *The Excursion,* Book 9, *Complete Poetical Works of William Wordsworth with an introduction by John Morley* (London: Macmillan, 1900), p. 528.
233 "Wordsworth received him kindly": KC, II, pp. 143–4.
234 "How is Keates": Wordsworth, *The Letters of William and Dorothy Wordsworth,* vol. 2, p. 861.
234 "Sad—sad—sad . . . What can we say?": LJK, I, p. 299.
235 "Mediators and Personages": LJK, II, p. 103.
235 "Mr. Keats, seemingly, can think or write of scarcely anything else": CH, p. 237.
236 *Encyclopædia Britannica*: CH, p. 367.
238 The anonymous critic in the *Monthly Review* bewailed: CH, p. 162.
238 "stimulating properties of a Christmas riddle": CH, p. 178.
238 The punning echo in "O Attic shape! Fair attitude!": Jeffrey N. Cox, *Poetry and Politics in the Cockney School,* p. 169.

241 "pretty-faced": Byron, *Beppo,* stanzas 11–12, *Lord Byron: The Major Works,* p. 319.

241 "I have never yet been able": LJK, I, p. 185.

242 "the excellence of every Art": LJK, I, p. 192.

244 "The attribution of truth to representational art": Helen Vendler, *The Odes of John Keats,* p. 147.

244 "though he is frequently involved in ambiguity": CH, p. 160.

244 "a peculiar satisfaction . . . priority": Quoted in David Blayney Brown, with Robert Woof and Stephen Hebron, *Benjamin Robert Haydon: Painter and Writer, Friend of Wordsworth and Keats,* p. 47.

245 "soul-soothing art": *Complete Poetical Works of William Wordsworth,* p. 404.

8. "TO AUTUMN"

248 Edmund Spenser's Elizabethan lines: quoted in Vendler, *The Odes of John Keats,* p. 243.

248 "greatest": Christopher Ricks, *Keats and Embarrassment,* p. 208.

248 "So compact, masterful, and yet gentle": Ibid.

248 "irritable state of health": LJK, II, p. 129.

248 "Within these two months I have written 1500 Lines": LJK, II, p. 139.

249 "I look upon fine Phrases like a Lover": Ibid.

249 As Helen Vendler once pointed out: Jack Stillinger, *John Keats: Poetry Manuscripts at Harvard,* p. xv.

250 "fatigue and trouble": LJK, II, p. 160.

250 "I know you will not be quite prepared for this": LJK, II, p. 119.

250 "for some Cash": LJK, II, p. 120.

251 "How beautiful the season is now": LJK, II, p. 167.

251 "most naturally, subtly, and unmisgivingly": Ricks, *Keats and Embarrassment,* p. 208.

252 "not less than 200,000": *Gentleman's Magazine,* September 1819, LXXXIX, ii, p. 269.

252 "subtly queasy": Tom Paulin, *The Day-Star of Liberty: William Hazlitt's Radical Style,* p. 47.

252 "with its hewn flagstaffs and torn banners": Ibid.

253 "You will hear by the papers of the proceedings": LJK, II, p. 194.

254 "All civiled [*sic*] countries": LJK, II, pp. 193–4.

254 Andrew Motion pointed out that gleaning: Andrew Motion, *Keats,* p. 462.

255 "and many other works held in superstitious horror": LJK, II, p. 194.

257 "marvellous Boy": *Wordsworth's Poetical Works,* p. 175.

258 "the purest writer in the English Language": LJK, II, p. 167.

259 "Sands the destroyer of Kotzebue": LJK, II, p. 194.

262 "unparalleled touch in the face of death": Stillinger, *John Keats: Poetry Manuscripts at Harvard,* p. xxi.

262 "spiritual triumph": Gittings, *The Odes of Keats,* p. 16.

263 "knowledge of contrast, feeling": LJK, II, p. 360.

263 "to venture on the common": LJK, II, p. 179 (to Dilke).

264 "I have no trust whatever on Poetry": LJK, II, p. 179.

264 "deep in love": LJK, II, p. 132.

264 "I love you too much to venture to Hampstead": LJK, II, p. 160.

265 "character and self-control": Matthew Arnold, quoted in Marquess, *Lives of the Poet,* p. 72.

9. "BRIGHT STAR!"

267 However, a manuscript version: For the dating of the manuscript, see *Poems,* p. 708.

267 "I have seen your Comet": LJK, II, p. 127.

267 "I will imagine you Venus tonight": LJK, II, p. 133.

268 "the first love most of us dream of enjoying": Jane Campion, Introduction, *So Bright and Delicate: Love Letters and Poems of John Keats to Fanny Brawne,* p. vii.

268 "I never knew before, what such a love": LJK, II, p. 126.

269 "Nothing strikes me so forcibly with a sense of the rediculous": LJK, II, p. 187.

269 "always seemed a cold, conventional mistress": LJK, I, p. li.

269 "a lady with whom a Poet so sensitive": William Dilke to Sir Charles W. Dilke, February 12, 1875, KC, II, p. 338.

270 "all the advances to him": Ibid.

271 "Mrs. Brawne, who took Brown's house": LJK, II, p. 8.

271 "I find . . . I am to be invited to Miss Millar's": Ibid.

272 positions of administrative power in Jamaica and Barbados: Joanna Richardson, *Fanny Brawne,* p. 3.

273 "Shall I give you Miss Brawn?": LJK, II, p. 13.

274 "the happiest day I had ever then spent": Edgcumbe (ed.), *Letters of Fanny Brawne,* p. 41.

274 "Miss Brawne and I have every now and then": LJK, II, p. 59.

275 "beautiful Girl whom I love so much": LJK, II, p. 122.

275 "at least touch my lips where yours have been": LJK, II, p. 123.

276 "ensure me an employment & maintenance": LJK, II, p. 125.

276 "I look not forward with any pleasure": LJK, II, p. 133.

277 "My dearest Lady, I am glad I had not": LJK, II, p. 122.

278 "not seventeen": LJK, II, p. 13.

278 "We might spend a pleasant year at Berne or Zurich": LJK, II, p. 138.

279 "Better be imprudent moveables": Ibid.

279 "But if you will fully love me": LJK, II, p. 126.

279 "I am indeed astonish'd to find myself so careless": LJK, II, p. 133.

279 "When I come to town I shall have a little talk with you": LJK, II, p. 136.

280 "So you intend to hold me to my promise": LJK, II, p. 137.

280 "Remember I have no idle leisure to brood over you": LJK, II, p. 140.

280 "I like [Miss Brawne] and I cannot help it": LJK, II, p. 177.

281 "It is quite a settled thing between Keats": KC, I, p. li.

281 "longed for": William Michael Rossetti, *The Life of John Keats*, p. 36.

281 "early marriage": Ibid.

282 "As his love for you formed so great a part of him": Quoted in Marquess, *Lives of the Poet*, p. 50.

282 "tattlers, and inquisitors into my conduct": LJK, II, p. 293.

283 "I was more generous ten years ago": Draft reply of December 1829 to Brown, M. B. Forman, *The Letters of John Keats*, p. lxiii.

284 "I asked hurriedly, 'What is the matter'": Brown, *Life of John Keats*, p. 64.

284 "They say I must remain confined to this room for some time": LJK, II, p. 250.

285 "How illness stands as a barrier betwixt me and you!": LJK, II, p. 263.

286 "My book has had good success among literary people": LJK, II, p. 321.

286 "I am nervous": LJK, II, p. 263.

288 "I am greedy of you": LJK, II, pp. 290–91.

289 "I cannot exist without you": LJK, II, p. 223.

289 "more and more concentrated in you": LJK, II, pp. 311–12.

290 "very poorly": LJK, II, p. 297.

290 Haydon wrote again: see LJK, II, p. 308.

290 "nervous": LJK, II, p. 313.

291 "They talk of my going to Italy": LJK, II, p. 303.

292 "with us": Edgcumbe (ed.), *Letters of Fanny Brawne*, p. 21.

292 the claim that she cut off her hair: see Campion, Introduction, *So Bright and Delicate: Love Letters and Poems of John Keats to Fanny Brawne*, p. xiv.

292 put her hair in curling papers: For the detail about curling her hair, see Edgcumbe (ed.), *Letters of Fanny Brawne*, p. 40.

292 her own "red and black" dress: see Edgcumbe (ed.), *Letters of Fanny Brawne*, p. 50.

294 "one intense affection": Milnes, *Life, Letters and Literary Remains of John Keats*, vol. 1, p. 173.

294 "In life's battle": Quoted in Marquess, *Lives of the Poet*, pp. 66, 67, 68.

294 "man so perfect": Ibid.

295 "A manful kind of man": Ibid.

295 "a very tender circumstance": Hunt, *Lord Byron and Some of His Contemporaries,* p. 267.

295 "more than he could bear": Ibid.

EPITAPH: HERE LIES ONE WHOSE NAME WAS WRIT IN WATER

297 In two passages of later reminiscences: see Sharp, *The Life and Letters of Joseph Severn,* p. 48.

298 "endeared him to me for ever": LJK, I, p. 392.

298 "to wear a consumptive appearance": LJK, II, p. 310.

298 "the Bacchanal beside the Tuscan sea": *Blackwood's,* 10 (December 1821), pp. 696–70.

299 Ironically, shortly after Keats's death: *Literary Gazette,* no. 254, December 21, 1821, p. 772.

301 "Dear Sir": LJK, II, p. 331.

301 "In case of my death this scrap of Paper": LJK, II, p. 319; for the assignment of copyright, see LJK, II, pp. 334–6.

302 they forwarded a further £150: see KC, I, pp. 147–8.

303 "plentiful shower of tears": LJK, II, p. 353.

303 "I am horror struck": Ibid.

303 "cant": Gittings, *The Living Year,* Appendix D, p. 232.

303 "disgusting": Ibid.

303 "load of WRETCHEDNESS which presses upon me": LJK, II, p. 351.

304 "I dare not fix my Mind on Fanny": LJK, II, p. 350.

305 "vomited near two Cup-fuls of blood": KC, I, p. 176.

305 "black and thick in the extreme": Ibid.

305 "in perpetual hunger or craving": LJK, II, p. 362.

305 "the continued stretch of his imagination [had] killed him": KC, I, p. 180.

305 "the exciting and thwarting of his passions": KC, II, p. 92.

305 "I should have had her": LJK, II, p. 351.

305 "I make bread and milk three times a day for Keats": Grant F. Scott (ed.), *Joseph Severn: Letters and Memoirs,* p. 128.

306 "here I am by our poor dying friend": LJK, II, pp. 375–6.

307 "He is gone—he died with the most perfect ease": Scott (ed.), *Joseph Severn: Letters and Memoirs,* pp. 136–7.

307 "To-night he has talked very much to me": KC, II, p. 91.

308 "I wish to believe in immortality": LJK, II, p. 293.

310 "delicate and fragile": Shelley, *Selected Poems and Prose,* p. 492.

310 "murderer": Ibid.

310 "pale flower": *Adonais,* stanza vi.

310 "broken lily": *Adonais,* stanza vii.

310 "a portion of the loveliness": *Adonais,* stanza xliii.

311 "Neither name nor date is requisite": Sharp, *The Life and Letters of Joseph Severn,* p. 107.

311 "an eyesore to me": Sharp, *The Life and Letters of Joseph Severn,* p. 165.

311 "sort of profanation": *New Letters of Charles Brown to Joseph Severn,* ed. Grant F. Scott and Sue Brown, Romantic Circles Electronic Edition, https://www.rc.umd.edu/editions/brownsevern/letters/26nov 1836.html.

311 "posthumous existence": LJK, II, p. 359.

Bibliography

Askwith, Betty, *Keats* (London: Collins, 1949).

Bari, Shahidha K., *Keats and Philosophy: The Life of Sensations* (London: Routledge, 2012).

Barnard, John, *John Keats* (Cambridge: Cambridge University Press, 1987).

———, "Keats's Letters," in Susan J. Wolfson (ed.), *The Cambridge Companion to Keats.*

———, "Which Letters Did Keats Take to Rome?," *Keats–Shelley Journal,* vol. 64 (2015), pp. 72–91.

———, "The Harvard Manuscript of Keats's 'On First Looking into Chapman's Homer,' Joseph Severn, Leigh Hunt, and Its Transmission into Print," *Romanticism,* vol. 25, no. 2 (2019).

Bate, Walter Jackson, *John Keats* (Cambridge, Mass.: The Belknap Press of Harvard University Press, 1963).

Becker, Michael G., et al., *A Concordance to the Poems of John Keats* (London and New York: Routledge, 1981).

Blanning, Tim, *The Romantic Revolution* (London: Weidenfeld & Nicolson, 2010).

Blunden, Edmund, *Keats's Publisher* (London: Jonathan Cape, 1936).

Brown, Charles Armitage, *Life of John Keats,* ed. Dorothy Hyde Bodurtha and Willard Bissell Pope (London: Oxford University Press, 1937).

Brown, David Blayney, with Robert Woof and Stephen Hebron, *Benjamin Robert Haydon: Painter and Writer, Friend of Wordsworth and Keats* (Kendal: The Wordsworth Trust, 1996).

Bush, Douglas, *John Keats: His Life and Writings* (London: Weidenfeld & Nicolson, 1966).

Butler, Marilyn, *Jane Austen and the War of Ideas* (Oxford: Clarendon Press, 1987).

Byron, George Gordon (Lord Byron), *Byron's Letters and Journals,* ed. Leslie

A. Marchand, 12 vols. (Cambridge, Mass.: The Belknap Press of Harvard University Press, 1973–1982).

———, *Lord Byron: The Major Works,* ed. Jerome J. McGann (Oxford: World's Classics, 1986).

Campion, Jane, Introduction, *So Bright and Delicate: Love Letters and Poems of John Keats to Fanny Brawne* (London: Penguin, 2009).

Chantler, Ashley, with Michael Davies and Philip Shaw (eds.), *Literature and Authenticity 1780–1900: Essays in Honour of Vincent Newey* (London and New York: Routledge, 2011).

Clark, Tom, *Junkets on a Sad Planet* (Santa Rosa, Calif.: Black Sparrow Press, 1994).

Clarke, Charles Cowden, *Recollections of Writers* (London: Sampson Low et al., 1878).

Colvin, Sidney, *Keats* (London: Macmillan and Co., 1898).

Coote, Stephen, *John Keats: A Life* (London: Hodder & Stoughton, 1995).

Cornwall, Barry (Bryan Waller Procter), *A Sicilian Story, with Diego de Montilla, and Other Poems,* 2nd edition (London: Ollier, 1820).

———, *Dramatic Scenes and Other Poems.* 2nd edition (London: C. and J. Ollier, 1820).

Cox, Jeffrey N., *Poetry and Politics in the Cockney School* (Cambridge: Cambridge University Press, 1998).

Dart, Gregory, *Metropolitan Art and Literature, 1810–1840: Cockney Adventures* (Cambridge: Cambridge University Press, 2012).

Davies, Damian Walford, and Richard Marggraf Turley (eds.), *The Monstrous Debt: Modalities of Romantic Influence in Twentieth-Century Literature* (Detroit: Wayne State University Press, 2006).

Davis, Susan L., "John Keats and 'The Poison': Venereal or Mercurial?," *Keats–Shelley Journal,* vol. 53 (2004), pp. 86–96.

Dyer, George, *Poetics: or, Series of Poems and Disquisitions on Poetry* (London: J. Johnson, 1812).

Edgcume, Fred (ed.), *Letters of Fanny Brawne to Fanny Keats* (London: Oxford University Press, 1936).

Erlande, Albert [pseud. Albert Jacques Brandenbourg], *The Life of John Keats* (London: Jonathan Cape, 1929).

Everest, Kelvin, *John Keats* (Tavistock: Northcote House, 2002).

———, "John Keats," entry in the *Oxford Dictionary of National Biography* (2004).

Ford, George H., *Keats and the Victorians: A Study of His Influence and Rise to Fame 1821–1895* (New Haven, Conn.: Yale University Press, 1944).

Forman, M. B., *The Letters of John Keats,* 4th edition (Oxford: Oxford University Press, 1952).

Ghosh, Hrileena, and Nicholas Roe, "Formative Years and Medical Training," in Michael O'Neill (ed.), *John Keats in Context.*

Gilbreath, Marcia, "The Etymology of Porphyro's Name in Keats's 'Eve of St. Agnes,'" *Keats–Shelley Journal,* vol. 37 (1988), pp. 20–25.

Gittings, Robert, *John Keats: The Living Year* (London: Heinemann, 1954).

———, *The Keats Inheritance* (London: Heinemann, 1964).

———, *The Mask of Keats: A Study of Problems* (London: Heinemann, 1956).

———, *John Keats* (London: Heinemann, 1968; London: Penguin, 1979).

———, *The Odes of Keats & Their Earliest Known Manuscripts in Facsimile* (London: Heinemann, 1970).

——— (ed.), Introduction, *Letters of John Keats: A Selection* (London: Oxford University Press, 1970).

Graham, William, *Last Links with Byron, Shelley and Keats* (London: Leonard Smithers and Co., 1898).

Harris's List (London: H. Ranger, 1788).

Hay, Daisy, *Young Romantics: The Shelleys, Byron and Other Tangled Lives* (London: Bloomsbury, 2010).

Haydon, Benjamin Robert, *Autobiography and Journals of Benjamin Robert Haydon,* ed. Malcolm Elwin (London: Macdonald, 1950).

———, *Neglected Genius: The Diaries of Benjamin Robert Haydon,* ed. John Jolliffe (London: Hutchinson, 1990).

Hayter, Alethea, "The Laudanum Bottle Loomed Large: Opium in the English Literary World in the Nineteenth Century," *Ariel* II, no. 4 (1980).

Hazlitt, William, *Table-talk: Or, Original Essays,* 2 vols. (London: Henry Colburn, 1822).

———, *Liber Amoris and Related Writings,* ed. Gregory Dart (Manchester: Carcanet, 2008).

Hewlett, Dorothy, *Adonais: The Life of John Keats* (London: Hurst & Blackett, 1937).

Hilton, Boyd, *A Mad, Bad and Dangerous People? England 1783–1846* (Oxford: Oxford University Press, 2006).

Hinckley, Edward B., et al., "On First Looking into Swedenborg's Philosophy: A New Keats-Circle Letter," *Keats–Shelley Review,* vol. 9, no. 1 (Winter 1960).

Homans, Margaret, "Keats Reading Women, Women Reading Keats," *Studies in Romanticism,* vol. 29, no. 3 (Fall 1990), pp. 341–70.

Howells, R. J., *Rousseau: La Nouvelle Héloise* (London: Grant and Cutler, 1986).

Howitt, William, *Homes and Haunts of the Most Eminent British Poets,* 5th edition (London: Routledge, 1848).

Hunt, Leigh, *Lord Byron and Some of His Contemporaries* (London: Henry Colburn, 1828).

———, *Poems of Leigh Hunt, with prefaces from some of his periodicals,* ed. Reginald Brimley Johnson (London: Dent, 1891).

———, *Selected Writings,* ed. David Jesson Dibley (Exeter: Carcanet, 1990).

Jugurtha, Lillie, *Keats and Nature* (New York: Peter Lang, 1985).

Kandl, John, "The Politics of Keats's Early Poetry," in Susan J. Wolfson (ed.), *The Cambridge Companion to Keats.*

Kelley, Theresa M., "Keats and 'Ekphrasis,'" in Susan J. Wolfson (ed.), *The Cambridge Companion to Keats.*

Leadbetter, Gregory, "The Hunt Circle and the Cockney School," in Michael O'Neill (ed.), *John Keats in Context.*

Lemprière, John, *Bibliotheca Classica; or, A Classical Dictionary, Containing a Full Account of Proper Names Mentioned in Ancient Authors* (London: T. Cadell, 1788).

Livesley, Brian, *The Dying Keats: A Case for Euthanasia?* (Leicester: Matador, 2009).

Lowe, Derek, "Seeing Through the 'Burden of the Past': Superior Belatedness in Keats's 'On First Looking into Chapman's Homer,'" *Keats–Shelley Review,* vol. 29, no. 2 (2015).

Lowell, Amy, *John Keats,* 2 vols. (Boston: Houghton Mifflin Co., 1925).

Lundeen, Kathleen, "Keats's Post-Newtonian Poetics," *Keats–Shelley Journal,* vol. 44 (1995), pp. 102–16.

Mahoney, Charles W., "Imagination, Beauty and Truth," in Michael O'Neill (ed.), *John Keats in Context.*

Marquess, William Henry, *Lives of the Poet: The First Century of Keats Biography* (University Park and London: Pennsylvania State University Press, 1985).

Matthews, G. M. (ed.), *John Keats: The Critical Heritage* (London: Routledge, 1971).

Miller, Lucasta, *L.E.L.: The Lost Life and Mysterious Death of the "Female Byron"* (New York: Knopf, 2019).

Milnes, Richard Monckton (Lord Houghton), *Life, Letters and Literary Remains of John Keats* (London: Edward Moxon, 1848).

———, "Memoir," *The Poetical Works of John Keats* (London: George Bell and Sons, 1876).

Motion, Andrew, *Keats* (London: Faber and Faber, 1997).

Muir, Rory, *Gentlemen of Uncertain Fortune* (New Haven, Conn.: Yale University Press, 2019).

Murry, John Middleton, *Keats and Shakespeare: A Study of Keats's Poetic Life 1816 to 1820* (London: Oxford University Press, 1921).

O'Gorman, Francis, "Critical Reception 1821–1900," in O'Neill (ed.), *John Keats in Context.*

O'Keefe, Paul, *A Genius for Failure: The Life of Benjamin Robert Haydon* (London: The Bodley Head, 2009).

O'Neill, Michael (ed.), *John Keats in Context* (Cambridge: Cambridge University Press, 2017).

O'Sullivan, Michael, *Weakness: A Literary and Philosophical History* (London: Continuum, 2012).

Paulin, Tom, *The Day-Star of Liberty: William Hazlitt's Radical Style* (London: Faber and Faber, 1998).

Plumly, Stanley, *Posthumous Keats: A Personal Biography* (New York: W. W. Norton & Co., 2008).

Pope, Alexander, *Poetical Works,* ed. Herbert Davies with an introduction by Pat Rogers (Oxford: Oxford University Press, 1978).

Rewald, Sabine, *Rooms with a View: The Open Window in the 19th Century* (New York: The Metropolitan Museum of Art; New Haven, Conn., and London: Yale University Press, 2011).

Reynolds, Ian, "The Gravestone of John Keats: Romancing the Stone," https://wordsworth.org.uk/blog/2018/04/16/the-gravestone-of-john -keats-romancing-the-stone/.

Reynolds, Suzanne, " 'Some Scraps of Paper': The Autograph Manuscript of *Ode to a Nightingale* at the Fitzwilliam Museum," *Keats–Shelley Review,* vol. 33, no. 2 (2019).

Richardson, Benjamin Ward, *Disciples of Aesculapius, with a Life of the Author by His Daughter Mrs. George Martin,* 2 vols. (London: Hutchinson & Co., 1900).

Richardson, Joanna, *Fanny Brawne, "Fair Love" of Keats: A Biography* (Norwich: Jarrold and Sons, 1952).

———, *The Life and Letters of John Keats* (London: Folio Society, 1981).

Ricks, Christopher, *Keats and Embarrassment* (Oxford: Oxford University Press, 1974; Clarendon Press paperback, 1988).

Robinson, Mary, *Poems* (London: J. Bell, 1791).

Rodriguez, Andrés, *Book of the Heart: The Poetics, Letters and Life of John Keats* (Hudson, N.Y.: Lindisfarne Press, 1993).

Roe, Nicholas, *John Keats and the Culture of Dissent* (Oxford: Oxford University Press, 1997).

———, *John Keats: A New Life* (New Haven, Conn., and London: Yale University Press, 2012).

———, "Dressing for Art: Notes from Keats in the Emergency Ward," *TLS,* May 27, 2015, pp. 14–15.

———, "English Restored: John Keats's 'To Autumn,' " *Essays in Criticism,* vol. 67, no. 3 (July 2017).

——— (ed.), *John Keats and the Medical Imagination* (Basingstoke: Palgrave Macmillan, 2018).

Rollins, Hyder E. (ed.), *The Letters of John Keats 1814–1821,* 2 vols. (Cambridge, Mass.: Harvard University Press, 1958).

———, *The Keats Circle: Letters and Papers and More Letters and Poems of the Keats Circle 1814–1879,* 2 vols. (Cambridge, Mass.: Harvard University Press, 1965).

Rossetti, William Michael, *The Life of John Keats* (London: Walter Scott, 1887).

Schulkins, Rachel, *Keats, Modesty and Masturbation* (London: Routledge, 2016).

Scott, Grant F. (ed.), *Joseph Severn: Letters and Memoirs* (Aldershot: Ashgate, 2005).

Scott, Matthew, "Keats Criticism, 1900–1963," in O'Neill (ed.), *John Keats in Context.*

Scott, Matthew, and Sue Brown, eds., *New Letters of Charles Brown to Joseph Severn,* Romantic Circles Electronic Edition, https://www.rc.umd.edu/editions/brownsevern/letters/26nov1836.html.

Sharp, William, *Life and Letters of Joseph Severn* (London: Sampson Low et al., 1892).

Sheats, Paul D., "Keats and the Ode," in Wolfson (ed.), *The Cambridge Companion to Keats.*

Shelley, Percy Bysshe, *Adonais, An Elegy on the Death of John Keats,* facsimile of the 1821 edition, ed. T. J. Wise (London: The Shelley Society, 1886).

———, *Selected Poems and Prose,* ed. Jack Donovan and Cian Duffy (London: Penguin, 2016).

St. Clair, William, *The Reading Nation in the Romantic Period* (Cambridge: Cambridge University Press, 2004).

Stillinger, Jack, *"The Hoodwinking of Madeline" and Other Essays on Keats's Poems* (Urbana: University of Illinois Press, 1971).

——— (ed.), *John Keats: Poetry Manuscripts at Harvard, a Facsimile Edition Edited by Jack Stillinger with an Essay on the Manuscripts by Helen Vendler* (Cambridge, Mass.: Harvard University Press, 1990).

———, *Reading The Eve of St. Agnes* (Oxford: Oxford University Press, 1999).

Swann, Karen, "*Endymion*'s Beautiful Dreamers," in Wolfson (ed.), *The Cambridge Companion to Keats.*

Thomson, Heidi, "Fanny Brawne and Other Women," in O'Neill (ed.), *John Keats in Context.*

Trilling, Lionel, "The Poet as Hero: Keats in His Letters," in *The Opposing Self: Nine Essays in Criticism* (London: Secker & Warburg, 1955).

Turley, Richard Marggraf, *Bright Stars: John Keats, "Barry Cornwall" and Romantic Literary Culture* (Liverpool: Liverpool University Press, 2009).

——— (ed.), *Keats's Places* (Basingstoke: Palgrave Macmillan, 2018).

———, "Keats Criticism, Post 1963," in O'Neill (ed.), *John Keats in Context.*

Van Kooy, Dana, "Darien Prospects in Keats's 'On First Looking into Chapman's Homer,'" *Keats–Shelley Review,* vol. 29, no. 2 (2015).

Vendler, Helen, *The Odes of John Keats* (1998; Cambridge, Mass.: Harvard University Press, 1983).

———, *Coming of Age as a Poet: Milton, Keats, Eliot, Plath* (Cambridge, Mass.: Harvard University Press, 2003).

———, essay, *John Keats: Poetry Manuscripts at Harvard, a Facsimile Edition Edited by Jack Stillinger with an Essay on the Manuscripts by Helen Vendler* (Cambridge, Mass.: Harvard University Press, 1990).

Walsh, John Evangelist, *Darkling I Listen: The Last Days and Death of John Keats* (New York: St. Martin's Press, 1999).

Ward, Aileen, *John Keats: The Making of a Poet* (London: Secker & Warburg, 1963).

Wasserman, Earl R., *The Finer Tone: Keats' Major Poems* (Baltimore: Johns Hopkins University Press, 1953).

Watson, Lucy, *Coleridge at Highgate* (London: Longman, 1925).

Wells, Walter, *A Doctor's Life of John Keats* (New York: Vantage Press, 1959).

White, R. S., *John Keats: A Literary Life* (Basingstoke: Palgrave Macmillan, 2010).

Williams, Blanche Colton, *Forever Young: A Life of John Keats* (New York: G. P. Putnam's Sons, 1943).

Wolfson, Susan J., *Reading John Keats* (Cambridge: Cambridge University Press, 2015).

—— (ed.), *The Cambridge Companion to Keats* (Cambridge: Cambridge University Press, 2001).

—— (ed.), *John Keats: A Longman Cultural Edition* (New York and London: Pearson Education, Inc., 2007).

Wootton, Sarah, "Biographies and Film," in O'Neill (ed.), *John Keats in Context*.

Wordsworth, William, *Complete Poetical Works of William Wordsworth*, with an introduction by John Morley (London: Macmillan, 1900).

——, *The Letters of William and Dorothy Wordsworth*, ed. Ernest de Selincourt, 2 vols. (Oxford: Clarendon Press, 1935).

Wu, Duncan, "Keats and the 'Cockney School,'" in Wolfson (ed.), *The Cambridge Companion to Keats*.

——, Introduction, *Immortal Bird: The Nightingale in Romantic Poetry* (Rome: Keats-Shelley House, 2011).

Wunder, Jennifer N., *Keats, Hermeticism and the Secret Societies* (2008; Abingdon: Routledge, 2016).

Yeats, W. B., *The Collected Poems of W. B. Yeats* (1933; London: Macmillan, 1958).

Index

ILLUSTRATION CREDITS

A NOTE ON THE TYPE

This book was set in Adobe Garamond. Designed for the Adobe Corporation by Robert Slimbach, the fonts are based on types first cut by Claude Garamond (ca. 1480–1561). Garamond was a pupil of Geoffroy Tory and is believed to have followed the Venetian models, although he introduced a number of important differences, and it is to him that we owe the letter we now know as "old style." He gave to his letters a certain elegance and feeling of movement that won their creator an immediate reputation and the patronage of Francis I of France.

Composed by North Market Street Graphics,
Lancaster, Pennsylvania

Printed and bound by Lakeside Book Company
Harrisonburg, Virginia

Designed by Cassandra J. Pappas